BY AND FOR THE PEOPLE

Constitutional Rights in American History

Arthur S. Link

Princeton University

General Editor for History

BY AND FOR THE PEOPLE
Constitutional Rights in American History

Edited by

Kermit L. Hall

University of Florida

A Project of the
Organization of American Historians

Ad Hoc Committee on the Bicentennial of the Bill of Rights:
Paul L. Murphy, Chair; Mary K. B. Tachau; Gordon Morris
Bakken; Kathleen Kean; Michael Les Benedict; Sandra F.
VanBurkleo; and Benno C. Schmidt, Jr.

Harlan Davidson, Inc.
Arlington Heights, Illinois 60004

Library of Congress Cataloging-in-Publication Data

By and for the people : constitutional rights in American history : a
    project of the Organization of American Historians Ad Hoc
    Committee on the Bicentennial of the Bill of Rights / edited by
    Kermit L. Hall.
        p.   cm.
    Includes bibliographical references and index.
    ISBN 0-88295-878-X
    1. United States–Constitutional law–Amendments–1st–10th–
History.   2. Civil rights–United States–History.   I. Hall, Kermit.
KF4749.A2B9   1991
342.73′085–dc20
[347.30285]   91-7845
                                                                 CIP

Credit:
Courtroom illustrations throughout this volume were done by and are
under the copyright of Ida Libby Dengrove.

Manufactured in the United States of America
95 94 93 92 91   MG   1 2 3 4 5 6 7

Dedicated to the Memory of Mary K. B. Tachau
Teacher, Scholar, Citizen

Contributors

Gordon Morris Bakken is Professor of History at California State University, Fullerton. His many publications include *Rocky Mountain Constitution Making: 1850–1912* (1987).

David J. Bodenhamer is Professor of History and Director of POLIS, Encyclopedia of Indianapolis, at Indiana University at Indianapolis. He is the author of *The Pursuit of Justice: Crime and Law in Antebellum Indiana* (1986).

Lawrence Delbert Cress is Jay P. Walker Professor of American History and Chair of the Faculty of History at the University of Tulsa. His many publications include *Citizens in Arms: The Army and Militia in American Society to the War of 1812* (1982).

Paul Finkelman teaches at the Brooklyn Law School and is the author of *An Imperfect Union: Slavery, Federalism, and Comity* (1981), as well as numerous articles and edited works on slavery, race relations, and American legal history.

Kermit L. Hall is Professor of History and Law at the University of Florida. His most recent work is *The Magic Mirror: Law in American History* (1989).

Paula Petrik is Associate Professor of History and Associate Dean of the College of Liberal Arts and Sciences at the University of Maine, Orono, and the author of *No Step Backward: Women and Family on the Rocky Mountain Mining Frontier, Helena, Montana, 1865–1900* (1987).

Norman Rosenberg is Professor of History at Macalester College and the author of *Protecting the Best Men: An Interpretive History of the Law of Libel* (1986).

Melvin I. Urofsky is Professor of History, Virginia Commonwealth University. His many publications include *A March of Liberty: A Constitutional History of the United States* (1988).

Sandra F. VanBurkleo is Assistant Professor of History at Wayne State University. She is the author of "No Rights But Human Rights: The Emancipation of American Women," *Constitution* (Spring/Summer 1990).

Samuel Walker is Professor of Criminal Justice, University of Nebraska at Omaha. His many publications include *In Defense of American Liberties: A History of the ACLU* (1990).

Contents

Preface

This book is one of several projects sponsored by the Organization of American Historians' Ad Hoc Committee on the Bicentennial of the Bill of Rights. Instituted under the leadership of Mary K. B. Tachau, the Committee decided that one of the most appropriate ways in which the OAH could commemorate the nation's basic charter of freedom was to provide school teachers, college instructors, and the general reader with short, nontechnical introductions to the history of the Bill of Rights. These essays connect controversies over rights and liberties today to their historical antecedents as well as explain how social, political, and cultural changes have influenced our understanding of specific provisions of the Bill of Rights. All of these essays, therefore, frame their subjects against the larger canvas of American history. Each essay also includes bibliographical information about readily accessible scholarship and a descriptive summary of leading cases relevant to its subject. Three appendices—the complete text of the Constitution and the Bill of Rights, a chronological checklist of the relevant court cases (see inside covers), and a glossary of terms—complete the volume. These essays are not comprehensive, either in the sense that together they cover all aspects of the Bill of Rights or that individual essays treat fully each of their subjects. Rather, they provide a wealth of material that can be quickly digested.

Teachers have played an important part in the design of this volume, and at each stage the editor, the authors, and the Committee have sought their guidance. Kathleen Kean, a teacher at Nicolet High School in Glendale, Wisconsin, and a member of the Committee, provided valuable suggestions about the structure and presentation of the volume. In addition, during the summer of 1990 the first drafts of all of the chapters were presented to two teacher institutes, one conducted by John Patrick at Indiana University and the other at a National Endowment for the Humanities seminar at Carleton College. The authors incorporated almost all of the substantive and organizational suggestions made by the more than fifty teachers in those two institutes. The result, we think, is a volume that will better meet the needs of teachers and students than if scholars alone had worked on the project. Indeed, the Committee believes that only through collaborative efforts such as *By and For the People* can

teachers and professors make American history genuinely accessible to the students we all seek to teach.

The National Commission on the Bicentennial of the Constitution provided early funding for this volume. The Committee thanks the Commission for its support, not just of this enterprise but for all it has done to enhance teaching about the Constitution. The Committee also owes a large debt of gratitude to Arnita Jones of the OAH and her staff for their strong and helpful support of this project. Their enthusiasm proved a valuable asset in getting the project going and moving it along. Our general editor, Kermit L. Hall, also deserves high praise for his many hours of hard work in riding herd on the authors, editing their work, and providing the Introduction and the contextual essay which set up the volume. Maureen Hewitt, of Harlan Davidson, Inc., threw her energy and intelligence into the project in a way that benefited all of the authors. Such expertise and dedication contributed heavily to the unity and richness of the final product. We hope its use will increase the understanding of our heritage of rights and liberties.

Paul L. Murphy, Chair
Ad Hoc Committee on the
Bicentennial of the Bill of Rights

Kermit L. Hall

INTRODUCTION

Public opinion surveys since World War II have revealed a paradox about American attitudes toward civil liberties and civil rights. On the one hand, when Americans are read a specific provision of the Bill of Rights covering, for example, freedom of speech or press, a majority of them respond in a conditional, even hostile way. Survey after survey has shown that large groups of American citizens, when offered the opportunity to choose between specific libertarian and antilibertarian responses, often select the latter. Yet these same respondents routinely insist that the Bill of Rights comprises the most important provisions of the Constitution. What these surveys suggest, of course, is that the Bill of Rights has captured the loyalty of Americans even if they do not know exactly what it contains. This paradox eloquently affirms how fully these amendments have become embedded in our constitutional conscience. As the essays in this volume make clear, however, the history of liberty teaches that rights have been most vulnerable when we have taken them for granted and that there is little evidence that men and women are led *by nature* to yearn for freedom, much less to guarantee the liberties of other individuals.

What is the Bill of Rights?

The Bill of Rights consists of the first ten amendments to the Constitution. Of these ten, some scholars and lawyers insist that only the first eight properly constitute a bill of rights. They argue that the Ninth and Tenth amendments are general statements that outline the division of powers within the Constitution rather than identify specific liberties to be protected. The Ninth Amendment commands that the "enumeration in the Constitution of certain rights shall not be construed to deny or disparage

the history of liberty teaches that rights have been most vulnerable when we have taken them for granted

others retained by the people." Long neglected in constitutional law, the amendment, as the essays by Paula Petrik and Sandra VanBurkleo explain, has emerged in the last quarter century as one of the most influential bases for the so-called right to privacy. Advocates of abortion, birth control, and women's rights, for example, have turned to it to claim constitutional protections nowhere explicitly mentioned in the Constitution. The Tenth Amendment has had a far longer and even more disputed history. Since 1791 proponents of state power have invoked its wording—"powers not delegated to the United States, are reserved to the States respectively, or to the people"—in a less-than-successful effort to blunt the seemingly ever increasing concentration of power in the national government.

Are the Ninth and Tenth amendments part of the Bill of Rights? Kermit L. Hall's essay on "Framing the Bill of Rights" concludes that they clearly are. James Madison, the architect of the Bill of Rights as well as the Constitution, viewed both amendments as critical to fashioning written guarantees that would protect individual rights against encroachment by the new national government. Madison appreciated that in a federal system these structural amendments complemented the substantive and procedural rights specifically guaranteed in the first eight amendments.

Substantive and Procedural rights

This division between substantive and procedural rights, while not hard and fast, clarifies the framers' larger goals in adopting the Bill of Rights. Several of the essays in this volume, such as those by Norman Rosenberg on freedom of speech and freedom of the press and that by Melvin I. Urofsky on freedom of religion, remind us that Madison and his colleagues were at considerable pains to declare certain substantive rights, such as political expression and individual religious belief. All of these rights, of course, were covered in the First Amendment, which also guaranteed freedom of assembly and petition. Other amendments have importance because they require the government to follow certain processes when it brings its power to bear against an individual. Those amendments protecting the rights of the accused (the Fourth, Fifth, Sixth, and Eighth) are good examples. Samuel Walker's essay on "Rights Before Trial" explains how the Fourth Amendment's prohibition against "unreasonable searches and seizures" limits the discretion of criminal justice officials. The Sixth Amendment, which David Bodenhamer's essay covers in detail, requires officials to inform suspects of the nature of the accusation against them as well as their right to "assistance of counsel." The Fifth Amendment not only contains a prohibition against compulsory self-incrimination, but as Gordon Bakken explains in his essay on property rights, it also provides that the federal government cannot take "life, liberty, or property without due process of law" and cannot take private property for "public use, without just compensation." When viewed collectively, these substantive and procedural guarantees bridle the national government. The Bill of Rights, as the historian Leonard Levy reminds us, was "a bill of restraints."[1]

Incorporation and the Scope of the Bill of Rights

Initially, the Bill of Rights was a limitation on the federal government only, but over the past two hundred years the scope of its coverage has broadened considerably. The most controversial aspect of the Bill of Rights still concerns its application to the states and not just the federal government.

The first phrase of the First Amendment clearly indicates the Bill of Rights was originally meant to limit the new, central government. It reads: "*Congress* shall make no law...." Although the word Congress does not appear anywhere else in the other nine amendments, there is little doubt that they were meant to apply only against the national government. James Madison's original proposal for what became the Bill of Rights did include a provision that made the most important of those rights—religion, press, and trial by jury in criminal cases—apply directly against the states. The Congress, however, rejected Madison's wording.

Yet no sooner had the amendments been added to the Constitution than several spokesmen, including Madison himself, proposed extending certain provisions of the Bill of Rights against the states. Chief Justice John Marshall first adjudicated the issue in *Barron v. Baltimore* (1833). The case involved a Baltimore program to construct and repair city streets that diverted certain streams from their natural courses. The new stream flows began to deposit sand and debris near a wharf owned by John Barron, making the water too shallow for ships to approach. Barron sued for damages and ultimately appealed to the Supreme Court on the grounds that the city's action violated the Fifth Amendment provision that private property could not be taken for public use "without just compensation." The question in *Barron* was whether the Fifth Amendment, and by extension all of the first ten amendments, restricted local and state governments as well as the nation. Marshall observed in what was his last constitutional opinion before leaving the bench that the question was "of great importance, but not of much difficulty."[2] The amendments, he said, speaking for a unanimous Supreme Court, were intended to prevent the "general government" from infringing the liberties of the people and could not be used to limit state power.

Marshall's important precedent stirred protest from antislav-

Barron v. Baltimore, 1833

ery advocates. From the 1830s until the Civil War, southern states outlawed speech and publication critical of slavery, while proslavery advocates in several northern states sought through violence and intimidation to silence abolitionist speakers and newspaper editors. Abolitionist lawyers countered these actions by claiming in both state and federal courts that the First Amendment protected the rights of American citizens comprehensively. These arguments fell on deaf judicial ears, as did later protests by Republican party leaders, immediately following the War but before passage of the Fourteenth Amendment, that southern state governments violated the federal Bill of Rights by denying newly freed African Americans, white Republicans, and loyal citizens basic rights to free speech and press, to due process, and to bear arms.

See Incorporation doctrine

The adoption of the Fourteenth Amendment in 1868 opened a new and controversial chapter in the relationship of the Bill of Rights to the states. It did so because it raised the specter of "incorporation." This is the legal practice or interpretation by which the various rights guaranteed in the Bill of Rights could be merged into the new amendment. The amendment made all persons born or naturalized in the United States *citizens* of the United States as well as the state in which they reside. Furthermore, it provided that *no state* should abridge the privileges and immunities of citizens or deny due process or equal protection of the laws to any person. Several Republican senators who managed the progress of the amendment in Congress argued that the privileges and immunities of citizens of the United States included rights named in the Bill of Rights. While no Senator or Congressman explicitly contradicted this view, some of them did adhere to the position that the Fourteenth Amendment produced only a limited transformation in American federalism, one that did not include, that is, incorporate, the Bill of Rights. The issue of incorporation received little attention in the state debates over ratification of the Fourteenth Amendment, and the discussion that did take place is inconclusive.

Privileges and immunities clause

Slaughter House Cases, 1873

The matter first appeared on the Supreme Court's docket in the famous *Slaughter House Cases* (1873). The justices had to decide whether the Louisiana legislature could grant a monopoly on slaughtering animals, thereby depriving some butchers in the city of New Orleans of their livelihood. The butchers claimed that the right to conduct a trade was a property right protected, in this case against the state of Louisiana, by the due process clause of the Fifth Amendment as incorporated through the Fourteenth Amendment. A majority of the Court, however, rejected this position; thereafter, the Court issued a line of decisions in which the justices stripped the Fourteenth Amendment's privileges and immunities clause of any significant meaning.

Due process

The Court pointed out the logical inconsistency of incorporating the Bill of Rights into the Fourteenth Amendment in *Hurtado v. California* (1884). The case involved the fate of Joseph Hurtado, a murderer sentenced to death in California, who claimed that he had been unconstitutionally tried because he had not been indicted, as the Fifth Amendment required, by a grand jury. Among the five provisions of the amendment are ones that set forth certain procedural requirements, including indictment by a grand jury; another, as discussed earlier, specifies that persons cannot be deprived of life, liberty, or property without due process of law. A majority of the justices rejected Hurtado's plea. They subscribed to the rule of statutory construction that provides that no part of a document is superfluous. Hence, due process in the Fourteenth Amendment meant something different from the specific guarantees in the Fifth Amendment. Yet, the Court also adopted the view that words have the same meaning throughout a document; therefore, due process had to mean the same thing in both the Fifth and the Fourteenth amendments. Stymied, the Court decided there was no way to include either the specific procedural guarantees of the Fifth Amendment or, for that matter, any other portion of the Bill of Rights under the due process clause of the Fourteenth Amendment.

Hurtado v. California, 1884

The Rise of Selective Incorporation

By the end of the nineteenth century, the justices began a slow retreat from the *Hurtado* precedent. The occasion for this change was the Court's tender feelings toward the property rights of business, which many of the justices believed were threatened as a result of state legislation designed to curb the excesses of rapid industrialization. The Illinois legislature, for example, passed an act that required railroads to assume the costs of constructing crossing facilities and maintaining a flagman there. A majority of the Court in *Chicago, Burlington, & Quincy Railroad Co. v. Chicago* (1897) sustained the Illinois statute, but at the same time the majority also observed that under the due process clause of the Fourteenth Amendment, rather than a specific provision of the Bill of Rights, private property could not be taken by a state without just compensation—the same limitation that was imposed on the federal government by the Fifth Amendment. The justices' action, in short, while upholding the state law, nonetheless indicated a practical correspondence between the Fourteenth Amendment and the Bill of Rights.

Chicago, Burlington & Quincy Railroad Co. v. Chicago, 1897

Conflicts over civil liberties during and after World War I added further momentum in this direction. The decisive case was *Gitlow v. New York* (1925). Benjamin Gitlow, a labor radical, claimed on appeal to the Supreme Court that his conviction un-

Gitlow v. New York, 1925

der a New York criminal anarchy statute denied him freedom of speech guaranteed by the First Amendment. The Court sustained the law, but in his majority opinion Justice Edward T. Sanford declared: "For the present purposes, we may and do assume that freedom of speech and of the press—which are protected by the First Amendment from abridgement by Congress—are among the fundamental personal rights and 'liberties' protected by the due process clause of the Fourteenth Amendment from impairment by the states."[3] The Court adopted this position because it was determined to uphold the New York state law, which the conservative justices believed was essential to quelling labor upheaval. If it had embraced the view that the First Amendment was not incorporated through and under the Fourteenth Amendment, then it would not have had jurisdiction to hear the case to begin with.

Shortly thereafter the process of selective incorporation began. The Court in 1931 actually incorporated the First Amendment into the due process clause of the Fourteenth Amendment in *Stromberg* v. *California*. The justices voided a California statute as a violation of free speech which prohibited the display of a red flag as an emblem of anarchism and opposition to organized government. In the same year, the Court in *Near* v. *Minnesota* held unconstitutional a Minnesota statute providing for the suppression of any malicious, scandalous, or defamatory newspaper publication. A year later, in *Powell* v. *Alabama*, the justices for the first time included one of the criminal procedure guarantees of the Bill of Rights under the Fourteenth Amendment's due process clause. The justices held that the refusal of the state of Alabama to grant African American boys convicted of raping two white girls access to counsel violated their right to counsel under the Sixth Amendment.

The Court in 1937 added still another twist to the development of the selective incorporation doctrine. In *Palko* v. *Connecticut*, the justices upheld the retrial of Frank Palko for first degree murder after the prosecution had successfully overturned his second degree murder conviction before the Connecticut Supreme Court. Palko claimed that his trial and conviction a second time violated the double jeopardy provision of the Fifth Amendment. Justice Benjamin Cardozo, writing for the majority, sustained the second conviction by drawing a distinction between provisions of the Bill of Rights which had been (and could be) incorporated under the Fourteenth Amendment because they were "fundamental principles of liberty and justice which lie at the base of all our civil and political institutions" and all other rights which, while certainly important, were not essential to a scheme of "ordered liberty."[4] Since freedom of speech and press, according to Cardozo, were critical to the enjoyment of all other liberties, they

Stromberg v. California, 1931

Near v. Minnesota, 1931

Powell v. Alabama, 1932

Palko v. Connecticut, 1937

Double jeopardy

were incorporated into the due process clause of the Fourteenth Amendment. But most other provisions, especially those dealing with the rights of the accused, were not. In those instances, the states were free to disregard them.

The Almost Total Incorporation of the Bill of Rights

Cardozo's scheme of selective incorporation held sway for the next three decades despite constant pressure to nationalize the Bill of Rights. Justice Hugo L. Black, for example, argued repeatedly that the historical evidence surrounding passage of the Fourteenth Amendment showed conclusively that the framers of that amendment meant it to incorporate all of the Bill of Rights. Black staked out his position most fully in *Adamson* v. *California* (1948). Admiral Dewey Adamson was convicted of murder after a summation by the state prosecutor which, under a practice then permitted in California, called attention to the defendant's failure to take the stand in his own defense. The majority of the Court affirmed the conviction, but Black and three other justices dissented. Some of the justices who voted with Black went even further than he did, arguing that the due process clause of the Fourteenth Amendment included any right deemed to be fundamental, even if it was not enumerated in the Bill of Rights. This position, known as incorporation plus, meant that the justices could essentially read into the Constitution certain implied or inherent rights, even ones rooted in natural law. Black, who argued for a literal interpretation, rejected this kind of construction of the Constitution. If a right was not written down in the document, Black argued, it could not be utilized, but if it was spelled out then its command was absolute.

Adamson v. California, 1948

Scholars and a majority of the Court attacked Black's formulation as constitutionally unsound and historically inaccurate. Led by Justice Felix Frankfurter, they insisted that total incorporation would undermine a valuable feature of American federalism—the opportunity for each state to secure rights in the way best suited to its peculiar social and political circumstances. According to Frankfurter, the rights absorbed into the Fourteenth Amendment were merely similar to those listed in the Bill of Rights.

Despite this opposition, the process of selective incorporation has been so extensive that much of what Black hoped to achieve has, in fact, been accomplished. (See table.) The process gained impetus while Earl Warren was Chief Justice (1953–1969), especially in the area of criminal procedure, where the Court has historically been the most reluctant to apply incorporation. In *Mapp* v. *Ohio* (1961), for example, the Court finally applied full

Mapp v. Ohio, 1961

INTRODUCTION

Gideon v. Wainwright, 1963

Fourth Amendment protection involving illegal searches and seizures as extended to the states through the Fourteenth Amendment. Two years later, in *Gideon v. Wainwright*, the justices applied the full assistance-of-counsel clause of the Sixth Amendment to the states. Thereafter, selective incorporation of most of the rest of the Bill of Rights became the wave of the future.

The following major Bill of Rights provisions have been incorporated, in addition to those provisions discussed earlier that were incorporated in the 1920s and 1930s. The states are now constitutionally bound to observe the provisions involving:

1947	– separation of church and state	1964	– self-incrimination
1948	– public trial	1965	– additional but unspecified rights contained in the Ninth Amendment
1961	– unreasonable (but not reasonable) searches and seizures	1966	– trial by an impartial jury
1962	– cruel and unusual punishments	1967	– speedy trial
1963	– counsel in *all* criminal cases	1968	– trial by jury in all criminal cases
		1969	– double jeopardy

Since 1969 no further provisions of the Bill of Rights have been incorporated, and current Chief Justice William H. Rehnquist has shown little enthusiasm for doing more. Those provisions that remain unincorporated are: 1) grand jury indictment (Fifth Amendment), 2) trial by jury in civil cases (Seventh Amendment), 3) the excessive bail and fines prohibitions (Eighth Amendment), 4) the right to bear arms (Second Amendment), and 5) the safeguard against involuntary quartering of troops in private homes (Third Amendment).

Conservative jurists and politicians during the 1980s continued to attack the incorporation doctrine. They complained that the practice of incorporation was inconsistent with the wishes of the framers of the Constitution. Those framers, they argue, wanted to leave the states with a significant degree of discretion to protect the rights of their citizens. Former Attorney General Edwin Meese, who served during the administration of President Ronald Reagan, was the leading opponent of incorporation. The Reagan appointees to the Supreme Court, moreover, have shown little inclination to expand further the scope of federal protection for rights. Generally protected by the Supreme Court, the Bill of Rights seems secure but unlikely to undergo further expansion in the near future.

State Bills of Rights

Yet developments in the states suggest a somewhat different trend. Throughout most of American history, citizens have had

to rely on the protection of state bills of rights rather than that of the federal Constitution. The judges of many of the highest state courts of appeal have demonstrated a willingness to extend certain rights well beyond the scope of the federal Bill of Rights. Under the Supremacy Clause of Article VI, state courts are bound to interpret the Bill of Rights in the same way as the Supreme Court. But a number of state courts have given a more expansive interpretation of state bill-of-rights provisions that parallel similar clauses in the federal document, thereby providing additional protection to their citizens. Since 1969 more than 400 decisions by the highest appellate courts of the states have done exactly that. The United States Supreme Court, moreover, has accepted this practice so long as the state courts root their opinions entirely on independent state grounds—that is, on state law or state constitutions. While the federal Bill of Rights, as interpreted by the Supreme Court, has become a sort of national floor for rights, state bills of rights and state judicial interpretation of those bills of rights have become the ceiling. The states, of course, can increase the scope of rights but they cannot reduce them.

Interpreting the Bill of Rights

There can be little doubt that both America and the Bill of Rights have changed since 1791. As the essay by Paul Finkelman on the rights of African Americans and Paula Petrik on women's rights argue, neither of these groups enjoyed anything like full constitutional protection at the birth of the Bill of Rights. Today, of course, while racism and sexism remain, the formal legal structure is much different. There is broad agreement today that this expansion of rights to groups previously excluded is worthwhile, but there is also continuing debate about the role that justices of the Supreme Court should play in bringing about that change. How, in short, should the justices interpret the Bill of Rights as it enters its third century? Given the changes in our geographical size, population, and ethnic and racial diversity, is it practical to suppose that rights have the same meaning today that they did two-hundred years ago?

The evolution of the Bill of Rights in the hands of the Supreme Court of the United States, as the essays in this volume indicate, has generated considerable controversy. Lawrence Cress's study of the origins and development of the right to bear arms nicely illustrates how eighteenth-century words can take on a different meaning when placed in a twentieth-century context. As one reads this and the other essays, one needs to be aware of the broad outlines of the continuing controversy over how to interpret the Bill of Rights, since that debate relates to the authority of

the states . . . can increase the scope of rights but they cannot reduce them

justices to do what they have historically done—to protect various kinds of rights from governmental interference. On the one side are the "originalists," perhaps best represented by Edwin Meese. In 1985 he made an influential speech before the American Bar Association in which he urged the justices to interpret rights in such a way as to take account of what the framers of the Constitution originally intended. Meese was particularly critical of the broad expansion of rights carried out through the incorporation doctrine while Earl Warren was Chief Justice. "Under the old system," Meese quipped, "the question was *how* to read the Constitution; under the new approach, the question is *whether* to read the Constitution."[5] He urged the justices to adhere closely to the text of the Constitution, including the Bill of Rights, and to employ a jurisprudence of "original intention." As the scholar Murry Dry has noted, for "Attorney General Meese and his supporters, the choice is between courts that say what the law is, which is their job, and courts that make law and policy, which is the job of legislatures."[6] By adhering to the wishes of the framers and by being bound by the words of the document itself, the true meaning of rights would be developed.

Meese's originalism has drawn a strong counterattack from the other, nonoriginalist school of constitutional interpretation. Former Supreme Court Justice William Brennan, for example, insisted that justices had to be actively engaged in protecting individual rights and insuring that political and social minorities were not ruthlessly subjected to majority will. Brennan claims that the historical record is invariably obscure and subject to differing interpretations. Reliance on the words of the Bill of Rights are only partially helpful, moreover, since they are broadly stated generalities rather than crisp commands, a condition that the framers of the Bill of Rights and the Constitution intentionally fostered. Finally, Brennan argues that the framers intended that the authority of law would be pitted against the will of popular majorities as a way of protecting minority rights. Thus, judges must take an active role in interpreting rights in their contemporary context. For Justice Brennan, "the choice is between being ruled by the dead hand of the past or the living present."[7]

Conclusion

The essays that follow raise this interpretive issue again and again. The reader should reflect not just on the ways in which the substantive and procedural guarantees of the Bill of Rights have worked, but the ways in which the justices of the high court have given meaning to them. Throughout, this question should be asked: How do we expect rights to be protected? Because, as all of these essays reveal, the real test of how well the Bill of Rights

"Under the old system," Meese quipped, "the question was *how* to read the Constitution; under the new approach, the question is *whether* to read the Constitution."

KERMIT L. HALL

has restrained government is not in its words but in the way in which it has been put into action. Government, the framers of the Bill of Rights believed, was an instrument of man, "its sovereignty held in subordination to his rights."[8] The Bill of Rights, therefore, means that the individual citizen is free to the extent that government is not.

Notes

[1]Leonard W. Levy, *Constitutional Opinions: Aspects of the Bill of Rights* (New York: Oxford University Press, 1986), p. 131.

[2]*Barron v. Baltimore*, 32 U.S. 254 (1833).

[3]*Gitlow v. New York*, 268 U.S. 665 (1925).

[4]*Palko v. Connecticut*, 302 U.S. 328 (1937).

[5]As quoted in Murry Dry, "Federalism and the Constitution: The Founders' Design and Contemporary Constitutional Law," *Constitutional Commentary* 4 (1987): 234.

[6]Ibid.

[7]Ibid.

[8]Levy, *Constitutional Opinions*, p. 134.

Cases

Adamson v. California, 322 U.S. 46 (1948). A deeply divided Supreme Court rejected Justice Hugo Black's vision of total incorporation of the Bill of Rights through the due process clause of the Fourteenth Amendment.

Barron v. Baltimore, 7 Peters 243 (1833). John Marshall for a unanimous Court held that the Bill of Rights applied only against the national government and not the states.

Chicago, Burlington, & Quincy Railroad Co. v. Chicago, 166 U.S. 226 (1897). An almost unanimous Supreme Court upheld an Illinois statute which required railroads to assume costs of constructing crossing facilities and maintaining flagmen, as reasonable exercises of the police power. But the Court also provided that certain individual property rights might be protected through the Fourteenth Amendment against interference by state legislatures.

Gideon v. Wainwright, 372 U.S. 335 (1963). Relying on the equal protection clause of the Fourteenth Amendment, a unanimous court held that counsel should be appointed for indigent defendants in criminal proceedings.

Gitlow v. New York, 268 U.S. 652 (1925). The Court sustained a New York state criminal anarchy statute at the same time that it accepted the proposition that the First Amendment guarantees of free speech extended through the Fourteenth Amendment to the states.

Hurtado v. California, 110 U.S. 516 (1884). The Supreme Court refused to incorporate the Fifth Amendment guarantees for the rights of the accused by means of the due process clause of the Fourteenth Amendment.

Mapp v. Ohio, 367 U.S. 643 (1961). Held that the constitutional guarantees against illegal search and seizure in the Fourth Amendment extended to the state of Ohio through the Fourteenth Amendment.

Near v. Minnesota, 283 U.S. 697 (1931). Through the incorporation of the First into the Fourteenth Amendment, the Supreme Court invalidated a Minnesota law authorizing the closing of publications alleged to be guilty of false charges against public officials.

Palko v. Connecticut, 302 U.S. 319 (1937). A nearly unanimous Supreme Court upheld a state law providing for a second trial in a criminal case, where the second conviction resulted in a more severe sentence, as not double jeopardy under state law where it might be under the Bill of Rights. Only those parts of the Bill of Rights essential to ordered liberty were incorporated under the Fourteenth Amendment.

Powell v. Alabama, 287 U.S. 45 (1932). A divided Supreme Court held in one of the "Scottsboro cases" that the right to counsel in felony cases was guaranteed to defendants under the Fourteenth Amendment.

Slaughter House Cases, 16 Wallace 36 (1873). A divided Supreme Court rejected the view that the Fourteenth Amendment extended its protection to all of the privileges and immunities of citizens.

Stromberg v. California, 283 U.S. 359 (1931). The Court invalidated a California "red flag" statute as unconstitutionally denying to American citizens the right to freedom of expression, including unpopular radical opinions and symbols.

Suggested Readings

Raoul Berger, *Government by Judiciary: The Transformation of the Fourteenth Amendment* (Cambridge: Harvard University Press, 1977). A critical attack on the proposition that the framers of the Fourteenth Amendment meant to incorporate the Bill of Rights.

KERMIT L. HALL

Berger argues, as well, that the modern Supreme Court has played fast and loose with the Bill of Rights by failing to take proper account of what its framers intended its scope to be.

Richard C. Cortner, *The Supreme Court and the Second Bill of Rights: The Fourteenth Amendment and the Nationalization of the Bill of Rights* (Madison: University of Wisconsin Press, 1981). The best analysis of the development of the incorporation doctrine and its implications for judicial power and liberty. A required book for anyone even remotely interested in the subject.

Michael Kent Curtis, *No State Shall Abridge: The Fourteenth Amendment and the Bill of Rights* (Durham, N.C.: Duke University Press, 1966). An excellent analysis of the question of whether or not the framers of the Fourteenth Amendment meant to incorporate the Bill of Rights. Curtis believes that they did.

Daniel A. Farber and Suzanna Sherry, eds., *A History of the American Constitution* (St. Paul, Minn.: West Publishing Company, 1990). A collection of primary materials with commentary by the editors, the final section of which provides an excellent introduction to the complex issues of original understanding, judicial activism, and the Bill of Rights.

Leonard Levy, *Constitutional Opinions: Aspects of the Bill of Rights* (New York: Oxford University Press, 1986). A series of brilliant essays that boldly support the idea that judges have a responsibility to protect individual liberty through an expansive reading of the Bill of Rights.

Herbert McClosky and Alida Brill, *Dimensions of Tolerance: What Americans Believe About Civil Liberties* (New York: Russell Sage Foundation, 1983). A fine analysis of contemporary attitudes toward civil liberties, which concludes that it is easier to teach intolerance than tolerance.

Paul L. Murphy, *The Constitution in Crisis Times, 1918–1969* (New York: Harper & Row, 1972). A fine synthesis of Bill-of-Rights developments during the twentieth century.

I

Kermit L. Hall

FRAMING THE BILL OF RIGHTS

Liberty Prior to the Constitution

The framers of the Bill of Rights in 1789 believed that the power of government was and would continue to be a constant threat to individual liberty. The events leading to the American Revolution and later the struggle over ratification of the federal Constitution had taught them precisely that lesson, but so too did English constitutional history, the common law tradition, colonial experience with self-government, and the development of state bills of rights during the American Revolution. In short, the decision to add a bill of rights to the Constitution echoed an already well-established American practice of using written documents to protect fundamental and inalienable rights.

This tradition of liberty stretched back to at least 1215, when the English barons had forced King John to sign the Magna Carta or Great Charter. That document applied only to the barons rather than to the English population as a whole, and most of its provisions clarified the feudal rights and duties that bound the king and the barons to one another. In this sense, the Magna Carta differed from modern bills of rights which succinctly enumerate a broad range of rights. Nonetheless, the Magna Carta did include provisions that guaranteed certain rights in the criminal justice process, the most notable of which was trial by a jury of one's peers. This tradition of protecting the rights of the accused was further amplified in the English Bill of Rights of 1689,

...the power of government was and would continue to be a constant threat to individual liberty

which Parliament passed in the wake of the Glorious Revolution. The Bill of Rights broadened the scope of the Magna Carta by extending the protection of rights to the English population as a whole and by adding provisions that prohibited standing armies in time of peace, protected the right to petition the king, and offered a limited form of freedom of speech. It also strengthened and extended the protections afforded the accused by providing that bail would not be excessive, that punishments would be neither cruel nor unusual, and that excessive fines would not be imposed. Taken together, therefore, the Magna Carta and the English Bill of Rights formed an important part of the colonists' inheritance of liberty.

The English common law was a second source for colonial American rights. The common law was "common" because it spread throughout England, not because it served the lower social orders. It had a customary quality that evolved from its day-to-day application in royal and local courts in England. Unlike their counterparts in French and Spanish settlements in America, English colonists were full citizens, which allowed them to claim protection of the common law. English authorities in the mid-eighteenth century, in an ultimately futile effort to keep the empire intact, insisted that the common law did not extend to the colonists, but by then the colonists had already selectively absorbed common law principles into their legal culture. This common law tradition, even more than the Magna Carta, produced the core idea that informed colonial understanding about rights: everyone was to be subjected to the same legal processes. As with the Magna Carta, the common law stressed the rights of the accused: the right to trial by a jury; the right to a speedy trial; prohibition of bills of attainder, *ex post facto* laws, and cruel and unusual punishment; and the guarantee of *habeas corpus*. But the common law also protected the rights of widows and the poor, the right to compensation for the taking of private property, and the understanding that a judge would not sit in judgment of any case in which he had an interest.

Bills of Attainder
Ex post facto
Habeas corpus

The colonists sought to prevent imperial encroachment on many of these rights by putting them into writing. The results were documents that functioned as charters of liberty. The Massachusetts Body of Liberties (1641), for example, codified and summarized legislation passed during the previous twenty years and added a few additional liberties. For all intents and purposes this was the first bill of rights in American history, even though its provisions were sandwiched into a regular law code. In Pennsylvania, William Penn, who had endured the hardships of political persecution in England, helped to fashion the Charter of Liberties (1682) and the Frame of Government (1682), both of which protected the rights of colonists from governmental inter-

the core idea that informed colonial understanding about rights: everyone was to be subjected to the same legal processes

vention. A year later, the colony of New York adopted a Charter of Liberties and Privileges.

The colonial experience with written protections for rights paved the way for the creation of state bills of rights during the American Revolution. Most of the political leaders who launched the states on their new course doubted the wisdom of resting individual rights solely upon the common law. They wanted, instead, more explicit protections in writing that would be backed by the force of constitutional sanction. The most important event in this process was the adoption by Virginia, the most powerful of the colonies and one of the leaders in the movement toward revolution, of a Declaration of Rights in 1776. Written by George Mason, the Declaration contained sixteen articles, nine of which contained basic principles of a free republic (human equality, popular sovereignty, right of revolution, majority rule, separation of powers, subordination of military to civil authority, and recurrence to fundamental principles[1]) and the other seven of which enumerated the rights of citizens, including a right of religious belief added at the insistence of a youthful James Madison. The Virginia Declaration of Rights provided lawmakers in other states with a handy model that they altered to suit their own circumstances.

Like the Virginia Declaration of Rights, the other state bills of rights usually appeared in a separate section that preceded their constitution. This disjunction between the listing of rights and the organization of government itself left open the question of whether the bills of rights were part of the ruling document. Moreover, before 1798 most state legislatures promulgated these bills of rights without any form of popular ratification, a practice that raised doubts about whether the documents could limit the legislative bodies that created them. In practice, however, these first bills of rights did act as powerful restraints, principally because they read as *declarations* rather than *enactments* of rights. That distinction meant that the specified rights were drawn from a fundamental source that made them inherent, inalienable, and self-evident. Such rights were beyond the reach of government.

Congress itself supplied a final precedent for the Bill of Rights through the Northwest Ordinance of 1787, the first federal document to contain a bill of rights. The Ordinance outlined the process by which territories would become states, and among these were requirements that the new territories and later states would respect the rights of their citizens. To extend "the fundamental principles of civil and religious liberty," Congress included articles that guaranteed territorial inhabitants habeas corpus, trial by jury, representative government, judicial proceedings according to the common law, and just compensation for private property taken for a public purpose. The ordinance also pro-

...the specified rights were drawn from a fundamental source that made them inherent, inalienable, and self-evident

tected private contracts, outlawed sex discrimination in land ownership, banned slavery, and established religious liberty.

The importance of this early American tradition of linking rights and fundamental law is readily apparent in the federal Bill of Rights. The first ten amendments to the federal Constitution contain twenty-seven separate rights. Six of these rights, or about 20 percent, first appeared in the Magna Carta. Twenty-one, or about 75 percent, had their initial formulation in colonial documents written before the 1689 English Bill of Rights. Even more impressive, all but the Ninth Amendment could be found in several of the state constitutions written between 1776 and 1787. The framers of the Bill of Rights, while certainly a part of the stream of English legal history, drew most fully from their own experience rather than simply recapitulating rights from the Magna Carta, the common law, and the English Bill of Rights.

The Question of Rights in the Constitutional Convention

The framers of the Constitution in 1787 worried incessantly about protecting liberty from encroaching governmental power, but most of them concluded that a separate bill of rights was unnecessary. The issue was first formally raised in the Constitutional Convention on August 20, when Charles Pinckney of South Carolina submitted a plan for consideration by the Committee on Detail. Pinckney's plan included provisions aimed at insuring the liberty of the press, keeping troops from being quartered in time of peace, and prohibiting religious tests for holding public office. Pinckney's ideas were rejected by both the Committee on Detail and later by the Committee on Style. In some measure, the lateness with which they were presented created difficulties. But even more important, several of the most prominent figures in the convention believed that they were superfluous. James Madison, for example, argued that since the Constitution was one of strictly enumerated powers, the federal government was necessarily prevented from passing legislation that would trample individual rights.

Madison's position, however, did not soothe the concerns of those delegates already opposed to the work of the convention. On September 12, only a few days before the convention adjourned, George Mason of Virginia, who would refuse to sign the Constitution, and Elbridge Gerry of Massachusetts raised the issue once again, but without success. Two days later Pinckney moved "to insert a declaration 'that the liberty of the Press should be inviolably observed.' "[2] Roger Sherman of Connecticut countered that such a provision was "unnecessary" because the "power of Congress does not extend to the Press."[3] With the defeat of that proposal, Gerry and Mason headed off in another direction, hoping to persuade the Convention to agree to amend the ratification procedure to permit the state ratifying conventions to propose amendments which would be decided upon by a second general convention. That motion lost as well.

The absence of a bill of rights complicated significantly the process of ratifying the new Constitution. Within hours of the delegates signing the Constitution, George Mason published a pamphlet entitled "Objections to this Constitution of Government," the central theme of which was that the absence of a "declaration of rights" made the Constitution unacceptable. Without limitations, Mason believed, the federal government would infringe the basic rights of the citizenry. "[T]he laws of the general government," Mason warned, "being paramount to the law and constitution of the several States, the Declarations of Rights in the separate States are no security."[4]

These arguments were picked up by the Antifederalist opponents of the Constitution and repeated throughout the state ratification debates. For ten months the overriding political question in America was whether the new constitution would be ratified and the chief impediment to its acceptance was the lack of a bill of rights. Beginning with the Massachusetts ratifying convention in February 1788, the Antifederalist succeeded in putting the Federalist supporters of the document on the defensive. Thomas Jefferson, who was in Paris at the time, applauded the new constitution, but he expressed disappointment to his friend James Madison that the document did not include "a bill of rights providing clearly & without the aid of sophisms" for the civil rights Americans had come to believe was their birthright.[5]

While the federal convention had withheld from the ratifying conventions the power to propose amendments, the conventions adopted the tactic of offering "recommendatory amendments." The issue of a bill of rights was particularly important in the crucial states of New York and Virginia. In the latter, Alexander Hamilton tried to hold the line against any addition of a bill of rights, observing to the delegates in that state's ratifying convention that the Constitution was one of delegated powers, hence, "why declare that things shall not be done which there is no power to do?"[6] But such logic proved unpersuasive, and other Federalist leaders such as James Madison quickly realized that without some accommodation the possibility existed that the entire document might not gain ratification. Madison, therefore, took the lead in urging the ratifying conventions to offer "recommendatory alterations."[7]

Madison was impressed by the strength of demands in his home state for the addition of a bill of rights, which was the one issue that seemed to coalesce the various opponents of the Con-

the absence of a bill of rights complicated significantly the process of ratifying the new Constitution

stitution. Virginia, like New York, voted to ratify the Constitution, but both state conventions did so with the proviso that the first Congress would consider the addition of a bill of rights. In essence, the Federalists in general and Madison in particular had gained ratification by promising to address the issue of a bill of rights later. To keep his promise, however, Madison had to secure a seat in the federal Congress. He originally planned to serve in the Senate, but his old political nemesis, Patrick Henry, arranged for the Virginia legislature to select two Antifederalist senators. Madison then won a close race against James Monroe for a seat in the House of Representatives. As part of his campaign, Madison pledged support for a bill of rights.

The Congressional Debates over the Bill of Rights

When the first Congress met, seven state conventions had submitted demands for amendments as a condition of their ratification. What forced the Congress to take these demands seriously was the continuing threat of a second constitutional convention. On May 5, 1789, Virginia submitted an application to Congress for just such a convention, and New York followed with a similar application the next day. Moreover, two states, North Carolina and Rhode Island, refused to ratify the Constitution at all.

James Madison's initial attempt on June 8 to propose the adoption of a bill of rights received mixed reviews. In part the members of Congress were anxious to get the new government up and running, and the organization of the judicial branch, the fixing of taxes and tariffs, and the establishment of the armed forces seemed much more important than dealing with a bill of rights. Some of the strongest opposition to Madison's call for a bill of rights came from the Antifederalist critics of the Constitution, who now worried that the adoption of a bill of rights would secure the strong central government that they did not want. By 1791, therefore, political positions on the issue had been reversed, with the Federalists convinced that only through the addition of a bill of rights would it be possible to preserve the new union.

Madison's original proposal, which borrowed liberally from the Virginia Declaration of Rights, listed nine amendments that ran to some twenty-six paragraphs. Madison's proposal began by affirming the people as the source of all power and asserting that government was bound to offer its citizens life, liberty, the right to acquire property, and the right to pursue "happiness and safety."[8] The next set of amendments drew heavily from state bills of rights, since they held out guarantees of freedom of religion, speech, press, peaceable assembly, petition for grievances, the right to bear arms, and a disavowal of the quartering of troops in

"why declare that things shall not be done which there is no power to do?"

peacetime. Thereafter, Madison listed the most extensive part of his proposal, which dealt with the rights of the accused. These included double jeopardy, self-incrimination, the due process of law in matters involving both life and property, excessive bail, searches and seizures, speedy public trials, confrontation by accusers, and aids to accused persons in need of witnesses or counsel. Madison also provided that the absence of a right from the list "shall not be so construed as to diminish the just importance of other rights retained by the people or...enlarge the powers delegated by the constitution."[9] While these declarations of rights applied only against the federal government, Madison also included a provision that "[n]o State shall violate the equal rights of conscience, or the freedom of the press, or the trial by jury in criminal cases."[10] Madison also provided for grand juries and trial by jury when the amount in controversy exceeded a certain sum. Criminal trials were to be held in the vicinity of the crime and to be heard by an impartial jury. Madison also retained for the people a right to a jury trial in common law, noncriminal cases. Madison closed with two provisions: one called for keeping the legislative, executive, and judicial branches separate; the other declared that all powers neither delegated elsewhere nor prohibited to the states should remain reserved to the states.

One of the key arguments advanced by Madison was that the Bill of Rights would offer additional *legal* protection against excessive legislative power. Since these guarantees would go into the Constitution, Madison believed that "independent tribunals of justice will consider themselves in a peculiar manner the guardians of those rights."[11] Madison intended that the newly created federal courts would protect individual rights against the popular branches of government.

After more than a month, a House select committee composed of one member from each state began to deliberate Madison's proposals. We know little about the actual workings of this committee, although the product of its labors was quite similar to what Madison had proposed, indicating that Madison played a critical part in the committee's drafting process. Roger Sherman, from Connecticut and a member of the Committee, prepared his own draft bill of rights, which paralleled Madison's but differed in several noteworthy ways. Sherman's draft prohibited Congress from granting monopolies, and it also contained natural rights language similar to the early state declarations of rights. An even more important difference was that Sherman wanted to place the amendments as separate articles following the already ratified Constitution, with each of the amendments standing alone as an independent provision. Sherman argued that the ratified Constitution embodied the will of the people and that will established the sole authority to amend the document. Hence, no changes

Madison believed that "independent tribunals of justice will consider themselves in a peculiar manner the guardians of those rights"

KERMIT L. HALL

could be made in the body of the Constitution; instead, amendments could only be added to it. Madison disagreed. He thought that by inserting the new amendments in the already existing Constitution there would be no "unfavorable comparisons" between the original document and subsequent amendments. Sherman's opposition against interlineation ultimately prevailed, and the amendments were added separately following the Constitution's main body. The House formally approved the committee's report on August 24, 1789.

The Senate made few substantive changes in the House Committee report. Senators altered the apportionment article and rejected the article that would have extended the most important provisions of the Bill of Rights against the states. The Senate also rejected the article requiring strict separation of powers in the national government and language protecting conscientious objectors from having to serve in the military. The most important debates in the Senate turned on what eventually became the First Amendment. Several alternative wordings were presented and rejected, before the Senate amended the House version to read: "Congress shall make no law establishing articles of faith, or a mode of worship, or prohibiting the free exercise of religion."[12]

A conference committee resolved the differences between the House and Senate versions and arranged the amendments in the order they were eventually sent to the states. The first amendment dealt with reapportionment of the legislature, the second with legislative salaries, and then the other ten which became the Bill of Rights. The committee changed the reapportionment article to limit the ultimate number of representatives to not more than one for every fifty thousand people. Criminal defendants were entitled to not only a speedy and public trial, but to one by "an impartial jury" in the district where the crime was committed. Finally, the conference committee agreed on the wording of what would become the First Amendment.

Ratification

President George Washington on October 2, 1789, transmitted twelve proposed amendments to the states, but nearly two years passed before ten of these amendments became part of the nation's fundamental law. Even though the records of the state legislative debates over ratification of the proposed amendments are almost nonexistent, we know that the outcome was never in doubt. Rhode Island (July 7, 1790) and North Carolina (December 22, 1789) ratified the amendments in order that they could become full members of the Union. Antifederalists in Virginia put up strong resistance. Senator William Grayson of that state

the most important debates in the Senate turned on what eventually became the First Amendment

wrote to Patrick Henry that the proposed amendments were "good for nothing...and will do more harm than benefit."[13] Grayson and Henry continued to urge the calling of a second constitutional convention in the hope of shoring-up state government in the face of increasing federal power. But on December 15, 1791, Virginia became the eleventh state to ratify the first ten amendments, thereby fulfilling the constitutional requirement that three-quarters of the states approve amendments to the Constitution.

Except for Virginia, we know almost nothing about the state ratification process. The states kept few records of their ratification debates; only the simple recording of votes is available today. We know, however, that there were important objections to two of the amendments, one dealing with a fixed schedule apportioning seats in the House of Representatives and the other prohibiting senators and representatives from altering their salaries until an election of members of the House had intervened. Neither of these dealt with personal rights. The first was rejected because the apportionment formula appeared to disadvantage several of the most important states; the second dropped by the way because its wording provided that sitting senators, with six year terms, could have their salaries raised after an election for members of the House, which occurred every two years.

The states of Massachusetts, Georgia, and Connecticut failed to ratify the new Bill of Rights once Virginia's legislature acted. In the case of Massachusetts the matter seems to have been a clerical error, since that state's legislature never formally enacted a bill signifying assent although both of its houses had voted in favor of it. At the time, legislators in Connecticut and Georgia thought that further action on their parts was unnecessary. All three states in 1939, the 150th anniversary of the creation of the Bill of Rights, added their symbolic ratifications.

Conclusion

The Bill of Rights resulted from the rich mixing of English history, practical colonial experience, and the tough political realities of winning broad support for the new Constitution. It was also a product of the social system of the framers, none of whom seriously believed that its protections extended to African Americans, Native Americans, and even white women. Yet it would be wrong to view the Bill of Rights as politically expedient, racist, and sexist. To the contrary, Madison's handiwork bequeathed a legacy of freedom the envy of the rest of the world because it anchored individual liberty in written constitutional guarantees that could be protected by an independent judiciary. Initially, of course, Madison hoped for amendments that would harness not

Madison's handiwork bequeathed a legacy of freedom the envy of the rest of the world

KERMIT L. HALL

only federal but state power; instead, he and the other framers settled on a genuinely federal system of protecting individual rights. Together, state and federal bills of rights formed an umbrella of protection for most citizens in which the states rather than the federal government initially had the foremost responsibility for protecting the day-to-day rights of citizens.

Since 1791, of course, America has changed and so too has the Bill of Rights. Once a document intended to protect citizens exclusively from encroachment by the federal government, it has become since the adoption of the Fourteenth Amendment in 1868 a powerful—and controversial—limit on the states as well.

Yet for all of the changes, a constant thread runs from the past to the present. The generation that fought the Revolution, framed the Constitution, and fashioned the Bill of Rights understood that human freedom was so precious that it had to be protected from government and that an enlightened and responsible citizenry would jealously guard that freedom. While we can never know for certain exactly what the framers of these amendments meant them to do, it seems clear that they believed that in the enduring struggle between individual liberty and governmental power, the former was much more likely to prevail if each succeeding generation could resort to the Bill of Rights. Today, therefore, we should appreciate that one of the most enduring legacies of the Bill of Rights is the responsibility it bequeaths to each new generation to maintain individual liberty.

Notes

[1] Recurrence to fundamental principles means that to be successful a republic must constantly refer back to certain ideals of equality and freedom. One of the purposes of early bills of rights was to emphasize and restate these principles. Such principles, of course, were beyond the reach of government to alter.

[2] Max Farrand, ed., *Records of the Federal Convention*, 4 vols. (New Haven: Yale University Press, 1966), 2: 617–18.

[3] Ibid.

[4] As quoted in Robert A. Rutland, *The Birth of the Bill of Rights, 1776–1791* (Boston: Northeastern University Press, 1983), p. 120.

[5] Ibid., p. 129

[6] Clinton Rossiter, ed., *The Federalist Papers* (New York: New American Library, 1961), p. 513.

[7] James Madison to Edmund Randolph, April 10, 1788, in William T. Hutchinson et al., eds., *The Papers of James Madison*, 16 vols. to date (Charlottesville: University of Virginia Press, 1962–), 11: 19.

[8]Daniel A. Farber and Suzanna Sherry, eds., *A History of the American Constitution* (St. Paul, Minn.: West Publishing Company, 1990), p. 228.

[9]Ibid., p. 230.

[10]Ibid., p. 228.

[11]Ibid., p. 230.

[12]Ibid., p. 242.

[13]As quoted in Robert A. Rutland, "Framing and Ratifying the First Ten Amendments," in *The Framing and Ratification of the Constitution*, eds., Leonard W. Levy and Dennis J. Mahoney (New York: Macmillan Publishing Company, 1987), p. 315.

Suggested Readings

Willi Paul Adams, *The First American Constitutions* (Chapel Hill: University of North Carolina Press, 1980). Adams explains the important connection in late eighteenth-century America between individual liberty and state constitutions. The book is particularly useful when read in conjunction with Dumbauld and Rutland below.

Edward Dumbauld, *The Bill of Rights and What It Means Today* (Norman: University of Oklahoma Press, 1957). A valuable guide to the various state proposals, Madison's plan for the Bill of Rights, and its connection to the English Bill of Rights.

Leonard W. Levy, *Origins of the Fifth Amendment* (New York: Oxford University Press, 1968). Levy dissects the history of one of the most important parts of the Bill of Rights, revealing in the process the interaction of law and politics.

Donald S. Lutz, *The Origins of American Constitutionalism* (Baton Rouge: Louisiana State University Press, 1988). A brilliant discussion of the role of the Magna Carta and the common law in development of early American constitutionalism and the Bill of Rights.

Robert A. Rutland, *The Birth of the Bill of Rights, 1776–1791*, Classic Edition (Boston: Northeastern University Press, 1983). A skillful analysis of the political and personal struggles behind the Bill of Rights.

Bernard Schwartz, *The Bill of Rights: A Documentary History*, 2 vols. (New York: Chelsea House, 1971). Schwartz not only provides the major documentary evidence surrounding the creation of the Bill of Rights but offers useful commentary as well.

Bernard Schwartz, *The Great Rights of Mankind: A History of the American Bill of Rights* (New York: Oxford University Press, 1977). A splendid explanation of the framing of the first ten amendments accompanied by an analysis of post-1791 developments.

II

Melvin I. Urofsky

THE RELIGION CLAUSES

E very day that the Congress of the United States is in session both the Senate and the House of Representatives will begin their work with a prayer led by a priest, a minister, or a rabbi. Every day that thousands of public schools across the country are in session teachers in tens of thousands of classrooms may not begin their classes by leading their pupils in prayer. According to the Supreme Court, teacher-led prayers in public schools violate the First Amendment, while chaplain-led prayers in legislative chambers do not.

If this distinction appears confusing, it is not surprising, and Supreme Court rulings in the last forty years on the Religion Clauses of the First Amendment can be difficult to understand. Why is it permissible, for example, to allow a crêche in a public park but not in a public building? Why may the state provide construction loans to a religiously affiliated college but not to a parochial high school? Why must a state pay unemployment insurance benefits to a person who refuses to work for a private employer on his or her sabbath, but does not have to allow such a person paid leave for religious holidays?

When the Supreme Court began its modern interpretation of the Religion Clauses, Justice Hugo L. Black quoted Thomas Jefferson in declaring that the First Amendment required "a wall of separation between church and State." Thirty-five years later, critics of the Court claimed that Jefferson's metaphoric "wall of separation" had become as winding as the famous serpentine wall he designed at the University of Virginia. The Court's rulings on

. . . teacher-led prayers in public schools violate the First Amendment, while chaplain-led prayers in legislative chambers do not

the Religion Clauses are, in fact, fairly consistent, and inconsistencies derive at least in part from confusion over what the framers actually intended the Religion Clauses to mean.

The Original Intent of the Religion Clauses

The First Amendment declares that "Congress shall make no law respecting an establishment of religion, or prohibiting the free exercise thereof." In its most basic meaning, the Establishment Clause is the measure for any governmental program that in any way or form attempts to assist religion, while the Free Exercise Clause is the standard for any form of official interference in one's religious beliefs or practices. As with the other provisions of the Bill of Rights, the Religion Clauses originally applied only against the national government; since the Everson case in 1947, however, they apply to action by state governments as well.

In the past few years a lively debate has been going on over what the framers meant by the phrase "respecting an establishment of religion," and how one answers that question is of far more than academic interest. How one interprets original intent determines how one views a variety of governmental activities involving religion.

Nearly all the thirteen colonies had an officially established religion, supported by government revenues, and in some cases enforced by compulsory attendance laws. There is widespread agreement that, at the very least, those who wrote the First Amendment, as well as the states that ratified it, meant that there should be no official religion, no one church supported and endorsed by the government to the exclusion and detriment of all others.

Did they intend, however, that the words should be taken literally, that Congress shall make *no* law that in any way, shape, or form might affect religion? Or did they mean only that while government could not *prefer* one religious sect over another, it might provide some form of aid to all religions on an equal basis?

If the former interpretation is correct, then the Constitution bars not only any form of financial aid to support a religious program, but any form of religious activity such as prayer in any tax-supported institution. People who argue for a total and unqualified separation of the state and any religious activity are known as "absolutists."

"Nonpreferentialists" espouse the latter view and believe that Congress and the states may be lavish in their aid and public agencies may host religious events on the sole condition that the government treat all religions equally, in a "nonpreferential" manner.

The problem is that the written record regarding the drafting and ratification of the First Amendment is sparse. James Madison, who drafted the Bill of Rights, did not write "Congress shall not establish a religion." Rather, the wording is "Congress shall make no law respecting an establishment of religion," and there is no explanation of what this rather awkward phrase means.

Some scholars suggest that the framers recognized that the old form of establishment, that of a single official church, was already dead. Most of the states, following the Declaration of Independence, had disestablished their official religions, especially where it had been the Church of England. The unusual wording, therefore, reflects their concern that Congress not get involved in any way with any form of religious enterprise. As John Adams wrote, "I hope that Congress will never meddle with religion further than to say their own prayers, and to fast and give thanks once a year." In this view, the founders intended the wall of separation between church and state to be high and unbreachable.

The nonpreferentialists point out that at this time religion in a variety of ways permeated public life. Not all states had disestablished their colonial churches, and in many states the legislatures provided aid to all religions. Congress, in the Northwest Ordinance (1787), had declared that "religion, morality and knowledge [are] necessary to good government and the happiness of mankind." In this view, the wall of separation is low, designed only to prevent the establishment of a state religion, and that religion—on a nonpreferential basis—should be encouraged and supported by the government for the welfare of society.

The Development of Establishment Clause Doctrine

In recent years Supreme Court decisions have been marked by a debate between those justices who argue for a total separation of church and state, and those who believe that history requires an accommodation between the two. In the first modern case, *Everson* v. *Board of Education* (1947), Justice Black declared that the wall of separation "must be kept high and impregnable. We could not approve the slightest breach." However, a few years later, in what has been termed its first "accommodationist" ruling, the Court approved a released-time program allowing religious instruction during school hours but not on school grounds. In explaining the decision, Justice Douglas wrote that the First Amendment "does not say that in every and all respects there shall be a separation of Church and State." After all, he concluded, "we are a religious people whose institutions presuppose a Supreme Being" (*Zorach* v. *Clausen*, 1952).

This tension between separation and accommodation is evi-

Everson v. Board of Education, 1947

the founders intended the wall of separation between church and state to be high and unbreachable

Zorach v. Clausen, 1952

MELVIN I. UROFSKY

dent in subsequent cases; in some instances the Court has swung over to a rigid separationist view; in others it has gone in the opposite direction, allowing extensive collaboration between religion and the state.

In one of its most controversial decisions, the Court ruled that a state-mandated prayer used to open school days in New York violated the First Amendment. A prayer, by any definition, Justice Black declared, constituted a religious activity, and the First Amendment "must at least mean that [it] is no part of the business of government to compose official prayers for any group of the American people to recite as part of a religious program carried on by government." It made no difference whether the prayer was denominationally neutral. The nature of prayer is religious, and by promoting it, the state violated the Establishment Clause in fostering a religious activity that it determined and sponsored (*Engel v. Vitale*, 1962).

Engel v. Vitale, 1962

A year later, the Court also struck down mandatory Bible reading in the schools. In explaining the decision, Justice Clark noted that the neutrality commanded by the Constitution stemmed from the bitter lessons of history. Whenever there had been a fusion of church and state, there had also been persecution of all but those who adhered to the official orthodoxy (*Abington School Dist. v. Schempp*, 1963).

Abington School District v. Schempp, 1963

The two decisions caused an enormous controversy. Newspapers carried such banner headlines as "COURT OUTLAWS GOD," and clergymen denounced the rulings for "striking at the very heart of the Godly tradition in which America's children have for so long been raised." Although some church groups praised the ruling and argued that all religious activity should be private and untouched by the state, in almost every session of Congress since 1963, constitutional amendments to permit these activities have been proposed.

In the 1980s, it appeared that accommodationist sentiment on the Court had swung in the opposite direction. The Court held that paid legislative chaplains and prayers at the start of each session of the Nebraska legislature did not violate the Establishment Clause (*Marsh v. Chambers*, 1983). The following year the Court declared that the Constitution "affirmatively mandates" accommodation, and upheld the placing of a crèche at public expense in front of the Pawtucket, Rhode Island, city hall (*Lynch v. Donnelly*, 1984).

Marsh v. Chambers, 1983

Lynch v. Donnelly, 1984

Chief Justice Burger noted in the Marsh case that opening prayers had been common at the time of the drafting and adoption of the First Amendment, and had been a staple of national, state, and local government since the founding of the Republic. Similarly, school prayer and Bible reading had been part of American education since the seventeenth century. One might

THE RELIGION CLAUSES

well question why one practice should receive judicial sanction and the other continue to be disapproved.

The answer to some extent is found in the changing makeup of the American people as well as the special environment of a schoolroom. In the seventeenth and eighteenth centuries, the American people were relatively homogeneous. The small town and rural communities around the country did not contain a great deal of religious or ethnic diversity. When and where most children were Protestant, reciting the Lord's Prayer or several verses from the King James's version of the Bible offended no one. In modern urban America, the religious and ethnic mix in the nation's schools is quite varied. There is no common prayer or even a common Bible. As Justice O'Connor noted in *Lynch* and elsewhere, to impose any particular activity is to make all those who cannot in good conscience participate feel like outsiders.

There is also a difference between adult members of a state legislature, there by their own free will, and young boys and girls required to attend school. Children are not known for their non-conformity, and the fact that a teacher is leading a prayer puts pressure to conform on those who do not believe as well as those who do.

Finally, it should be mentioned that many people are unaware that the Supreme Court has never ruled that children may not pray in school. Students may pray silently any time the spirit moves them, and all teachers have seen this happen, often just before a test. It is one thing, however, to pray silently, individually, and voluntarily; it is another, as the Court has pointed out on a number of occasions, to be required to participate vocally, publicly, and involuntarily.

The Development of Free Exercise Doctrine

In many ways, the Free Exercise Clause is easier to understand than the Establishment Clause, because a broad range of opinion in the American public agrees that the government should not tell people what they should believe, or interfere with their religious practice. Problems arise only when practice touches upon some public concern.

The distinction between "belief" and "practice," central to Free Exercise questions, first arose over a century ago in connection with the Church of the Latter Day Saints. A federal law prohibited bigamy in U.S. territories, and at the time, the Mormons had only recently abandoned the practice of polygamy. One man who still believed in the old ways claimed that the law violated

his right to free exercise of religion; it interfered with his having more than one wife, which he considered a religious obligation.

In evaluating this claim, Chief Justice Morrison Waite wrote: "Suppose one believed that human sacrifices were a necessary part of religious worship, would it be seriously contended that the civil government [could] not interfere to prevent a sacrifice?" To permit sacrifices, on the basis of religious belief, would make religion superior to the law of the land. People can, therefore, believe whatever they want, free from governmental interference, but if attempting to act out these beliefs would harm others or significantly disturb social order, then the state may prevent that action (*Reynolds v. United States*, 1878).

Reynolds v. United States, 1878

However, for many religions, doctrine requires action, and the believers must live out their faith. During World War II, for example, many states required that all schools start their day with a salute to the flag, on the grounds that this would inculcate loyalty to the nation. But Jehovah's Witnesses, taking literally the biblical command against bowing to a graven image, refused to salute the flag. In the ensuing cases *Minersville School District v. Gobitis* (1940) and *West Virginia State Board of Education v. Barnette* (1943), a second standard emerged by which to measure Free Exercise claims.

Minersville School District v. Gobitis, 1940

West Virginia State Board of Education v. Barnette, 1943

The Religion Clauses are part of the First Amendment, which includes guarantees of speech, press, and assembly—all concerned with forms of expression. Just as the state cannot restrict speech except if it creates a "clear-and-present danger," so it cannot limit religious practice that by itself does not endanger the public. This test follows logically from the belief/action dichotomy, and expands the meaning of Free Exercise. A person can believe whatever he or she chooses to believe, and may carry those beliefs into practice so long as he or she not only does not harm but also does not endanger others.

Nor is the "truth" or "accuracy" of a person's belief open to question by the government. In the 1940s members of the "I Am" sect were convicted of mail fraud, and at their trial the prosecutor informed the jury that the sect claimed its members had been chosen as "divine" messengers of "Saint Germaine" and had been given the power to heal. Justice Douglas ruled that "Men may believe what they cannot prove. They may not be put to the proof of their religious doctrines or beliefs.... If one could be sent to jail because a jury in a hostile environment found those teachings false, little indeed would be left of religious freedom" (*United States v. Ballard*, 1944).

United States v. Ballard, 1944

There are times when the Free Exercise and Establishment Clauses come into conflict. What if in attempting to avoid interfering with a person's beliefs the state creates conditions that somehow favor that person? Does this cause a problem under the Establishment Clause? The Old Order Amish, for example, object on religious grounds to their children attending public school past the eighth grade. Most states require children to attend until they are of a certain age, and this often carries them past the eighth grade. By exempting the Amish children from the compulsory school law on Free Exercise grounds, as the Court did in *Wisconsin v. Yoder* (1972), does the state create a preference for that group that violates the Establishment Clause?

Wisconsin v. Yoder, 1972

Similarly, both Congress and the courts have held that conscientious objectors may be excused from military service if they object to war on religious grounds. Does a statute exempting religious pacifists constitute a "law respecting an establishment of religion"? Does a law that applies only to religious pacifists violate the free exercise of those who object to war on nonreligious grounds?

The one rule that, at least in the abstract, seems to be universally accepted is that any law that impinges on religious freedom must be content neutral, and regulations have to apply to all groups on an equal basis. For example, some religious groups may believe that they are required to proselytize, and they seek converts by handing out leaflets on street corners. Local governments may restrict such activities to certain areas at certain times, but these rules have to apply to all groups and be enforced in an even-handed manner.

This neutrality is a key idea of religious liberty that is sometimes difficult to understand because it is a relative concept. For the devout, neutrality may appear to be hostility, while for the nonbeliever anything that seems to aid religion may seem too much. We can see some of these problems in current issues growing out of the Religion Clauses.

Current Issues Involving the Religion Clauses

One of the most persistent issues has been public aid to religious schools. Those who favor such aid talk about the benefits to the pupils who, whatever their religion, will one day take their place as adult members of society; proper education of future citizens is a social responsibility, whether it takes place in a public or a parochial school. Those who oppose aid are not concerned that governmental monies will be used to teach secular subjects, but that by relieving the church schools of the cost of those secular subjects, the public purse will indirectly support religious instruction. In this area the debate between separationists and accommodationists, between preferentialists and nonpreferen-

regulations have to apply to all groups on an equal basis

tialists, has been intense and continuous for more than a quarter-century.

In attempting to resolve this issue, the Supreme Court has enunciated a three-pronged test, commonly called the *Lemon* test (*Lemon v. Kurtzman*, 1971). Public aid, whether from the state or federal governments, will be constitutionally permissible if: 1) there is a secular legislative purpose; 2) its primary effect neither advances nor inhibits religion; and 3) it does not foster excessive government entanglement with religion. Although this test seems straightforward enough, in practice it often takes on the semblance of the serpentine wall, because both legislators and judges differ on whether some practices are more secular than religious and what level of government involvement is "excessive." The *Lemon* test, for all that it is often cited by both the majority and the minority in school aid cases, is important because it remains the only standard the Court has ever agreed upon to use in measuring the legitimacy of aid programs.

Lemon v. Kurtzman, 1971

Justice White quite candidly explained the confusion over the issue in general and the *Lemon* test in particular. There is no "litmus-paper test to distinguish permissible from impermissible aid." The cases coming to the high court "are not easy; we are divided amongst ourselves. What is certain is that our decisions have tended to avoid categorical imperatives and absolutist approaches at either end of the range of possible outcomes. This course sacrifices clarity and predictability for flexibility." While flexibility is certainly a virtue, this approach often makes it difficult for both the layperson as well as the lawyer to understand how the Court reaches its decisions.

Public aid is one strand of Establishment Clause cases; a far more controversial area involves state sanction of specific religious practices. Although it has been almost three decades since the Court outlawed compulsory prayer and Bible reading in the schools, there is a significant minority in the country that has never stopped attempting to restore these practices. To get around the outright ban, they have attempted a variety of stratagems, including "voluntary" prayers and "moments of silence," and have invoked the Free Speech Clause to allow religious clubs access to school facilities.

The issue is one of definition. The Court has never prohibited private voluntary prayer, nor forbidden the reading of the Bible by individuals. It has been concerned with the voluntary nature of these prayers and at what point a moment of silence slides over into a moment when students feel overt or covert pressure to join in prayer. Several state legislatures have enacted statutes permitting moments of silence, but at least one statute required teachers to lead students in voluntary prayer. The Court saw this as compulsion (*Wallace v. Jaffree*, 1985).

"... our decisions have tended to avoid categorical imperatives and absolutist approaches at either end...."

Wallace v. Jaffree, 1985

Related to this question is display of religious symbols on public grounds, things such as Christmas trees or crèches or menorahs in city halls. To some people, these are religious symbols pure and simple, and their presence in a government building or park implies government sanction of the beliefs they symbolize—a clear crack in the wall of separation. Other people, while recognizing the religious nature of these items, also see them as part of the secular culture. In a pluralistic society such as ours, the argument goes, it is good for different groups to be able to share in each other's festivals and traditions. A third group claims that these are definitely religious symbols but that America is a "Christian nation" and should be proud to display the emblems of its faith. The Supreme Court, unfortunately, has been unable to come up with anything even remotely approaching a rule on this issue, and continued debate is likely.

Another current issue also involves what will be taught in the school classroom. The American tradition of public education has always centered on local control; the community elects the school board. While there may be state or even federal criteria that must be met, it has been assumed that the curriculum will reflect local values. But what if these local values include something that, in the eyes of many people, is a religious teaching?

The question lives in the ongoing debate between those who adhere to a literal belief in the biblical account of creation, and those who support the theory of evolution. The issue gained national prominence in 1925 with the trial in Dayton, Tennessee, of John Scopes, who was convicted of teaching evolution in violation of a state law. The Tennessee Supreme Court overturned the conviction on a technicality, and so the U.S. Supreme Court did not rule on this question until 1968. It then held that a requirement to teach the biblical story of creation constituted a teaching of religion and was thus unconstitutional (*Epperson v. Arkansas,* 1968).

Epperson v. Arkansas, 1968

Many people consider evolution the scientific explanation of how our world came to be as it is and the biblical account a myth. For fundamentalists, however, the biblical account is the truth, and the theory of evolution is false. This latter group has marshalled evidence to support what they call "creation science." They demand that it be taught at least alongside evolution, with students instructed that both are valid theories. This issue, of course, creates a problem for schools and teachers and highlights questions involving both the Establishment and Free Exercise Clauses.

See Edwards v. Aguillard, 1987

the Supreme Court . . . has been unable to come up with anything even remotely approaching a rule on this issue

Does imposing creation science on the curriculum constitute an establishment of religion? Does it impinge on the free exercise of those who do not share that belief? Does precluding that

MELVIN I. UROFSKY

teaching violate the free exercise of those who do believe? The Constitution requires that the state be neutral, but can it be in this situation? The Court has held that the state cannot inquire into the "truth" of one's belief, yet science and its teaching require that truth be tested.

Conclusion

There are no easy answers to the questions posed throughout this chapter. Moreover, changes in personnel on the Court, or even the facts of a particular case, may turn an accommodationist minority in one decision into a majority in the next. Unless one espouses a strict absolutist view or a very lenient accommodationist position, the issues related to the Religion Clauses will rarely be easy to resolve.

Does it really make sense, for example, to say that the nexus between the state and a religious symbol is so thin that it is alright to have a crèche in a public park (*Lynch v. Donnelly*, 1984) yet the connection is so direct as to forbid a menorah or a crèche in a public building? (*Allegheny County v. ACLU Greater Pittsburgh Chapter*, 1989). State aid to religiously affiliated colleges is sometimes justified because college students are older and more mature than high school students, and therefore will not be influenced as much by the pervasive religious motifs of such schools (*Hunt v. McNair*, 1973). Unemployment insurance is an entitlement (*Sherbert v. Verner*, 1963; *Hobbie v. Unemployment Appeals Commission of Florida*, 1987) and as such cannot be limited because of religious affiliation. But in terms of one's everyday religious obligations, is it not as important to secure paid leave for religious holidays? (*Ansonia Board of Education v. Philbrook*, 1986).

The Religion Clauses of the First Amendment protect the American people in one of their most prized liberties, the freedom to believe or disbelieve without interference from the government. Yet America has always been a nation in which religion has permeated the social fabric, and its people have always considered religious activities part and parcel of its national heritage. In interpreting the Religion Clauses the Supreme Court has attempted to find rules that will on the one hand prevent the government from invading the religious freedom of its citizens, while on the other avoid setting up the state as an enemy or advocate of religion. Maintaining that balance is a difficult task that will no doubt continue to raise many difficult questions.

Allegheny County v. ACLU, Greater Pittsburgh Chapter, 1989

Hunt v. McNair, 1973
Sherbert v. Verner, 1963
Hobbie v. Unemployment Appeals Commission of Florida, 1987

Ansonia Board of Education v. Philbrook, 1986

Abington School District v. Schempp, 374 U.S. 203 (1963). Held that mandatory daily Bible reading in public schools violated separation of church and state.

Cases

Allegheny County v. ACLU, Greater Pittsburgh Chapter, 57 U.S.L.W. 5045 (1989). Ruled that a menorah and a crêche displayed in public buildings violated separation of church and state.

Ansonia Board of Education v. Philbrook, 479 U.S. 60 (1986). Held that school systems did not have to provide paid leave for the observation of religious holidays.

Edwards v. Aguillard, 482 U.S. 578 (1987). Voided state law requiring teaching of "evolution science" as a violation of the Establishment Clause.

Engel v. Vitale, 370 U.S. 421 (1962). Held that compulsory school prayer was unconstitutional, as a violation of separation of church and state.

Epperson v. Arkansas, 393 U.S. 97 (1968). Struck down law prohibiting teaching of evolution as violation of Establishment Clause.

Everson v. Board of Education, 330 U.S. 1 (1947). Upheld use of public transportation for parochial school students while at the same time articulating the idea of a high wall of separation between church and state. Also applied the Religion Clauses to the state as well as the federal government.

Gobitis (see **Minersville School District v. Gobitis.)**

Hobbie v. Unemployment Appeals Commission of Florida, 480 U.S. 136 (1987). Reaffirmed ruling of *Sherbert* that persons refusing to work on their sabbath could not be denied unemployment compensation benefits.

Hunt v. McNair, 413 U.S. 734 (1973). Upheld use of state building loan funds for religiously affiliated colleges.

Lemon v. Kurtzman, 403 U.S. 602 (1971). Established tripartite test for constitutionality of state aid to religious schools.

Lynch v. Donnelly, 465 U.S. 668 (1984). Held that display of a crêche in a public park did not violate the Establishment Clause.

Marsh v. Chambers, 463 U.S. 783 (1983). Upheld practice of state assembly of starting every session with a chaplain-led prayer.

Minersville School District v. Gobitis, 310 U.S. 586 (1940). Upheld power of state to require daily flag salute over objections of Jehovah's Witnesses who claimed this violated their religious beliefs.

Reynolds v. United States, 98 U.S. 145 (1878). Established dichotomy between religious belief and action, and ruled that while government may not restrict belief, it may curtail action to protect public safety and order.

Sherbert v. Verner, 374 U.S. 398 (1963). Held that it would be a violation of the Free Exercise Clause for a state to refuse unemployment compensation benefits to persons refusing to work on their sabbath.

United States v. Ballard, 322 U.S. 78 (1944). Held that the state may not inquire into the accuracy or content of religious beliefs.

Wallace v. Jaffree, 472 U.S. 38 (1985). Held that state could not establish prayers in school under guise of "voluntary" moment of silence.

West Virginia State Board of Education v. Barnette, 319 U.S. 624 (1943). Reversed *Gobitis,* and held that compulsory flag saluting violated free exercise rights of Jehovah's Witnesses.

Wisconsin v. Yoder, 406 U.S. 205 (1972). Held that state compulsory school attendance law violated Old Order Amish right, under Free Exercise Clause, not to send children to public schools beyond seventh grade.

Zorach v. Clausen, 343 U.S. 306 (1952). Upheld released-time programs for religious instruction, provided such programs took place off school grounds.

Suggested Readings

Thomas J. Curry, *The First Freedoms: Church and State in America to the Passage of the First Amendment* (New York: Oxford University Press, 1986). Discusses the different ties and tensions between religion and authority during the colonial era and the first years of independence.

Leonard W. Levy, *The Establishment Clause and the First Amendment* (New York: Macmillan, 1986). The best single overview of problems arising under the Establishment Clause, but written from a definite absolutist position.

David Manwaring, *Render Unto Caesar: The Flag Salute Controversy* (Chicago: University of Chicago Press, 1962). Places the flag salute cases in the broader context of a nation at war as well as the emerging jurisprudence of the First Amendment.

William Lee Miller, *The First Liberty: Religion and the American Republic* (New York: Knopf, 1986). Another balanced look at the complex relations between religion and authority in early America.

Rodney K. Smith, *Public Prayer and the Constitution* (Wilmington: Scholarly Resources, 1987). Good overview of the cases and issues involved, as well as the conflicting constitutional positions.

Wayne R. Swanson, *The Christ Child Goes to Court* (Philadelphia: Temple University Press, 1989). Case study of *Lynch v. Donnelly.*

III

Norman Rosenberg

FREEDOM OF SPEECH

Framing Some Basic Issues

People have used various models for trying to explain freedom of speech and to resolve First Amendment disputes. Seeking to illustrate Franklin Roosevelt's "Four Freedoms," the artist Norman Rockwell even attempted to visualize the practice of free speech. Though normally a fast worker, he labored over his project, unable to find a framework. Ultimately, he embraced a familiar model, the New England town meeting. Supplementing legal treatises and court opinions, Rockwell's "Freedom of Speech" (1943) quickly became part of First Amendment folklore.

The town meeting does capture one aspect of public speech—its ideal relationship to self-government. In Rockwell's picture, a plaid-shirted worker holds the floor. With the town's annual report tucked in his pocket, he enthralls his better-dressed audience. Perhaps they admire his ideas and grasp of issues; or, perhaps, they listen out of respect for the process by which free debate informs public decision making. The calm and reasoned speech of every individual, Rockwell's canvas suggests, provides the basis for government by the people.

Though an evocative symbol, used by many legal writers, the town-meeting ideal fails to ask, let alone answer, many important free-speech questions. Rockwell's picture, for example, lacks any public official empowered to stop speech that might endanger public safety and welfare. Since even the most fervent defenders of free speech draw some limits—at expression inciting people to rob and injure others, at vicious "fighting" epithets directed toward specific individuals, or at the disclosure of national security secrets, for example—when can public authorities legitimately restrain or penalize "dangerous" speech? With its preplanned agenda and strict rules of order, the town-meeting model offers very little guidance here.

Similarly, most town meetings seem too homogeneous to test, in any serious way, the social limits to speech. Over the course of American history, people espousing unorthodox ideas have struggled to find platforms from which to speak. Can speech be considered "free" when many people lack easy access to effective public forums? Moreover, what happens when emotional speech provokes the kind of disorder unknown to most, rationally ordered, town meetings? Does "free" speech stop when action ensues? In what ways should audience reactions, especially when hostile, affect constitutional guarantees for speech?

Controversies over limiting speech, then, have invariably raised questions of social and political power. The power to give voice to discontents has helped to define both the people who have been able to speak out and those who have primarily listened. Moreover, in contrast to communication through the mass media, the traditional speech situation allowed little time for reflection and reconsideration. For most of American history, speakers and listeners have met within a limited time and space. If audiences were receptive, orators could soar towards eloquence, or sink into demagoguery; if listeners were hostile, speakers risked being pressured into silence or provoked to anger. The expression that has tested the limits of free speech historically has been the kind that aroused communities, angered powerful people, and challenged major public policies. Despite the appeal of tidy models such as the town meeting, the story of speech that *really* mattered has been marked by fights over what tales could be told and what ideas should be heard.

Free-Speech Fights, 1791–1860

From the earliest days of the republic, conflicts over *who* could say *what* to *whom* and in what *contexts* have helped citizens construct the boundaries of everyday life and constitutional government. Although Federalist partisans primarily aimed the Sedition Act of 1798 against Jeffersonian publications, the concept of seditious libel—the idea that public officials and governmental authority itself could be injured by words alone—extended to "speech." This sedition law made it a crime to utter, as well as print, libelous falsehoods against government, the president, or members of Congress. The 1790s thus ended with widespread controversy over freedom of speech.

Federalists espoused a theory of speech—and of public life—that was overtly elitist. Because "licentious" political criticism,

Seditious libel, Libel law

the power to give voice to discontents has helped to define both the people who have been able to speak out and those who have primarily listened

they insisted, tended to destroy respect for authority and to undermine social order, public officials needed broad powers over "dangerous" and "offensive" speech. By inflaming passions and spreading misinformation, speech critical of government could aid the schemes of wily demagogues.

Fighting to save their party from sedition prosecutions and construct a less elitist political culture, Jeffersonians urged more limited use of controls. Even when exaggerated and intemperate, speech rarely threatened public safety and tranquility; in most cases, exposure to dissenting ideas helped educate and enlighten ordinary citizens. Legal restraints over speech, especially by distant national officials, represented a most dangerous use of governmental power. Did not the remote chance of critical speech fomenting unrest pale before the immediate danger of corrupt officials using sedition laws to stifle legitimate criticism?

Cases under the Sedition Act dramatized the passion that surrounded fights over political speech. In 1799, for example, Federalists in Massachusetts prosecuted an obscure Jeffersonian activist, David Brown, for helping to raise a "liberty pole." Colorfully decorated stakes, which symbolized the anti-authoritarian spirit of the American Revolution, these poles were examples of what constitutional lawyers now call "expressive conduct," a combination of speech and action roughly analogous to the contemporary use of placards by pickets or flag burnings by political demonstrators. Furious that liberty poles had remained part of popular political culture, Federalists condemned them for promoting political discord and popular discontent. For helping to raise a liberty pole—and for denouncing a crowd of hostile Federalist spectators—David Brown received the stiffest sentence handed down under the Sedition Act. Lacking money to pay his fine, he remained incarcerated until pardoned by President Thomas Jefferson in 1801.

Expressive conduct

Prosecutions against speech, however, proved as futile as the Federalists' legal sallies against Jeffersonian writers. The Sedition Act not only failed to tame everyday political invective, but the measure's unpopularity contributed to the Federalist Party's electoral defeat in 1800. Consequently, few political figures, especially at the national level, wanted to risk being labeled enemies of free speech. By the 1830s people aligned with the major parties could safely denounce, in the bitterest of terms, their rivals. According to one observer of pre–Civil War politics, speakers hurled enough dirt to "make at least one good sized mountain, and some half-dozen hills besides, under which numerous unfortunate candidates lie buried"[1]

expression that has tested the limits of free speech historically has been the kind that aroused communities, angered powerful people...

Not everyone, however, could speak so freely, especially on controversial issues such as slavery. African-American slaves, of course, lacked virtually all of the liberties enjoyed by free whites, including freedom of speech. Slave-holding interests, worried that critical discussions might jeopardize their peculiar institution, tightly controlled all types of public speech in the antebellum South.

Proslavery forces also attempted to extend restrictions to the free states. In the 1830s, southerners and their northern supporters tried to prevent Congress from receiving antislavery petitions and prompted a long-running constitutional battle. Antislavery forces denounced as a gross violation of free speech the Congressional effort to "gag" citizens by refusing to consider their petitions. Finally, in 1844, Congress voted to accept the petitions, reversing its own earlier policies.

This national petition struggle seemed tame when compared to the free-speech contests that antislavery people fought in local communities throughout the antebellum North. Usually directed by community leaders, large and often angry mobs mobilized to silence antislavery speakers. Risking injury and even death, antislavery people successfully made their ability to speak a crucial test of the degree of liberty in any community. After being warned out of one northern town, for example, the famous abolitionist Theodore Dwight Weld scolded his audience. They were no better than slaves if they permitted the town's elite to curtail his right to speak and their liberty to listen. Would a free people, he taunted, ever allow such a violation of free speech? His appeal to popular ideas about liberty of speech worked: Weld continued his lectures, before larger crowds.

Free-Speech Fights, 1860–1917

Not all free-speech battles ended so easily or happily, and the legacy of the nineteenth and early twentieth centuries proved a mixed one. Many men and women—including labor activists, early feminists, and various political outsiders—rarely found safe platforms, and they often risked public and private penalties when they did manage to speak out. In addition, over the course of the nineteenth century, the dominant political culture repudiated the elitist ideas of the Federalists in favor of a powerful, new "democratic" justification for suppressing speech.

Liberal-democratic theory could easily justify restrictions on speech. If political authority rested upon the principle of majority rule, were not controls on speech, when adopted and enforced by the people's representatives, perfectly legitimate exercises of the general community's policing powers? Why should the speech "rights" of a few individuals, especially those outside the political and cultural mainstream, outweigh the democratically articulated sentiments of the vast majority? Virtually everyone praised free speech as an abstract ideal; many simply refused to protect ex-

risking injury and even death, antislavery people successfully made their ability to speak a crucial test of the degree of liberty in any community

pression that challenged dominant community values. Thus, most courts and "right-thinking" people generally accepted legal restrictions on "radical" and "offensive" expression.

In the late nineteenth and early twentieth centuries, members of the labor movement frequently led the opposition to this orthodoxy. As part of the often violent struggle to organize the immigrant-based industrial workforce, unions challenged dominant free-speech theory and community practices. In reply, anti-union interests mobilized their forces, including private goon squads and public laws, in order to stifle union activists. Labor speakers found streets and public parks, as well as private auditoriums, often closed to them. Communities passed local ordinances that banned public speaking without a permit. Under such licensing systems, local authorities could limit access to public forums, such as streets and parks, and people who spoke without permits could be arrested for "disorderly conduct."

The labor movement also tested the boundaries of "speech": Where should the line between free speech and provocative action be drawn? Union members, for example, viewed the picketing of businesses with which they had labor disputes as protected expression. In contrast, business leaders saw picketing, and other union demonstrations, as coercive action, not expressive conduct. A few incidents—such as the Haymarket rally of 1886, which ended with a bomb attack upon the police (allegedly by anarchists)—helped to link labor activities with illegal violence. This popular identification carried over into the law courts when labor activists asserted free-speech claims. Judges invariably upheld trespassing convictions against union pickets and routinely issued injunctions—court orders prohibiting workers from gathering—against pro-union demonstrations.

Other activists joined labor in struggles to expand the bounds of protected speech. Prominent feminists, for example, battled local speech restrictions in their crusades for women's suffrage and better access to birth control information. In time, a familiar ritual, the "free speech fight," emerged. Union members, especially the radical "Wobblies" of the International Workers of the World (IWW), would directly challenge local ordinances requiring permits or authorizing suppression of "disorderly conduct." IWW members streamed into towns throughout the West, violated ordinances against public speaking, and tried to overflow the sheriff's jail with arrested Wobblies. Although this tactic dramatized speech issues to a larger public, it also exposed participants to retaliatory violence from police officers and hostile mobs. Similarly, birth-control activists, such as Emma Goldman and Margaret Sanger, risked their freedom by deliberately violating local ordinances regulating public speaking. Governmental officials rarely sided with free-speech advocates, but a growing core of middle-class reformers, especially the Free Speech League, supported efforts to change legal and popular ideas.

Between 1798 and 1917, state and local officials led the attack against dissenting speech; United States' entry into World War I, however, began an unprecedented assault on speech that officials in Washington considered hostile to majoritarian sentiments and national security. From 1917 through 1920, the Democratic administration of Woodrow Wilson centralized the localistic tradition of harassing "aliens" and dissenters, using the national government as a powerful new arm of suppression. After years of fending off local authorities, for example, Emma Goldman and many radical labor leaders succumbed to this new, wartime "national security" state: Citing their criticisms of the war effort as justification, the Wilson administration deported Goldman, imprisoned labor leaders such as Eugene Debs, and effectively crushed the IWW.

Despite more than a century of free-speech struggles, national officials still enjoyed ample legal support for suppressing dissenting speech. Rejecting, for instance, claims that Goldman was merely urging people to consider dodging the military draft, a federal judge ruled that free speech meant discussing issues "in [a] lawful and orderly fashion," not "counseling disobedience of the law," especially in time of war.[2] The Supreme Court applied a similar line of reasoning in upholding the conviction of Debs and other antiwar protesters: Although their speech did not directly incite violations of law, it did present a "clear and present danger" of producing attitudes that might impede the war effort.

The end of World War I did not halt national action against dissenting speech. During the "Red Scare" of 1919, Wilson's attorney general, A. Mitchell Palmer, rounded up thousands of alleged radicals, especially those with recent immigrant backgrounds. The war and Red-Scare eras also gave impetus to a new, national bureaucracy—reorganized as the Federal Bureau of Investigation (FBI) by 1924—that soon exercised surveillance over many types of political speech.

Free-Speech Fights and the First-Freedom Ideal, 1920–1940

In a reciprocal process, though, invention of national-security and surveillance bureaucracies stimulated new, nationwide initiatives to control state power over speech. Emerging from the free-speech struggles of 1917–20, the American Civil Liberties Union (ACLU) picked up the reformist mantle of the Free Speech League. A small group of people who challenged measures that they considered constitutional violations, the ACLU provided legal support during many post–World War I speech battles.

a federal judge ruled that free speech meant discussing issues "in [a] lawful and orderly fashion," not "counseling disobedience of the law," especially in time of war

NORMAN ROSENBERG

In contrast to their limited part in earlier free-speech issues, Supreme Court justices also came to play influential roles after 1920. Not only did the Court hear appeals in speech cases involving the national government, but it ruled for the first time, in *Gitlow v. New York* (1925), that First Amendment guarantees also limited state action against political expression. Supreme Court opinions became major statements about the meaning of free speech. By the time of Norman Rockwell's 1943 painting, the idea that "Freedom of Speech" constituted the "first freedom," the basis for exercising other fundamental political liberties, enjoyed wide appeal.

Gitlow v. New York, 1925

In 1927, Justice Louis Brandeis authored a classic judicial defense of this "first freedom" ideal. In many ways, his oft-quoted prose in *Whitney v. California* anticipated the visual imagery of Rockwell's picture: Free speech supported the larger processes of self-government. The antidote to outrageous speech was not "enforced silence" but counterspeech, calm and rational arguments that suggested better policies. The law should silence obstreperous dissenters only when speech could reasonably be linked to a clear and present danger of a serious and very immediate peril. Ironically, Brandeis asserted these ideals in an opinion that upheld the conviction of an IWW supporter for simply belonging to an organization that allegedly urged violence and not for inciting (or even advocating) violence herself.

Whitney v. California, 1927

In subsequent years, people had numerous opportunities to test the first-freedom ideal. Labor-union activists, civil-rights workers, and political radicals asked familiar questions—about limiting governmental powers, providing dissenters with access to public forums, and confronting threats from hostile audiences— in new contexts. The labor-organizing drives of the 1930s, for example, altered the balance of political power so that union members found that laws curtailing political expression no longer tilted so radically against them. Encouraged by small victories, free-speech activists asked new questions, especially of the Supreme Court.

The "Free Flow" of Ideas and More Protected Speech, 1940–1980

By the 1940s, the Supreme Court had assumed special responsibility for trying to protect controversial speech. It generally disappointed, however, those who believed that any national commitment must continue during even the most dangerous of times. When considering expression that allegedly threatened national security, for example, the Supreme Court accepted a wider range of restraints than in other types of speech cases. During the Cold War era of the 1940s and 1950s, people linked to left-wing organizations and "un-American" ideas risked legal action and loss of their livelihoods, especially if their public expression put them in the limelight. Consequently, fear of sanctions may have caused people, during the Cold War years, to refrain from speaking out on controversial issues. And even after concern about subversive activity largely passed, people who worked for branches of the national-security bureaucracy faced various legal restraints if they wanted to discuss critically policies they considered unwise and immoral. Tensions between the First Amendment and claims of national security have continually posed controversial free-speech questions.

In cases without national-security implications, however, the Court chipped away at, or simply cut down, many traditional barriers to expression. For example, it consistently ruled that the threat of disorder cannot justify denying controversial speakers access to public platforms or stopping their speeches. Even abusive remarks to police officers came to enjoy some constitutional protection. The Court also scrutinized municipal ordinances requiring parade and speaking permits; regulations must advance some general public purpose, such as prohibiting noisy demonstrations late at night, and not provide subterfuges for silencing controversial speech. Similarly, "private" areas that serve "public" purposes, such as shopping malls, cannot arbitrarily exclude everyone with a political message. Although the Court generally refused to place nonpolitical speech on the same high constitutional ground as political expression, it came to extend considerable protection to commercial advertising and even sexually explicit expression.

This trend represented no sudden discovery of the "true" principles of free speech. Rather, the continuing swirl of free-speech battles, along with an appreciation for diversity of the nation's sociocultural milieu, helped to produce new ideas about the role of public discourse. In contrast to dominant opinion during the nineteenth and early twentieth centuries, when authorities invoked the power of electoral majorities to justify prosecution of minority viewpoints, a variant on the first-freedom ideal stressed the importance of protecting the speech of individuals and dissenting minority groups against temporary majorities. According to this view, both a concern for allowing minority groups to speak out and a general interest in promoting the "free flow" of individual ideas overrode complaints that certain kinds of speech challenged the preferences of the majority or offended some people's sensibilities. In addition, this view emphasized the importance of preventing local groups from interfering with the path of speech through a *national* marketplace of ideas. Thus, the Supreme Court often reiterated a goal of seeing that debate on public issues "should be uninhibited, robust and wide-open."[3]

the continuing swirl of free-speech battles... helped to produce new ideas about the role of public discourse

NORMAN ROSENBERG

This approach repudiated the theory behind the Federalists' Sedition Act of 1798—that speech, by itself, can be a crime—and even went beyond Brandeis's views in *Whitney* v. *California*. Especially in the 1960s and 1970s, the Supreme Court proclaimed its commitment to encouraging the freest possible flow of diverse ideas and viewpoints. In *Brandenburg* v. *Ohio* (1969), for example, it unanimously overturned the conviction of a Ku Klux Klan member who had suggested force as a way of reversing civil-rights policies and ruled that even the advocacy of violence, in the absence of any direct incitement to imminent lawlessness, constituted protected political speech. Two years later, in *Cohen* v. *California* (1971), a majority of the court ruled that authorities could not prosecute a person with a jacket that denounced with a famous four-letter word the military draft for the Vietnam War. One person's vulgarity might be another's lyric, the Court's majority opinion observed. And in one of the most divisive freespeech fights of recent history, the Court refused to allow a town that had many survivers of Hitler's death camps to ban a deliberately provocative parade by neo-Nazis.

Brandenburg v. Ohio, 1969

Cohen v. California, 1971

Why Speech Deserves Special Protection: Recent Debates

Protecting "offensive" and "dangerous" speech—as part of larger commitments to promoting a diversity of individual viewpoints and encouraging the free flow of ideas—prompted renewed public debates during the 1980s and early 1990s. Many people, scattered all across the political spectrum, asked hard questions about whether or not the first-freedom and free-flow ideals always translated into wise public policy. Beginning in the 1980s, amidst concern about violence against women and rising ethnic conflict, even some self-styled liberals and progressives proposed various types of laws that could, they hoped, stem the flow of "hateful" ideas and "abhorrent" images of others. Since these kinds of "verbal assaults" would likely not gain protection if directed at specific individuals, why should defamation of groups be judged any different? According to this view, the traditional faith that counterspeech could confront vicious gender and ethnic slurs ignored the systematic exclusion of women and minorities from major speech forums. What did communities stand to gain by tolerating speech by the intolerant, by protecting bigoted expression that the vast majority would, one hopes, never translate into social programs? Had protection of extremist expression really helped to change, in any way, existing distributions of political and social power?

These debates over why communities should protect unorthodox speech worried people committed to extending the first-freedom principle. New legal controls, however well intentioned, represented a capitulation to fear, an abandonment of faith in the marketplace of ideas, and a surrender to the march of censorship. Who could guarantee, for example, that restraints against "offensive" speech would not dilute legal protection for other types of expression? Might not crusades against commercial porndealers encourage censorship of artistic and cultural works, especially those by artists who challenged the status quo?

In this new context, not surprisingly, the Supreme Court spiced, rather than soothed, public debates. Much of the controversy during the 1980s and early 1990s centered on cases involving "offensive" speech and expressive conduct. In 1988, for example, the Court ruled that even an advertisement parody, in *Hustler* magazine, claiming an incestuous relationship between a prominent minister and his mother qualified as protected speech. And in two 5–4 decisions, the Court reaffirmed protection for expressive conduct and struck down both state and national laws against flag burning. The flag cases, *Texas* v. *Johnson* (1989) and *United States* v. *Eichman* (1990), prompted calls for a constitutional amendment that would authorize protective legislation for Old Glory and led to protracted conflicts over the consequences of protecting such expression.

Texas v. Johnson, 1989 and United States v. Eichman, 1990

The Supreme Court, however, did not consistently rule in favor of free-speech claims. It upheld a conviction against KKK members who were protesting, in highly offensive ways, the impact of Vietnamese immigrants upon Texas's fishing economy; it supported suspension of a high-school student who had given an assembly speech filled with sexually suggestive metaphors; and it approved a local ordinance that banned certain kinds of picketing in residential neighborhoods. Did these decisions, as many hoped and others feared, represent the beginning of a new spirit of skepticism, by a majority of the Court, about the benefits to be gained from the free flow of speech?

Conclusion

Recent controversies thus recall earlier free-speech fights. Lines of arguments and claims of fundamental principles might change, but political battles over the meaning of constitutional guarantees still mark debates about the First Amendment. No free-speech models, simple formulas, or neutral principles seem available to answer difficult questions. As in the past, differences over what kinds of speech merit protection remain part of larger political struggles in which people fight to define, ultimately through the force of law, the bounds of community and the texture of everyday life.

in this new context, not surprisingly, the Supreme Court spiced, rather, than soothed, public debates

NORMAN ROSENBERG

[1] Quoted in Norman L. Rosenberg, *Protecting the Best Men: An Interpretive History of the Law of Libel* (1990), 143–44.

[2] Quoted in Paul L. Murphy, *World War I and the Origin of Civil Liberties in the United States* (1978), 213.

[3] This famous phrase is by Justice William Brennan in *New York Times v. Sullivan*, 376 U.S. 254, 270 (1964).

Notes

Cases

Brandenburg v. Ohio, 395 U.S. 444 (1969). The Court unanimously overruled *Whitney*, holding that government could not punish political speech, even if it advocated violence, unless there was also a specific incitement to imminent lawlessness.

Cohen v. California, 403 U.S. 15 (1971). The Court upheld the right of an anti-Vietnam demonstrator to wear a jacket that denounced the draft with a four-letter epithet. The fact that this example of "expressive conduct" might offend some people could not justify prosecution of a political demonstrator for disturbing the peace.

Gitlow v. New York, 268 U.S. 652 (1925). The Court upheld the conviction of a socialist writer under a state criminal anarchy law, but it also ruled that the First Amendment applied to state, as well as national, restrictions on speech and press.

Texas v. Johnson, 57 U.S.L.W. 4770 (1989) and **United States v. Eichman,** 58 U.S.L.W. 4744 (1990). By two 5 to 4 votes, the Court struck down laws punishing the burning of the U.S. flag, holding that these flag burnings represented constitutionally protected examples of free speech.

Whitney v. California 274 U.S. 353 (1927). The Court unanimously upheld conviction of a member of the IWW under a state syndicalist law. Case is best known for the concurring opinion of Justice Louis Brandeis who authored a famous defense of the importance of free speech.

Suggested Readings

Lee Bollinger, *The Tolerant Society: Freedom of Speech and Extremist Speech in America* (New York: Oxford University Press, 1986). A spirited defense of the decision to protect "offensive" speech in the case of a neo-Nazi march through a town heavily populated by Jewish Holocaust survivers.

Nat Hentoff, *The First Freedom: The Tumultuous History of Free Speech in America* (New York: Delacorte, 1980). A popular history by a prominent civil libertarian who espouses the "first freedom" ideal.

Harry Kalven, Jr., *A Worthy Tradition: Freedom of Speech in America* (New York: Harper & Row, 1988). A landmark study of Supreme Court decisions, from 1920 to 1974, on First Amendment issues by a renowned legal scholar who strongly supported civil liberties positions.

Catherine A. MacKinnon, *Feminism Unmodified: Discourses on Life and Law* (Cambridge, Mass.: Harvard University Press, 1988). A series of essays, many of which criticize First Amendment decisions that protect pornography, by a prominent feminist scholar.

Paul L. Murphy, *The Meaning of Free Speech: First Amendment Freedoms from Wilson to Roosevelt* (Westport, Conn.: Greenwood, 1972). A superb account of various free-speech battles of the 1920s and 1930s

Paul L. Murphy, *World War I and the Origin of Civil Liberties in the United States* (New York: W.W. Norton & Co., Inc., 1979). A thoughtful and important analysis, by a leading constitutional historian, of the rise of a national surveillance state and the countervailing emergence of new ideas about free speech.

Robert C. Post, "The Constitutional Concept of Public Discourse: Outrageous Opinion, Democratic Deliberation, and *Hustler Magazine* v. *Falwell*," 103 *Harvard Law Review* 603–86 (1990). A challenging article by a First Amendment scholar who raises important questions about conflicts between individual speech interests and community values.

Norman L. Rosenberg, *Protecting the Best Men: An Interpretive History of the Law of Libel* (Chapel Hill: University of North Carolina Press, 1990). An overview of libel law which includes broader material on changes in the socioeconomic and cultural background of free-speech battles.

Rodney A. Smolla, *Jerry Falwell* v. *Larry Flynt: The First Amendment on Trial* (New York: St. Martin's Press, Inc., 1988). An expert but popularly oriented analysis of an important free-speech battle by a law professor who specializes in First Amendment issues.

IV

Norman Rosenberg

FREEDOM OF THE PRESS

The American press draws upon a complex mix of public values, historical memory, socioeconomic power, and constitutional law to protect its freedom. As a general matter, the idea of a "free" press seems uncontroversial; yet, people who one day praise the press's contributions to public debate and popular enlightenment can suddenly condemn the ways in which certain publications deal with specific issues and ask legal institutions to tame journalistic excesses and media power.

In considering how Americans have understood freedom of the press as a fundamental constitutional value, three general historical eras come into focus: 1) the 1790s and the crisis over the Sedition Act of 1798; 2) the broad sweep of history from about 1800 to 1920, a period in which the press expanded its influence and enjoyed relative freedom from legal restraints; and 3) the post–1920 era, a time in which *both* new governmental restraints and stricter constitutional protections became part of the history of freedom of the press.

The Sedition Act of 1798: The Origins of Controversy

The 1790s proved an important decade for the press. The beginning of organized, two-party competition between Federalists and Jeffersonian-Republicans enlivened political journalism and provoked controversy over the meaning of freedom of the press. Both parties financially supported printers, and, in return, journalists supplied newspapers and pamphlets that endorsed ideas and candidates favored by their patrons. Political friends were lauded; enemies were denounced, often in the harshest of terms. The later ideal of an independent press simply did not exist.

Eventually, many Federalists feared that "licentious" political journalism threatened their party's—and the nation's—future. Committed to a system in which only the "best" people, generally the wealthy and socially prominent, held office, Federalists viewed Jeffersonians as plotting to overturn public policies and even the constitutional order. Legal controls over corrupt journalists, Federalists argued, would not destroy freedom of the press but would protect journalistic integrity and safeguard the entire community's interest in meaningful public debate; the law should prevent clever writers from perverting the press and fooling citizens into supporting unqualified leaders or into opposing wise governmental policies.

During a period of tension between the United States and France, Federalists in Congress enacted the Sedition Act of 1798. Although the Franco-American foreign-policy crisis justified this sedition law, Federalists also aimed it at Jeffersonian journalists. Any writer found guilty of "seditious" criticism of the government, the president, or members of Congress could be fined and sentenced to jail. The fact that the sedition law would expire automatically, after the national election of 1800, only heightened Jeffersonian suspicions about Federalist motives.

Seditious libel, Libel law

The Sedition Act provoked fierce controversy. It translated into a statute the common law of seditious libel—the idea that critical words, by themselves, could harm political leaders and governmental authority and that the law should protect the reputation of both individual officials and the government itself. But sensitive to criticism that seditious libel isolated public officers from legitimate criticism and endangered freedom of the press, Federalists also included two reforms associated with the 1735 prosecution of John Peter Zenger in colonial New York in the Sedition Act. The law permitted defendants to offer proof of the truth of their publications as a defense and empowered juries, rather than judges, to determine whether or not a defendant's publication met the legal definition of seditious libel. Federalists thus claimed that the Sedition Act struck a perfect balance: It simultaneously protected freedom of the press, curbed the excesses of licentious writers, and advanced the larger public interest in sound, responsible journalism.

Zengerian Reforms

Experience quickly proved the limited value of the Zengerian reforms during a time of international crisis and domestic political conflict. Most judges and officers of the national court system belonged to the Federalist Party. As a result, the juries selected to hear sedition prosecutions also tended to be Federalist partisans, and Jeffersonian defendants watched their trials end with verdicts of guilty. Some prominent Jeffersonians received large fines, and several went to jail.

In retrospect, though, the Sedition Act rebounded against the Federalist Party. Because of the rapid spread of printing presses and political publications, the law of 1798 offered a crude and clumsy way of dealing with an organized, popularly based opposition party. Most Federalists soon realized that expanding their own network of printers and newspapers, in order to respond to Jeffersonian criticism in kind, provided a better means of swaying popular opinion than legal prosecutions. Unfortunately for their party, Federalists discovered this too late; popular resentment against the Sedition Act contributed to the Federalist Party's electoral defeat in 1800.

Prosecutions against the press also helped to undermine the very First-Amendment principles that Federalists meant the Sedition Act to protect. Because the Zengerian reforms proved of little practical value when Jeffersonian writers faced Federalist juries, Jeffersonians raised new questions about freedom of the press. In a torrent of pamphlets and newspaper articles, they challenged Federalist ideas. Some argued that political comments such as the complaint that President John Adams dined with the "ridiculous pomp" of an aristocrat represented matters of opinion, not questions that could be settled by introducing evidence of truth in a court of law. Except when published from malicious motives, these Jeffersonians argued, all opinions about politics and politicians should be privileged from libel suits. Equally as disturbing to Federalists, other Jeffersonian writers insisted that even false statements of fact about governmental policies and public officials should be exempt from legal penalties. Why, for example, should a republican nation with guarantees of a free press retain traditional restrictions on political publications?

Despite all of the controversy, the Sedition Act expired as scheduled in 1801, and the Supreme Court never heard a case that tested its constitutionality. The demise of this law, however, hardly ended arguments about freedom of the press.

Debates over Freedom of the Press, 1800–1920

In the short run, ironically, Federalists won the legal argument. After 1801, only the most radical Jeffersonians still espoused the free-press ideals of 1798 to 1800. In the dominant legal view, people who edited newspapers or ran printing presses possessed very dangerous instruments. The press could destroy individual political reputations and undermine the public's interest in reading enlightened and uncorrupted publications; consequently, it should

most Federalists soon realized that expanding their own network of printers and newspapers . . . provided a better means of swaying public opinion than legal prosecutions

be absolutely responsible, under the law, for all libelous misstatements of political fact.

During the nineteenth century, most state courts, the places in which the vast majority of free-press cases were tried, followed Federalist ideas about the role of the press. Federalists such as Alexander Hamilton successfully argued that libelous falsehoods should not be permitted to corrupt political debate; when journalists printed what might be a libel about government or political leaders, they must be ready to supply evidence of truth. Unless the law protected the "best" candidates and officials from unscrupulous writers, people who valued their good reputations might simply avoid public life. Following Hamilton's lead, many states further required the press to demonstrate "good motives" and "justifiable ends," even when called into court for publishing unpleasant truths about political officials. In theory, then, libel laws tightly restrained the political press.

If Federalists won their legal battle, however, they lost the journalistic war. Between about 1830 and 1890, journalism changed dramatically, and these changes influenced popular ideas about freedom of the press. Beginning in the 1830s, people interested in politics faithfully read their party's newspapers; political newspapers and other publications became part of the social process by which public opinion took shape. At the same time, inexpensive, mass-circulation newspapers sprang up in the nation's largest cities. These independent "penny presses" of the pre–Civil War era downplayed political-party news in favor of human-interest and crime stories; they offered readers kaleidoscopic glimpses of the dizzying whirl of city life. Even the bloody Civil War (1861–1865) aided this communication revolution: New technologies such as the telegraph allowed reporters to speed political and battlefield news to their readers. Similarly, war brought only intermittent censorship; the Civil War years, historians generally agree, produced a comparatively mild system of legal restraints.

During the second half of the nineteenth century, the press continued to expand. Although smaller newspapers remained tied to political factions, the idea of independent journalism took firm hold. By the 1890s, the New York *Times* offered a powerful journalistic model. Under its motto, "All the News Fit to Print," it featured careful, cautious reporting of public affairs. Sometimes dull but pledged to accuracy and the ideal of neutrality, the *Times* claimed to be the "paper of record" for public issues and events.

Newspapers owned by publishers such as Joseph Pulitzer and William Randolph Hearst offered competing models. Aggressively pursuing or "creating" (according to their critics) stories, they pushed the idea of "news" and of a free press much further than papers such as the *Times*. Anything—from events preceding

many states further required the press to demonstrate "good motives" and "justifiable ends"

NORMAN ROSENBERG

the Spanish-American War of 1898 to brawls in a rough urban neighborhood—could be translated into shocking exposés by the "popular press." Publishers like Hearst and Pulitzer made previously private events public knowledge and elevated the routines of daily life into spectacular, larger-than-life tales.

This style of journalism, sometimes called "muckraking," produced numerous calls for legal restraints. Denouncing popular newspapers for converting private incidents, especially the problems of prominent people, into public news, some legal writers urged a new right of privacy that would award monetary damages for newspaper stories that maliciously invaded family life. At the same time, critics of the popular press also urged the public to support more vigorous enforcement of libel laws, in either private libel suits by individuals or in governmental prosecutions for seditious libel.

Lawmakers also condemned "offensive" and "radical" publications. During the late nineteenth century, for instance, many states joined the national government in legislating against "obscenity," including publications by feminists in the birth control movement. Later, following President William McKinley's assassination in 1901, a series of state "syndicalist laws" and "criminal anarchy" laws targeted various radical papers. Calls for additional legal controls against more mainstream, commercial publications, however, generally went unheeded. Despite the Federalist tilt to the statutory and case law of most states, popular political culture accepted a much greater freedom than the law technically allowed the press. Prosecutions for seditious libel and (the much more common) civil libel suit for money damages by prominent politicians could occasionally trouble individual newspapers and writers, but they failed to affect the day-to-day tone of political journalism. Electoral politics regularly featured colorful, as well as vicious, commentary. Despite repeated calls for tougher libel and new privacy laws, the credo of American politics seemed to be "every good libel deserves another." Certainly, American writers faced far fewer legal restraints than their counterparts in other industrial nations such as Great Britain and Germany. This legacy would be sorely tested, however, during and after World War I.

Freedom of the Press Disputes, 1920 to the Present

After 1920, the growing power of media corporations together with other fundamental changes in American life renewed calls for legal restraints. Tensions associated with industrialization and successive waves of immigration made the United States a heterogeneous, often unruly, society. At the same time, political leaders expanded the nation's growing power onto the world stage. In

popular political culture accepted a much greater freedom than the law technically allowed the press

light of fierce struggles over both domestic and foreign policies, some people worried that an overly critical press might threaten social order and even the nation's security.

Issues of Concern

Two primary areas of concern emerged. First, new printing technologies permitted insurgent labor and radical political movements to produce, quickly and cheaply, their own publications. Conflicts involving small, maverick publishers raised particularly difficult questions.

Radical publications increasingly tangled with the national government. Focusing on dissenters against United States entry into World War I, Congress enacted a new sedition law, in 1918, that made antiwar criticism a criminal offense. Using this measure, Woodrow Wilson's administration prosecuted publications by radical political and labor organizations; it also used its postal authority to ban many radical and antiwar materials from the mails. World War I showed how easily claims of national security could justify legal controls over dissenting presses.

The wartime period, then, inaugurated a new pattern of action by the national government. Throughout the 1920s and 1930s, smaller publishers often became targets for legal action. And, on the eve of World War II, Congress passed the Smith Act, which made it a crime to conspire to overthrow the government and to print materials that might aid such a conspiracy. After World War II, officials in Washington spent a good deal of time examining, and occasionally prosecuting, leftist publications, especially those of the Communist Party. Attempts to "protect national security" produced legal and political confrontations that recalled a question first raised during the 1790s: To what extent should the law protect publications demanding radical political and social change? Also, in the new context of cultural diversity, should the law seek to control publications that preached racial and ethnic hatred?

At the same time, the growth of large, independent publishing empires raised a second set of free-press questions. Though controlled by people firmly opposed to radical socioeconomic change, the mass media still clashed with powerful public figures over public policy and personal issues. President after president, for example, feuded with various editors and reporters. In their search for readers and corporate profits and in their pursuit of independent journalism, even establishment newspapers eventually came in conflict with governmental officials. Moreover, as the powers of government, especially at the national level, extended to all manner of domestic and international "problems," the media's adversaries asked new questions about the ways in which state authority intersected with claims of freedom by the

throughout the 1920s and 1930s, smaller publishers often became targets for legal action

NORMAN ROSENBERG

press. If an activist government could constitutionally regulate the activities of other large and socially powerful businesses, why should those who made money by publishing news and opinion enjoy special exemptions from public controls? Did the First Amendment really make the press so special? Confronting these kinds of difficult questions, people turned toward the Supreme Court of the United States for answers.

The Supreme Court: The First Free-Press Decisions

After 1920 the Supreme Court considered a number of cases involving freedom of press and articulated several basic, often-quoted principles. First, in *Gitlow v. New York* (1925), a prosecution against a socialist writer under a state criminal anarchy law, the Court ruled that the First Amendment's free-press guarantee limited the power of the states as well as that of the national government; only those state syndicalist laws that met First Amendment standards could restrict the flow of information and ideas through the press. As the principle of *Gitlow* was expanded to other types of regulatory measures, the Supreme Court, for the first time in the nation's history, came to play an important role in First Amendment debates.

Gitlow v. New York, 1925

Seven years after *Gitlow*, the Court joined the controversy over "offensive" publications filled with ethnic slurs. *Near v. Minnesota* (1931) involved a state law that allowed judges to halt further publication by newspapers they found to be "public nuisances." By a vote of 5 to 4, the Court decided that the First Amendment prohibited this type of judicial "prior restraint" against a small, anti-Semitic newspaper that blamed Minneapolis's political troubles on "Jewish gangsters." Under *Near*, "offensive" publications still could be prosecuted or sued after publication, but courts could not stop a newspaper from printing political criticism simply because of a judge's fear, on the basis of its previous stories, that it might endanger the public welfare or upset individuals and groups.

Near v. Minnesota, 1931

Many of the Court's most difficult free-press decisions involved claims of national security. The Justices were continually divided over dealing with publications that allegedly threatened the nation's security. A popular legal formula, which limited penalties to publications that created a "clear and present danger" of some substantial "evil," sounded much better in theory than in practice. Did, for example, the literature of the tiny and isolated Communist Party of the post–World War II era offer such a danger? The FBI, federal prosecutors, and a majority of the Supreme Court generally thought that they did. But civil liberties groups doubted that the remote danger posed by communists and other radicals justified the dangerous precedent of allowing governmental restraints on the press. In most cases, the Court's critics ob-

the justices were continually divided over dealing with publications that allegedly threatened the nation's security

served, judges could find some alleged danger that seemed evil enough, at least at the time, to justify denial of First Amendment claims by unorthodox publications.

Similarly, disagreement continued over cases in which the mainstream press became caught up in political and social struggles. Championing the public's "right to know," journalists of the 1960s and 1970s rediscovered the crusading style of Pulitzer and Hearst: They sought greater access to information on foreign and domestic issues, to materials which governmental officials considered "secret," and to the so-called whistle blowers and leakers who were ready to reveal alleged misdeeds within sprawling governmental bureaucracies. At the same time, radical groups, anxious to gain power and change public policies, looked to the media as the quickest way to carry their messages to the broadest possible audience. Critics once again charged journalists with "making," rather than simply reporting, the news, and with undermining the social order.

New York *Times v.* Sullivan and New York *Times v.* United States

As a result of its inevitable involvement in political struggles over domestic and foreign policy, even the cautious New York *Times* became a defendant in two dramatic free-press cases.

In the first, *New York* Times v. *Sullivan* (1964), a southern official successfully sued the paper for publishing a political advertisement, by civil rights advocates, that contained libelous falsehoods about his role in desegregation efforts. If the $500,000 judgment against the *Times* were upheld, other southern segregationists might be encouraged to use libel suits as a way of curtailing the national media's role in the civil rights debate. The Supreme Court thus saw the libel suit in *Sullivan* raising the same basic question as the Sedition Act of 1798: Could governmental officials use any kind of libel law to punish the press for discussing political issues?

The Court answered no. Although an Alabama jury had found the *Times* responsible for the libel, the Court declared that the First Amendment prohibited such a finding. In supporting its decision, the Court appealed to history. Any legal procedure that resembled the Sedition Act of 1798 and broadly protected government or public officials from criticism violated a central meaning of the First Amendment.

In effect, the Court in *Sullivan* sided with Jeffersonian critics of the Sedition Act. If juries could determine the "truth" of political statements, fear of libel suits might threaten the press's ability to respond to controversial issues and interfere with the free flow of political ideas. According to the Court, "unpleasantly sharp attacks on government and public officials" were inevitable in a free society.

New York Times v. Sullivan, 1964

Cases such as *Sullivan* also suggested a repudiation of the old Federalist view of the press: Rather than a dangerous instrument to be contained, the press represented a potential good, and it deserved special legal protection. In *Sullivan* and subsequent media cases, the Court emphasized that, except for knowingly libelous statements against specific officials, the press's contributions to public enlightenment outweighed any interests in strictly protecting the good name of government or even the individual reputations and privacy of public figures. Freedom of the press could not survive if publishers were required, even years after a story had appeared, to justify their political writings.

The value of the media to political debate became a central issue in a second important case that also repudiated the principles of the Sedition Act. In 1971, the *Times* and several other newspapers began to print excerpts from a secret government report, the "Pentagon Papers," that criticized American policies during the Vietnam War. President Richard Nixon immediately sought a court order to halt publication of the embarrassing excerpts; if excerpts continued to run, the government argued, national security, and even the safety of troops still in Vietnam, might be endangered.

In *New York* Times v. *United States* (1971), three justices agreed with the government, but the majority rejected the argument for censorship. In one sense, this case followed *Near* v. *Minnesota* in condemning prior restraints. In a larger historical view, though, the "Pentagon Papers case" renounced the premise of the Sedition Act and the Federalist view of political journalism. Governmental officials, no matter how important the interests they claimed to represent and no matter how pure their proclaimed motives, simply could not be trusted with power to censor the press, save in the most pressing of military situations and other acute emergencies.

New York Times v. United States, 1971

Recent and Contemporary Issues

New York Times v. *Sullivan* and the Pentagon Papers case only begin to suggest the controversial and complex issues of recent years. In one sense, Court decisions such as *Sullivan* offered new legal protections; but in an age when the media, even at the high school level, could easily become the stormcenter of broader social and cultural conflicts, even favorable legal decisions seemed to generate many times their weight in further litigation. New constitutional protections, in other words, hardly insulated the press from additional legal conflicts.

Consider, for example, recent debates over libel law. Journalists have complained about the popularity of libel suits among politicians and media celebrities and about soaring legal costs; even if a publication wins its case, it still suffers considerable legal

. . . the press's contributions to public enlightenment outweighed any interests in strictly protecting the good name of government. . . .

Milkovich v. Lorain Journal, 1990

Hazelwood School District v. Kuhlmeir, 1988

expenses. Even one costly libel suit can mean disaster for a small publisher. Worse, attempts to clarify and expand the *Sullivan* libel decision seemed to produce overly complex rules that proved difficult to apply.

Milkovich v. *Lorain Journal* (1990) epitomized recent trends in libel law. Here, a high-school wrestling coach sued a sports columnist who suggested that the coach had "lied" during hearings into responsibility for a post-meet brawl. After many years of complex and expensive legal appeals, courts in Ohio finally dismissed the coach's suit on the grounds that the critical sports column was merely one writer's "opinion" and, therefore, immune from any libel action. But a majority of the Supreme Court rejected this view; they held, instead, that the column also "implied" libelous facts for which even an opinion writer might be responsible in a libel suit. Although the columnist could claim all the journalistic protections mandated by *Sullivan*, the case still had to go back to the Ohio courts for more litigation over factual issues. In contrast, the dissenting justice, William Brennan, wanted to end the Milkovich case once and for all; he insisted that all comments about the coach's actions represented mere "conjecture," a legitimate form of journalistic commentary that should be protected against libel claims.

Apart from libel, other free-press issues have emerged in recent years. Fearing further rending of the social and cultural fabrics, for example, many people challenged extension of broad First Amendment protection to "fringe" publications that preached race hatred, demeaned ethnic groups and women, and espoused violent political change. Equally troublesome questions involved the role of television and powerful newspapers when they covered issues already fraught with dangerous ethnic and social tensions. Should inflammatory journalism, especially when aimed at better television ratings and higher circulation figures, be called to account for contributing, even if only indirectly, to ethnic and social strife? And to take only one more example, people also differed over the constitutional status of student-run publications. In *Hazelwood School District* v. *Kuhlmeir* (1988), the Supreme Court upheld a high school principal's power to exercise prior restraint over two stories, related to sexuality issues, written for a school-sponsored newspaper. Does this ruling, that administrators "need not tolerate" publications that clashed with a school's "basic educational mission," erode the freedom of student journalists?

Cases such as *Milkovich* and *Hazelwood* raise important questions about the future direction of free-press debates. Do decisions such as these suggest that a majority of the Court may be seeking to establish some clear limits on freedom of the press? Are they signs that the press might have to tailor its coverage and

NORMAN ROSENBERG

commentary on public events more with an eye toward avoiding legal costs than with a clear view toward informing the public or stimulating public debate?

Conclusion

Answering free-press questions has never been easy. Neither specific disputes nor even broader principles can be discovered by appealing to the First Amendment or other legal texts. Over the course of American history, ideas about the role of the press and about legal limits on its "freedom" have grown out of the complex interaction between the media and legal institutions. And this interaction, in turn, has always taken place within the broader social, political, and cultural milieu in which both the press and the law must operate.

Gitlow v. New York, 268 U.S. 652 (1925). Court upheld use of a state criminal anarchy law against a socialist publication, but it also ruled that the First Amendment applied to state as well as national laws affecting speech and press.

Hazelwood School District v. Kuhlmeir, 433 U.S. 299 (1988). The Court upheld, as a permissible act of censorship, a high-school principal's elimination of two stories from a school-sponsored newspaper that was connected to a journalism class.

Milkovich v. Lorain Journal, 58 U.S.L.W. 4846 (1990). The Court refused to accept the media's theory that columnists were not accountable for libelous "opinions"; instead, the majority held that opinion columns that "implied" factual situations might be sued, though libel plaintiffs would still have to meet the standards set down in *Sullivan* (see above) and subsequent libel cases.

Near v. Minnesota, 283 U.S. 397 (1931). By a 5 to 4 vote the Court declared a state law that authorized judges to ban the future issues of publications they found to be "public nuisances" was an unconstitutional prior restraint.

New York Times v. Sullivan, 376 U.S. 254 (1964). The Court belatedly declared the expired Sedition Act of 1798 unconstitutional and limited the ability of public officials to sue the press for libel to cases in which publications contained known or reckless libelous falsehoods.

New York Times v. United States, 403 U.S. 713 (1971). By a 6 to 3 vote, the Court rejected the government's attempt to secure

Cases

a court order halting further publication of a secret government report on policies in Vietnam; such a court order, the majority held, would be an unconstitutional prior restraint.

Suggested Readings

Harry Kalven, Jr., *A Worthy Tradition: Freedom of Speech in America* (New York: Harper & Row, 1988). An analysis of First Amendment cases from 1919 to 1974 by a leading Supreme Court scholar.

Leonard W. Levy, *The Emergence of a Free Press* (New York: Oxford University Press, 1985). The classic historical account of ideas and practices during the colonial period and the early years of the republic.

Paul L. Murphy, *World War I and the Origin of Civil Liberties in the United States* (New York: W.W. Norton & Co., Inc., 1979). A first-rate historical analysis of the simultaneous rise of surveillance institutions and new First Amendment ideas.

Norman L. Rosenberg, *Protecting the Best Men: An Interpretive History of the Law of Libel* (Chapel Hill: University of North Carolina Press, 1990). An overview of libel law, from the colonial era to the 1980s, which looks at social, political, and cultural influences.

Michael Schudson, *Discovering the News: A Social History of American Newspapers* (New York: Basic Books, Inc., 1978). An excellent overview of the nineteenth century journalist models by a leading media scholar.

James Morton Smith, *Freedom's Fetters: Alien and Sedition Laws and American Civil Liberties* (Ithaca, NY: Cornell University Press, 1956). The fullest and best historical discussion of the free-press debates of 1798 to 1800.

Rodney A. Smolla, *Suing the Press: Libel, the Media and Power* (New York: Oxford University Press, 1986). A lively and authoritative analysis of recent libel cases by a law professor who specializes in free-press questions.

V

Lawrence Delbert Cress

THE RIGHT TO BEAR ARMS

I n June 1776, the Virginia Declaration of Rights proclaimed "that a well-regulated Militia, composed of the body of the people, trained to arms, is the proper, natural, and safe defence of a free State."[1] About two months later, Pennsylvania declared that "the people have a right to bear arms for the defence of themselves and the state." Both states actually juxtaposed the right to arms alongside a perceived threat to liberty posed by standing armies. They wanted and needed to assure the "strict subordination" of military to civil power. The language of Virginia and Pennsylvania's resolutions provided models for subsequent revolutionary declarations. Delaware, Maryland, and New Hampshire incorporated Virginia's explicit endorsement of the militia into their constitutions, while the renegade republicans of Vermont borrowed freely from Pennsylvania's more open-ended declaration. North Carolina guaranteed the right to arms "for the defence of the State." Massachusetts used similar language: "The people have a right to keep and bear arms for the common defence." The Congress of the United States borrowed from the states when it formulated and approved what became the Constitution's Second Amendment: "A well regulated militia being necessary to the security of a free state, the right of the people to keep and bear arms shall not be infringed."

Did George Mason, the author of the Virginia document, and his revolutionary colleagues all agree about the intent of these guarantees? Had these states proclaimed the citizenry—trained, armed, and organized in the militia—the guarantor of

Militia

Standing armies

civil defense and public liberties? Or did Pennsylvania and Vermont—or Massachusetts and North Carolina for that matter—guarantee an individual right to arms independent of a person's service in a militia? Had Congress, in blending these provisions, sought to guarantee an individual right to arms or to ensure a viable militia? Or had it tried to do both? In recent years historians, constitutional scholars, and politicians have argued over the meaning of the Second Amendment. Some have claimed the amendment guarantees an individual right to own firearms. Others have argued that the amendment proclaims a collective right whose privileges are restricted to those in a trained and disciplined militia. Still others have called for a dual interpretation, arguing that the Founders sought both to underscore the importance of the militia in a free society and to ensure the right of individuals to protect themselves. What, then, were the intellectual roots of the Second Amendment? And how have the courts interpreted its meaning during the past two hundred years?

English Roots

The notion of an armed citizenry was supported by the framers of the Constitution, who drew on centuries-old arguments to make their case. Niccolò Machiavelli, the great Florentine political theorist, linked republican liberties to an armed citizenry willing and able to defend the state. "Never did anybody establish a republic," he wrote in *The Art of War*, "who did not suppose that the same persons who inhabited it would need with their weapons to defend it."[2] The republican theorist, James Harrington, who wrote during England's tumultuous mid-seventeenth century and was familiar to Americans of the revolutionary generation, took a similar position. The propertied and enfranchised militiaman both assured national security and deterred the intrigues of ambitious, centralized political power. Harrington's intellectual heirs, the radical Whigs, expected the militia to guarantee political liberties too. In the years surrounding the Glorious Revolution of 1688, Algernon Sidney and others linked the rise of tyranny with the militia's decay. John Trenchard, an Englishman later well known in the colonies as the coauthor with Thomas Gordon of *Cato's Letters*, began his career writing pamphlets proclaiming the dangers of standing armies and praising the locally organized, propertied citizen militia as the only force compatible with the security and the liberties of a free people.

Calls for militia reform in the decade after William and Mary assumed the English throne in 1688 underscored the relationship between bearing arms and liberty. Trenchard and his colleagues sought to arm and organize the industrious and propertied men

Radical Whigs

of the realm. They believed that in the ancient republics "arms never lodged in the Hands of any who had not an Interest in preserving the public Peace." To the contrary, "a general Exercise of the best of their People in the use of Arms, was the only Bulwark of their Liberties." They felt that lesser men were unreliable defenders of the public interest, lacking both the means and the leisure to understand and serve the "Public Good." "Most Men do as much Mischief as lay in their Power," reminded Trenchard; it was best to "take away all Weapons by which they may do either themselves or others an Injury."[3]

Trenchard's counsel would have surprised few of his contemporaries. The militia's misuse by royal authorities and its subsequent decline during the Restoration (1660–1688) had troubled both the royal court's friends and foes, if only because militia leadership and local authority went hand in hand. James II's preference for hired professional troops had reminded everyone of the dangers standing armies posed to freedom. Neither would Trenchard's limited notion of the right to arms have raised concern. Game laws, which restricted the use and ownership of private arms, dated to the fourteenth century in England. As recently as 1671, legislation had radically restricted the right to own arms while simultaneously expanding the power of the local gentry to enforce arms restrictions. Still, Trenchard's sense that militia service was a duty inherent in citizenship may have struck some people as out of step.

By the late seventeenth century many in England considered an army under parliamentary control compatible with liberty and national security. England's Bill of Rights (1689) prohibited the monarchy from raising an army in peacetime without Parliament's consent, but it did not require militia service of citizens. Reacting to James II's recent attempt to disarm his Protestant opposition, Parliament affirmed only "that the subjects which are Protestants may have arms." Parliament, it appears, rejected an effort to link access to arms with service for the "common defence," preferring language more in tune with the realm's long tradition of regulating private arms. "Protestants may have arms," the revolutionary settlement announced, "for their defence" but only as is "suitable to their conditions and as allowed by law." Rather than a fundamental individual right to arm for self-defense, the Bill of Rights assured a class of citizens, Protestants of "suitable condition," access to arms unless Parliament legislated otherwise. Existing law, which remained in force through the American Revolution, placed the property requirement for gun ownership at a level some fifty times higher than required for voting. At the end of the seventeenth century, less than 1 percent of Englishmen living on the land had a legitimate right to arm.

The revolutionary settlement left radical Whig spokesmen

"Most Men do as much Mischief as lay in their Power," reminded Trenchard

THE RIGHT TO BEAR ARMS

unsatisfied. They insisted that the absence of a viable militia endangered traditional English liberties. Trenchard and Gordon's *Cato's Letters*, James Burgh's *Political Disquisitions*, and a host of other tracts and essays appeared on both sides of the Atlantic during the eighteenth century arguing, for instance, that "if the militia be not upon the right foot"—that is, well trained—and "consisting. . .of men of property," then "the liberty of the people must perish."[4] The noted jurist William Blackstone lent the authority of his *Commentaries on the Laws of England* to the opposition claim as well. Individuals might take up arms for self-preservation "when the sanctions of society and laws" fail "to restrain. . .oppression"; such a circumstance, however, was beyond his comprehension. The militia, he argued, was "the constitutional security, which our laws have provided for the public peace, and for protecting the realm against foreign or domestic violence."[5]

The Revolutionary Era

Radical Whig tracts circulated widely in the mid-eighteenth century, offering Americans a critique of the danger imperial policy posed to liberty in the colonies. The British military occupation of Boston in 1768 and again in 1774, to say nothing of the Boston Massacre, left little doubt that hired soldiers could be agents of political oppression. "Our times prove Mr. Trenchard a True prophet," declared a dissident essayist on the eve of the revolution. Certainly the rebellious colonies responded to the mounting crisis in a fashion Trenchard and his colleagues would have approved. Among the petitions and resolutions passed during the winter of 1774–1775 demanding the repeal of the Coercive Acts, several county assemblies and provincial conventions roundly condemned standing armies, resolving—in language that foreshadowed the Second Amendment—"that a well-regulated Militia, composed of the gentlemen, freeholders, and other freemen, is the natural strength and only stable security of a free Government."[6] At the same time, the Continental Congress urged provincial assemblies to "disarm all such as will not associate to defend the American rights by arms."[7]

Like Trenchard, Americans were ready to "disarm" persons whose actions threatened the public good while at the same time expecting the citizenry to "associate" in defense of their liberties. Indeed, by the early 1770s, the militia had become synonymous with the body politic and inseparably entwined with the preservation of English liberties in the colonies. The anniversary of the Boston Massacre never passed without an orator proclaiming that "the true strength and safety of every commonwealth or limited monarchy is the bravery of its freeholders, its militia."[8] A widely read attack on the Boston Port Act reminded colonists that "the sword should never be in the hands of any, but those who have an interest in the safety of the community." Liberty depended on a "well disciplined militia, composed of men of fortunes, of education, and virtue."[9] An appropriately constituted militia enhanced more than military prowess, however. Regular training in arms had "a natural Tendency to introduce and establish good Order, and a just Subordination among the different Classes of People in the Community."[10] The parade field, in short, reinforced the social and political relationships that ensured order and a respect for authority in a free society.

The militia proved a disappointing defender of republicanism when war broke out with Great Britain. To secure independence, Americans, like their English counterparts a century before, turned to men willing to embrace, at least for the duration of the war, the values and discipline of professional soldiers. Nevertheless, as we have seen, state constitutions from Massachusetts to the Carolinas linked the citizen in arms with liberty and military service, reflecting the strong influence of radical Whig thought. Language differed, but the point was the same: Only the citizenry, trained, armed, and organized in the militia, could be depended upon to preserve republican liberties.

Unlike the English Bill of Rights, American revolutionary constitutions linked citizenship with the responsibility to bear arms for the common defense. Provisions exempting individuals from that responsibility make that clear. New Hampshire's Bill of Rights, the last written during the Confederation period and as such a compendium of previous thinking on the matter, provides a case in point. It declared the importance of "a well regulated militia [to the] defence of a state" while it exempted from service any "person...conscientiously scrupulous about the lawfulness of bearing arms." In other words, the individual right of conscience was asserted against the collective responsibility of the citizenry for the common defense. Not surprisingly, the state assessed fees, known as equivalents, so that someone else could be hired to "bear arms" in the conscientious objector's place.

Ratification and Bearing Arms

The issues that informed the states' declarations of rights—the militia's centrality to free government, the threat of standing armies, the free exercise of conscience in matters of militia service, the subordination of military to civil authority—shaped the debate over the new federal Constitution. Federalists and Antifederalists alike identified the preservation of free institutions with a strong militia. Antifederalists, however, rejected the idea that the distant national government could represent the popular will

...the individual right of conscience was asserted against the collective responsibility of the citizenry for the common defense

and, therefore, feared the militia powers granted to a remote and potentially arbitrary Congress. George Mason's approach to this concern conveniently summarizes the sentiments that led to the Second Amendment. He sought first to convince convention delegates to adopt a separate bill of rights explicitly affirming the militia's place in the new order. Failing that, he moved to amend the statement of Congress's authority to organize, arm, and discipline the militia with language identifying that prerogative as intending to secure "the liberties of the people against the dangers of standing armies in time of peace."[11] Though the convention rejected his proposal—despite the support of James Madison, who would later draft the Bill of Rights—Mason persisted. On the eve of Virginia's ratification convention, he and other Antifederalists sought to graft the essence of the commonwealth's Article 13 to the new Constitution.

The issue at hand was the preservation of a viable—that is armed and disciplined—militia; no one criticized the Constitution's failure to guarantee an individual's right to arm. "The militia may be here destroyed," Mason warned Virginia's ratification convention, "by rendering them useless, by disarming them." Great Britain had long ago "disarm[ed] the people . . . by totally diffusing and neglecting the militia," raising a standing army in its place. If the new government did the same, the states would be helpless because "congress has the exclusive right to arm them." "Why," Mason asked, "should we not provide against the danger of having our militia, our real and natural strength, destroyed?" Predictably, Mason backed Patrick Henry's proposal giving each state "the Power to provide for organizing, arming and disciplining its own Militia, whensoever the Congress shall omit or neglect to provide for the Same."[12]

The claim that individuals had a right to arm for private ends surfaced before and several times during the debate over the Constitution. In 1776 Thomas Jefferson unsuccessfully urged that the right of freemen to use arms within their "own lands or tenements" be incorporated into Virginia's constitution. Pennsylvanians may have had a similar guarantee in mind when they adopted their Declaration of Rights ensuring "the people . . . a right to bear arms for the defence of themselves and the state." Pennsylvania's Antifederalists doubted that, though. The minority report of that state's ratification convention called for amendments to the federal Constitution both proclaiming the corporate responsibility to bear arms—using the language of their state's Declaration of Rights—and guaranteeing "that no law shall be passed for disarming the people or any of them." In Massachusetts, a similar proposal by Samuel Adams failed to get majority support. Only New Hampshire's ratification convention actually endorsed an individual right to arms. Among a series of amend-

the issue at hand was the preservation of a viable . . . militia; no one criticized the Constitution's failure to guarantee an individual's right to arm

LAWRENCE DELBERT CRESS

ments forwarded to the First Congress, it recommended that "Congress shall never disarm any citizen, unless such as are or have been in actual rebellion."

Madison took little note of these recommendations as he prepared the original draft of the Bill of Rights. Rather than guarantee an individual right to arm, Madison sought to ensure that Congress not purposefully neglect the militia and that Congress exempt conscientious objectors from militia service. The congressional committee charged with developing a slate of amendments accepted Madison's approach and recommended to Congress an explicit statement of the armed citizenry's collective importance to the constitutional order: "A well regulated militia, composed of the body of the people, being the best security of a free state, the right of the people to keep and bear arms shall not be infringed." The committee also proposed that "no person religiously scrupulous shall be compelled to bear arms."

The committee's recommendations passed largely unchallenged through the House and Senate. Debate focused on whether the amendment adequately protected the militia from federal neglect, the absence of a prohibition on standing armies during peacetime, and the appropriateness of an exemption for conscientious objectors. The amendment sent to the states— where it was approved unanimously and without recorded debate—lacked that last provision, but was otherwise altered only in that the militia was described as "necessary to" rather than the "best" form of national defense. This last change more accurately expressed the growing sentiment that in wartime regular soldiers also had an important role to play, even in the defense of a republic. On December 15, 1791, with Virginia's ratification, the Second Amendment became part of the Constitution: "A well regulated Militia, being necessary to the security of a free state, the right of the people to keep and bear Arms, shall not be infringed." The historic tie between republicanism and a vital militia had become part of the nation's higher law. Henceforth, Congress was prohibited from taking any action that might disarm or otherwise render the militia less effective.

For some, including Secretary of War Henry Knox, the amendment confirmed the deeply held belief that military service was a duty inherent in citizenship. His plan for the defense of the new nation, which had roots in peacetime military planning begun under the Articles of Confederation, sheds more light on the meaning of the Second Amendment. Critics of the new Constitution had insisted that "to preserve liberty, it is essential that the whole body of the people always possess arms, and be taught alike, especially when young, how to use them,"[13] Secretary Knox proposed to do just that.

Knox, like Trenchard and his colleagues a century before,

the committee also proposed that "no person religiously scrupulous shall be compelled to bear arms"

wanted citizens responsible for the republic's defense: "An energetic national militia is to be regarded as the capital security of a free Republic; not a standing army." "Every man," he advised the First Congress, which was laboring to implement its authority over the militia, "is firmly bound by the social compact to perform, personally, his proportion of military duty for the defence of the State." The recent war had confirmed that Americans were no more inclined to embrace the hardships of war than the subjects of an arbitrary monarch. Thus, he envisioned a system of military training camps to inculcate discipline, discourage idleness and dissipation, and impart an understanding of "the eminent advantages of free Government." Attendance would be compulsory. These academies of military and civic training promised for the United States the political and moral stability that had eluded past republics. In the militia Knox saw "an institution, under whose auspices the youth and vigor of the constitution could be revived with each successive generation." In well-informed and disciplined members of the community would be merged the best traits of citizen and soldier. A certificate of militia service would be "required as an indispensable qualification for exercising any of the rights of a free citizen."[14]

The Nineteenth Century and After

Knox's plan proved too ambitious for congressmen more concerned about the centralization of militia power than institutionalizing the citizen's duty to defend the state. While decentralization meant decay and neglect, and despite repeated reminders by presidents from Washington through Madison that "for a people who are free, and who mean to remain so, a well organized militia is their best security,"[15] Congress declined to act. Congress and the American people had other concerns. If, as some have suggested, the revolutionary era was the last act of the Renaissance, the Second Amendment may have been the last line. State constitutions written during the first half of the nineteenth century rarely included statements affirming the "people's" collective responsibility for the republic's internal and external security. Instead, those documents proclaim an individual's right to arm in self-defense and/or in defense of the state. Mississippi's constitution of 1817, for example, guaranteed both rights for "every citizen." Michigan reserved the same rights for "every person." Maine, like its parent state, Massachusetts, declared a right to keep and bear arms for the common defense, but that right belonged not to the "people," as John Adams had phrased it in 1780, but to "every citizen." Arkansas and Florida followed suit, defining citizenship more narrowly by limiting that right to "free white men." Rhode Island adopted a truncated ver-

if . . . the revolutionary era was the last act of the Renaissance, the Second Amendment may have been the last line

sion of the Second Amendment when it rewrote its constitution in 1842. In step with the times, it declared that "the right of the people to keep and bear arms shall not be infringed," mentioning neither the militia nor any other reason for an armed population.[16]

Meanwhile the foremost constitutional commentator of the period, Justice Joseph Story, bemoaned the militia's decline and with it "all the protection intended by [the Second Amendment] of our national bill of rights." Citing Blackstone, Story noted in his *Commentaries on the Constitution of the United States* that "the right of the citizens to keep and bear arms has justly been considered, as the palladium of the liberties of a republic; since it offers a strong moral check against the usurpation and arbitrary power of rulers." "The importance of a well regulated militia would seem so undeniable," the Supreme Court justice lamented, "how it is practicable to keep the people duly armed without some organization, it is difficult to see."[17]

Nevertheless, antebellum America accepted the demise of the militia "organization" in stride, looking instead to the individual to provide the "protection intended" by the Second Amendment. Even if one is willing to interpret the clauses in the Pennsylvania, Vermont, North Carolina, and Massachusetts constitutions as asserting an individual's rights to arms, as some have, it still must be acknowledged that only these states bothered to guarantee that right during the revolutionary era. For that matter, only one of the 124 amendments submitted to Congress as it prepared the Bill of Rights—that submitted by New Hampshire—sought protection for an individual's right to bear arms. Yet in the years before the Civil War, 70 percent of the states entering the Union, together with Connecticut and Rhode Island, guaranteed that right for individual citizens. Kentucky and Georgia courts even struck down gun-control legislation on the grounds that it "diminished" the constitutional right to arms guaranteed in their state constitutions.[18] Whatever the founders intended, on the eve of the American Civil War keeping and bearing arms connoted an individual right. That may explain in part why Americans, both in the North and South, opposed compulsory military service during the Civil War. Chief Justice Roger B. Taney, in a draft opinion on the constitutionality of Union conscription, took a slightly different position, however. Grounded in an earlier understanding of the Second Amendment, he argued that federal conscription "annulled" the rights guaranteed in the Second Amendment because conscription necessarily destroyed "the militia" which "belongs to the several states."[19]

The Second Amendment, then, rooted in a republican tradition that considered the armed citizen the heart rather than the

See Bliss v. Kentucky, 1822; Nunn v. Georgia, 1846

opponent of the state, found little nurture in a young American republic more interested in individual rights than collective responsibilities. Curiously, the courts, following Taney's lead, have rarely interpreted the Second Amendment and its cousins found in state constitutions as guaranteeing a private right to arms. Cases are admittedly rare, but they suggest nevertheless the continuing influence of classical republican thought on the United States judiciary. Defendants challenging state gun-control statutes passed after the Civil War frequently cited state and federal constitutional rights to arm. State courts consistently rejected these pleas, however, both on the grounds that the Second Amendment restricted only the national government and because, as a Tennessee court explained, "the right to bear arms for the common defense does not mean the right to bear them ordinarily or commonly, for individual defense."[20] Federal courts took similar positions during the Gilded Age, declining to apply the amendment to the states by incorporation through the Fourteenth Amendment. As a leading constitutional commentator of the period explained, the right to bear arms "extends no further than to keep and bear those arms which are suited and proper for the general defense of the community against invasion and oppression."[21] The Supreme Court, in *Presser* v. *Illinois*, even declared constitutional an Illinois law prohibiting the "drill or parade with arms" of any group "other than the regular organized volunteer militia of this State." "Military organization and military drill and parade under arms are subjects especially under the control of the government of every country," declared the Court. They were not "an attribute of national citizenship" to be exercised "independent of law."[22]

See Andrews v. Tennessee, 1871

Presser v. Illinois, 1886

In the only modern case addressing the Second Amendment, *United States* v. *Miller*, the Supreme Court joined many state courts in affirming the constitutionality of gun-control legislation. The National Firearms Act of 1934 did not infringe on the rights guaranteed by the Second Amendment, the Court ruled, because the weapons the law sought to control bore no "reasonable relationship to the preservation or efficiency of a well regulated militia."[23] While one might argue that the decision left room for the private ownership of any weapon in the military arsenal, that clearly was not the government's position. The solicitor general rested his argument on the view that "the Second Amendment refers to the militia—'the arms-bearing population of the state, organized under the law, in possession of weapons for defending the state, and accustomed to their use'—and not to isolated individual rights."[24]

United States v. Miller, 1939

the Second Amendment, then, ...found little nurture in a young American republic more interested in individual rights than collective responsibilities

After the *Miller* case in 1939, gun control disappeared from the national agenda for nearly thirty years. Motivated by rising crime rates and the assassinations of Robert F. Kennedy and Martin Luther King, Jr., Congress enacted strict controls in 1968 governing the sale of handguns, rifles, shotguns, and ammunition despite sentiment in some quarters that such legislation violated constitutional rights guaranteed by the Second Amendment. Though the Supreme Court never ruled on the constitutionality of those statutes, Congress repealed restrictions on the interstate sale of rifles and shotguns in 1986, responding to heavy pressure from lobbying groups. In recent years, however, lower courts have ruled on a variety of cases arising from fierce political and legal battles between the champions and opponents of gun control. Like the decisions handed down in the nineteenth century, the federal and state courts have consistently viewed the Second Amendment as "framed in contemplation not of individual rights but of the maintenance of the states' active, organized militias."[25] The Supreme Court's studious silence on the issue since the *Miller* case has lent even greater authority to nineteenth-century precedence. Most recently, the Supreme Court declined to hear a case challenging a local ordinance prohibiting the possession of handguns within the city of Morton Grove, Illinois. That ruling left standing a circuit court decision exempting state and local statutes from the prohibitions outlined in the Second Amendment. The Seventh Circuit Court of Appeals, quoting *Presser* and *Miller*, ruled that the Second Amendment "had no other effect than to restrict the power of the National Government" in matters concerning "those arms which are necessary to maintain well-regulated militia."[26]

See Burton v. Sills, 1968

See Quilici v. Morton Grove

Conclusion

The origins and development of the right to bear arms has a rich and complex history. Drawing on the intellectual heritage of classical republicanism, Americans of the revolutionary generation considered freedom best preserved by a locally organized and armed citizen militia. State constitutions incorporated that idea and provided the model for what became the Second Amendment. The notion that individuals had a fundamental right to arm themselves had its proponents among the Constitution's founders, but that extended understanding of personal freedom awaited the specific wording of nineteenth-century state constitutions for elevation to the status of higher law. By the eve of the Civil War, the individual's absolute right to bear arms had gained recognition in several states. Nevertheless, the state and federal courts with few exceptions, especially after the Civil War, have followed the original intent of the framers, even declining to incorporate the Second Amendment into the guarantees provided under the Fourteenth Amendment. The Supreme Court, perhaps by intentional default, has left local and state governments

the Supreme Court's studious silence on the issue . . . has lent even greater authority to nineteenth-century precedence

free to regulate gun ownership while prohibiting congressional action only in areas threatening the maintenance of a well-regulated militia.

Notes

[1]This and other quotations bearing on the origins of the Second Amendment not footnoted can be found in Bernard Schwartz, ed., *The Roots of the Bill of Rights* (5 vols., New York, 1980).

[2]Niccolò Machiavelli, *The Art of War*, in *Machiavelli: The Chief Works and Others*, translated by Allan Gilbert (Durham, 1965), II, 585–86.

[3][John Trenchard and Walter Moyle], *An Argument, Shewing, That a Standing Army is Inconsistent with a Free Government, and Absolutely Destructive to the Constitution of the English Monarchy* (London, 1697), 10–13, 19.

[4][James Burgh], *Political Disquisitions: or, An Enquiry into Public Errors, Defects, and Abuses* (London, 1774–1775), II, 400.

[5]William Blackstone, *Commentaries on the Laws of England* (Chicago, 1979 [facsimile of the 1st ed, 1765–1769]), I, 139, 157, 400.

[6]Maryland Convention, December 8, 1774, in Peter Force, comp., *American Archives: Fourth Series, Containing a Documentary History of the English Colonies in North America* (Washington, 1837–1846), I, 1032.

[7]Oliver Wolcott to Samuel Lyman, March 16, 1776, in Edmund C. Barnett, ed., *Letters of the Members of the Continental Congress* (Washington, 1921–1936), I, 397.

[8]H. Niles, *Principles and Acts of the Revolution in America: or, An Attempt to Collect and Preserve some of the Speeches, Orations, and Proceedings* (Baltimore, 1822), 17–20.

[9]Josiah Quincy, Jr., *Observations on the Act of Parliament Commonly Called the Boston Port-Bill: With Thoughts on Civil Society and Standing Armies* (Boston, 1774), 41–43.

[10]Timothy Pickering, "A Military Citizen," *Essex Gazette*, January 31, 1769.

[11]*Notes of Debates in the Federal Convention of 1787, Reported by James Madison* (Athens, Ohio, 1966), 639–40.

[12]Robert A. Rutland, ed., *The Papers of George Mason, 1725–1792* (Chapel Hill, 1970), III, 1074–75, 1079–81, 1117.

[13]"Letters from the Federal Farmer to the Republican," quoted in Sanford Levinson, "The Embarrassing Second Amendment," *The Yale Law Journal*, vol. 99 (1989), 649.

[14]*Annals of Congress*, 1 Cong., 2 sess., January 18, 1790, appendix, pp. 2088–2107.

[15]Thomas Jefferson's 1808 address to Congress, in James D. Richardson, *A Compilation of the Papers of the Presidents, 1789–1897* (Washington, 1896–1899), I, 454–55, for example.

[16]Robert J. Taylor, "American Constitutions and the Right to Bear Arms," *Proceedings* of the Massachusetts Historical Society, 95 (1983), 58–60.

[17]Joseph Story, *Commentaries on the Constitution of the United States; with a Preliminary Review of the Constitutional History of the Colonies and States, before the Adoption of the Constitution* (Boston, 1833), III, 746–47.

[18]*Bliss v. Commonwealth*, 2 Litt. 90–94 (Kentucky, 1822); *Nunn v. State*, 1 Kelly 243 (Georgia, 1846).

[19]Philip G. Auchampaugh, ed., "A Great Justice on State and Federal Power. Being the Thoughts of Chief Justice Taney on the Federal Conscription Act," *Tyler's Quarterly Historical and Genealogical Magazine*, 18 (1936), 80.

[20]*Andrews v. State*, 13 Heisk. 165–66 (Tenn., 1871).

[21]Thomas M. Cooley, ed., *Commentaries on the Laws of England*, by William Blackstone (Chicago, 1884), I, 143n.

[22]*Presser v. Illinois*, 6 *Supreme Court Reporter* 585 (1886).

[23]*United States v. Miller*, 59 *Supreme Court Reporter* 816 (1939).

[24]Memorandum for the Solicitor General, June 22, 1938, Department of Justice, 80–10–2, Box 13073.

[25]*Burton v. Sills*, 28 A. L. R. 3d 829 (New Jersey, 1968).

[26]*Quilici v. Morton Grove*, 695 *Federal Reports* 2d 261 (7th Circuit Court, 1982).

Cases

Andrews v. Tennessee, 13 Heisk. 165 (1871). Rejecting the application of the Second Amendment to the states, the Tennessee Supreme Court ruled that that state's constitutional guarantee of the right to bear arms was limited only to "arms [used] for the defense of the community."

Bliss v. Kentucky, 2 Litt. 90 (1822). Citing Kentucky's constitutional guarantee of "the right of citizens to bear arms in defense of themselves and the state," the Kentucky Supreme Court struck down a statute barring the wearing of concealed weapons. The "right of the citizens to bear arms," the court ruled, has "no limits."

Burton v. Sills, 28 A.L.R. 3d 829 (New Jersey, 1968). This case arose out of a challenge to a 1966 New Jersey gun-control statute. The New Jersey Supreme Court, citing the English common law, which did not "recognize any absolute right to keep and bear arms," the reliance of American colonists on the militia to deter tyranny, and federal judicial decisions addressing the Second Amendment. The court ruled that the Second Amendment "is not designed to secure personal liberties against intrusion by government but to protect one governmental unit, the state, against subjection by another unit, the Federal government."

Nunn v. Georgia, 1 Kelly 243 (1846). The Georgia Supreme Court upheld legislation regulating the wearing of concealed weapons, but it gave notice that legislative authority extended only to the regulation of the mode of bearing arms. Georgia's constitution left unlimited the right of citizens to bear arms.

Presser v. Illinois, 6 Supreme Court Reporter 585 (1886). This case marks the first federal statement that the Second Amendment applied only to the national government. This precedent for nonincorporation still stands.

Quilici v. Morton Grove, 695 Federal Reports 2d 261 (1982). The ruling of the Seventh Circuit Court of Appeals in this case and the acquiesence of the U.S. Supreme Court confirmed that the Second Amendment remains outside the incorporation provision of the Fourteenth Amendment.

United States v. Miller, 59 Supreme Court Reporter 816 (1939). The Court unanimously rejected a challenge to the National Firearms Act of 1934 based on the Second Amendment on the grounds that concealed weapons were not necessary to "assure the continuation and render possible the effectiveness of the Militia." The decision, the Supreme Court's only full statement on the Second Amendment, left open the possibility that private weapons with uses appropriate to military action were protected by the Second Amendment.

Suggested Readings

Lawrence D. Cress, "An Armed Community: The Origins and Meaning of the Right to Bear Arms," *Journal of American History,* 71 (1984), 22–42. This article analyzes the intellectual traditions underlying the Second Amendment and argues that the amendment was intended to guarantee a sound militia.

Stephen P. Halbrook, *That Every Man Be Armed: The Evolution of a Constitutional Right* (Albuquerque: University of New Mexico Press, 1985). The book contends that the Second Amendment endorses an individual right to arm.

LAWRENCE DELBERT CRESS

David T. Hardy, "The Second Amendment and the Historiography of the Bill of Rights," *Journal of Law and Politics*, IV (1987), 1–62. Hardy argues that the framers of the Second Amendment intended to guarantee a sound militia *and* the right of individuals to own guns.

J. G. A. Pocock, *The Machiavellian Moment: Florentine Political Thought and the Atlantic Republican Tradition* (Princeton: Princeton University Press, 1975). This lengthy study examines the development of classical republican thought from Machiavelli through the American Revolution.

Robert E. Shalhope, "The Ideological Origins of the Second Amendment," *Journal of American History*, 69 (1982), 599–614. Shalhope, like Cress, explores the intellectual roots of the Second Amendment, but Shalhope concludes that the amendment was intended to guarantee an individual right to arms.

VI

Samuel Walker

RIGHTS BEFORE TRIAL

I t is a hot summer night in a big city. Two police officers stop a young man in a low-income neighborhood.

What rights does the young man have? What powers do the police officers have? Do they need a reason to stop him? Does he have to answer their questions? Can they frisk him? What grounds would they need for arrest? If they arrest him, must they advise him of any rights? When? If the young man resists arrest, can they use force to subdue him? How much force? How long can he be held for questioning? Does he have a right to bail? If he tries to flee, can the officers shoot him? Even if he is unarmed?

Confrontations between police officers and citizens occur thousands of times every day and raise fundamental questions about individual rights. The same issues are raised in less dramatic situations, such as when officials investigate a suspected white-collar crime. This essay discusses the rights that individual citizens have in criminal proceedings before trial.

Pretrial rights are in many respects more important than rights at trial, simply because they affect far more people. The vast majority of the people stopped by the police are not arrested. About half of those who are arrested are released without being charged with any crime. Most of those who are prosecuted plead guilty rather than go to trial. Pretrial proceedings, in short, introduce a series of decision-points where rights may be violated. Such proceedings affect most of the people who have contact with the criminal justice system.

Pretrial proceedings raise the basic issue of constitutional government: how to balance freedom and order. On the one side

pretrial rights are . . . more important than rights at trial, simply because they affect far more people

stands the principle of individual freedom. The Bill of Rights exists to protect freedom by limiting the power of government officials. On the other side, however, the Constitution grants government certain powers for the purpose of maintaining an orderly society and promoting the conditions of freedom. Maintaining order includes enforcing the criminal law through appropriate police action. Maintaining the proper balance between these two goals is an extremely difficult problem.

The problem is particularly acute in the United States because of the high volume of serious crime. Its murder rate is ten times higher than that of England and its robbery rate is one hundred times higher than Japan's. High crime rates generate public demand for "tough" law enforcement. The police, under pressure to "get results," are tempted to use tactics that violate individual rights.

Constitutional Protection of Pretrial Rights

Specific Provisions of the Bill of Rights

Individual rights before trial are protected by the Fourth, Fifth, Sixth, Eighth, and Fourteenth amendments to the Constitution.

The Fourth Amendment guarantees protection against unreasonable searches and seizures. The Fifth Amendment prohibits double jeopardy and self-incrimination, and guarantees that "no person shall be deprived of life, liberty, or property, without due process of law." The Sixth Amendment guarantees a criminal defendant a speedy and public jury trial, the right to be informed of the charges and to confront accusors, and the right to assistance of counsel. The Eighth Amendment guarantees protection against "excessive bail" and "cruel and unusual punishments."

Double jeopardy

The Fourteenth Amendment guarantees that *no state* shall "deprive any person of life, liberty, or property, without due process of law; nor deny to any person within its jurisdiction the equal protection of the laws." Because state and local governments have the primary responsibility for crime control, the vast majority of arrests are made by local police, and the resulting cases are prosecuted in state courts, this amendment is extremely important for pretrial rights. Gradually, the Supreme Court "incorporated" provisions of the Bill of Rights into the due process clause of the Fourteenth Amendment and extended their protections to state and local criminal proceedings.

Due process

Origins of the Constitutional Protection of Pretrial Rights

Two considerations led the framers to place specific protections of pretrial rights in the Bill of Rights: a general sense of the rights of free people and the more immediate experience of the struggle for

pretrial proceedings . . . introduce a series of decision-points where rights may be violated

independence, which had resulted from incidents where those rights had been violated.

The framers drew upon the English heritage of individual liberty marked by such milestones as the Magna Carta (1215), the Petition of Right (1628), and the Bill of Rights (1689). The Magna Carta established the principle of limiting government power. While it contained no specific language related to pretrial rights, Section 39 provided that no "freeman" could be imprisoned except "by the law of the land." This phrase contained the germ of the concept of due process. Subsequent generations of English legal theorists gradually expanded the idea of individual rights in criminal proceedings. The Bill of Rights in 1689 added protections against excessive bail and "illegal and cruel punishments." Even though there were no specific prohibitions against unreasonable searches and seizures, by the sixteenth century English legal theorists began to argue that they were inherent in the tradition that began with the Magna Carta.

The American colonists inherited this legal tradition. Additionally, the first one hundred and fifty years of colonial experience reinforced their sense of being a free people. Specific guarantees of individual rights appeared in the earliest colonial governance documents. The Massachusetts Body of Liberties (1641) proscribed excessive bail and cruel bodily punishments.

To a great extent, the British left the colonies to their own devices during the first century and a half. Thus, when the British began to assert greater control in colonial affairs during the mid-eighteenth century, the Americans regarded this as an intrusion upon their liberties. Specific British practices sharpened their consciousness of the need to place formal restrictions upon government authority. The enforcement of new tax laws and the impressment of men into the navy, both accomplished through intrusive searches, were particularly offensive. A Massachusetts law passed in 1756 was the first document to affirm the idea that all searches must be limited by particularity—that a warrant had to specify the evidence to be seized.

When the colonies declared their independence in 1776, they included bills of rights in their new state constitutions. The Virginia Declaration of Rights was the first true bill of rights in this country. It included prohibitions on excessive bail and cruel and unusual punishment, protection against self-incrimination, and a guarantee that "no man be deprived of his liberty except by the law of the land." The section on searches and seizures declared that general warrants "ought not to be granted." There was no consistent pattern in the state bills of rights. The Pennsylvania constitution omitted prohibitions on excessive bail and cruel and unusual punishments but added the right to counsel and a stronger limitation on searches and seizures than that provided by the Virginia Declaration of Rights.

the first one hundred and fifty years of colonial experience reinforced [the] sense of being a free people

SAMUEL WALKER

The existence of the bills of rights provided a powerful precedent for similar protections in the U.S. Constitution, drafted in 1787. Madison fashioned the final Bill of Rights out of the language of the state constitutions and other recommendations from the states. In the case of the Fourth Amendment, Madison's final wording afforded the strongest protection to that time. His version substituted the stronger "shall not" prohibition for the more prevalent "ought not" wording.

The principle issue in the adoption of the Bill of Rights was not the language of the specific provisions but whether such a document was needed at all. Many of the framers argued that a federal bill of rights was not necessary since individual liberty was protected by the various state constitutions. Others worried that a list of specific prohibitions would mean that the federal government would have the implicit power to do anything not explicitly forbidden.

The enumerated pretrial rights in the final Bill of Rights were a radical affirmation of individual liberty. The list was far more comprehensive than any previous document in Anglo-American legal history. Nonetheless, it left many questions unanswered, questions with which subsequent generations have had to wrestle. The Fourth Amendment, for example, offered a general prohibition on unreasonable searches and seizures, but there was no clear understanding of what constituted an "unreasonable" search, nor was there any penalty stipulated for violating this provision.

While the framers were highly conscious of certain rights, they lived in a very different and much simpler world than today's. The growth of a complex urban-industrial society and the attendant bureaucratization of the administration of justice would introduce many new problems. In 1791 there were no large police forces in American cities. The subsequent development of law enforcement agencies, with officers patrolling throughout the community, would raise a host of new questions about the powers of law enforcement and the protection of individual rights. Modern technology—the telephone, the polygraph, sophisticated surveillance devices—would also introduce complex problems.

The Bill of Rights articulated a strong but general sense of pretrial rights. It remained for subsequent generations to define those rights in a complex and ever-changing world.

Implementation of Pretrial Rights

In practice, pretrial rights are protected through a variety of means that provide a complex and constantly changing "mix" of specific protections. The Bill of Rights defines a set of general principles. The Supreme Court interprets various provisions on a

the enumerated pretrial rights in the final Bill of Rights were a radical affirmation of individual liberty

case-by-case basis. Federal and state codes of criminal procedure offer even more specific guidelines. State courts interpret state constitutional protections. Finally, individual criminal justice agencies adopt their own policies and procedures. The Constitution is the supreme law of the land, and none of these other measures may violate a provision of the Bill of Rights—although each one may provide greater protections.

The Growth of Constitutional Protections

Constitutional protection of pretrial rights expanded relatively recently in American history. The greatest extension occurred in the 1950s and 1960s through a series of Supreme Court decisions under Chief Justice Earl Warren.

Through most of American history, constitutional guarantees played a very limited role in the criminal process. Defense lawyers vigorously represented their clients, usually by challenging evidence at trial or by questioning the instructions to the jury. The assertion of pretrial rights was extremely limited in two important respects. First, there were no definitive Supreme Court rulings. Until the middle of the twentieth century, the Bill of Rights was not applied to state and local proceedings. Second, very little attention was given to events that occurred prior to trial: police stops, frisks, interrogations at the police station, and the use of deadly force.

The Warren Court's expansion of pretrial rights began slowly in the 1950s and then increased rapidly in the 1960s. The Civil Rights movement was particularly important in sensitizing the Court to the problems of the poor and racial minorities at the hands of the criminal justice system. This led the Court to develop greater protections for individual suspects. The turning point was the *Mapp v. Ohio* decision of 1961 in which the Court adopted the "exclusionary rule," holding that evidence gathered in violation of the Fourth Amendment could not be used against criminal defendants. The Court not only interpreted the Fourth Amendment broadly, but also extended the protections of the Fourteenth Amendment to state and local cases. Over the next few years, the Court expanded constitutional protection of other pretrial rights. The most controversial decision was *Miranda v. Arizona* in 1966, where the Court held that the police were required to advise a suspect of the right to remain silent, the right to an attorney, and that an attorney would be provided if the suspect could not afford one. The "Miranda warning" was designed to protect a person against self-incrimination.

Mapp and *Miranda* were part of a larger group of decisions enlarging individual rights throughout the entire criminal justice system. Other decisions guaranteed the right to an attorney at trial, due process in juvenile court proceedings, and the constitu-

Mapp v. Ohio, 1961
Exclusionary rule

Miranda v. Arizona, 1966

tional rights of prisoners. The impact of these decisions has been called the "due process revolution."

The Warren Court's decisions on police behavior provoked a bitter reaction. Critics accused it of being too sympathetic to criminals and insensitive to the rights of law-abiding people and the victims of crime. With a new chief justice in 1969 and the addition of several conservative justices in the 1970s and 1980s, the Court became less sympathetic to the rights of criminal suspects and more willing to rule in favor of law enforcement officials. In 1984, for example, the Court created a "public safety" exception to the Miranda warning. The *New York* v. *Quarles* decision held that, to protect themselves, police officers could ask a suspect about the location of a gun without first giving the Miranda warning. The Court also endorsed the concept of "preventive detention," upholding a federal law allowing judges to deny bail to suspects they believed to be dangerous.

New York v. Quarles, 1984

Statutes and Codes of Criminal Procedure

The most detailed protections of individual rights are found in federal and state codes of criminal procedure. Rule #5 of the federal rules of criminal procedure, for example, provides that an arrested person must be taken "without necessary delay before the nearest available federal magistrate" and that the magistrate shall inform the defendant of the charge, the right to make no statement, the right to an attorney, and so on. This and other rules are designed to protect individual rights by specifically limiting the behavior of criminal justice officials. Each of the fifty states has its own code of criminal procedure.

Individual rights before trial can also be protected—or restricted—by statute. Bail is a good example. The right to bail was greatly expanded in the 1960s through federal and state bail reform laws that allowed defendants to be released on their own recognizance (that is, their promise to appear in court voluntarily). These laws sought to eliminate discrimination against poor people who were unable to raise money or property for bail. The same laws established specific criteria for determining eligibility for release on recognizance (such criteria as employment status or whether there are family members in the community). In the 1970s, however, a second bail reform movement began to restrict the right to bail. Federal and state "preventive detention" laws authorized judges to deny bail to persons deemed dangerous to the community.

Release on recognizance

Preventive detention

Administrative Policies

Individual rights can also be protected by policies adopted by criminal justice agencies. This approach is called administrative rulemaking. A good example involves police use of deadly force.

Administrative rulemaking

Fleeing felon rule

Tennessee v. Garner, 1985

Police powers

In the 1970s most big city police departments began to adopt policies limiting police use of deadly force to "defense of life" situations; also prohibited was the shooting of unarmed "fleeing felons." Most of these policies put more restrictions on police use of deadly force than the Supreme Court's decision in *Tennessee v. Garner* (1985), which declared the fleeing-felon rule unconstitutional.

State Constitutional Protections

Pretrial rights are also protected by state constitutions. Each state constitution has its own bill of rights, similar although not identical to that found in the U.S. Constitution. State constitutional protection of individual rights has been overshadowed by the prominent role of the U.S. Supreme Court. The role of state constitutions began to receive more attention in the 1980s as the Supreme Court moved in a more conservative direction. In some instances, state supreme courts affirmed greater protection of individual rights under the state constitution than the Supreme Court did under the federal constitution.

Controversies

The growth of constitutional protection of pretrial rights in the 1960s generated enormous controversy, involving three interrelated issues: the meaning of the specific provisions of the Bill of Rights; the role of the Supreme Court in American society; and the relationship between individual rights and effective crime control.

The Meaning of the Bill of Rights

The guarantees in the Bill of Rights are expressed in very general phrases such as "due process of law," "unreasonable searches and seizures," and "excessive" bail. Honorable people can and do disagree over the meaning of these phrases. What, for example, does "due process" mean? What kinds of searches are "unreasonable?"

There are no obvious answers to these questions. The language of the Constitution itself does not tell us, for example, whether the police have the right to conduct random traffic stops to administer sobriety tests. Are such stops, carried out with no specific regard to the individual's behavior, an unreasonable search? Or are they a reasonable exercise of police power for the purpose of promoting public safety? The concept of due process is particularly difficult to define. Virtually everyone agrees that it means that criminal proceedings should be "fair" and not "arbitrary." But people can and do disagree over what is fair or arbitrary with respect to particular actions.

Recent debates over the meaning of the Bill of Rights have been dominated by the concept of "original intent." Conservative legal scholars argue that particular sections of the Bill of Rights mean only what the framers intended them to mean. They accuse liberal justices and scholars of substituting their own social and political values for the original meaning in order to achieve the results they desire. Liberal scholars reply that it is proper for judges to interpret the Bill of Rights in light of changing social circumstances and values. Thus, for example, punishments that were considered acceptable in one era might be regarded as cruel and unusual in another.

The Role of the Supreme Court

Debate over the meaning of the Bill of Rights also inevitably involves the question of the role of the Supreme Court. The principal controversy is between the advocates of "judicial restraint" and "judicial activism." Advocates of judicial restraint argue that the Court should be very hesitant in ruling unconstitutional legislation or decisions by state courts. The advocates of judicial activism, on the other hand, argue that the Court has a special responsibility to give the principles of the Bill of Rights meaning through application in specific cases.

Judicial restraint
Judicial activism

This debate involves two distinct issues. With respect to legislation, the advocates of judicial restraint argue that the Supreme Court has a unique status as an unelected, undemocratic body in a democratic society. Thus, it should be very careful about substituting its judgment for majority will. If the majority wishes to deny bail to certain categories of people through preventive detention, the Court should accept their judgment. The advocates of judicial activism, on the other hand, argue that the very purpose of the Bill of Rights is to protect minorities and unpopular views against action by the majority.

The second issue is a matter of federalism, which has special relevance for pretrial rights. The advocates of judicial restraint argue that the federal Supreme Court should not intrude itself excessively in state matters, leaving them to state legislature and state courts. The advocates of judicial activism, on the other hand, argue that the Fourteenth Amendment "incorporates" the Bill of Rights and consequently gives the Supreme Court authority over violations of such rights, even at the state level. Significantly, the Court has never accepted the argument, advanced by Justice Hugo Black, that the Fourteenth Amendment incorporates the entire Bill of Rights. Instead, the Court has chosen a process of "selective incorporation."

Incorporation doctrine

Individual Rights versus Crime Control

Finally, issues of pretrial rights have been among the major controversies in American politics over the past thirty years.

Critics of the Warren Court accused it of demonstrating excessive concern for criminal suspects, defendants, and prisoners, and too little concern for the law-abiding majority and crime victims. The major Warren Court decisions coincided with a dramatic rise in serious crime beginning in the early 1960s. Critics argued that such decisions as *Mapp* and *Miranda* "handcuffed" the police and contributed to the rise in crime. Substantial criminological research, however, indicated that very few criminals successfully "beat the system" because of technicalities. In fact, some research indicated that the Court's decisions spurred reform by criminal justice agencies, including the professionalization of the police. Nonetheless, criticism of the courts for being "soft" on crime continued.

In the 1980s a crime victims movement emerged. President Ronald Reagan appointed a task force on the rights of victims which made a number of recommendations for change in federal, state, and local criminal justice agencies. Several states passed victims' rights legislation, including laws providing financial compensation to victims, guaranteeing victims the right to participate in all phases of the criminal process (and in some cases to make recommendations on sentencing their offenders), and relaxing the exclusionary rule. The Bill of Rights contains no provisions specifically or implicitly affirming the rights of crime victims, and consequently much of the energy of the victims' rights movement was directed toward eliminating such existing protections of the rights of criminal suspects as the exclusionary rule and the Miranda warning.

The criticisms of the Warren Court had a significant impact on American politics. Conservative presidential candidates made the Court's criminal justice decisions major campaign issues. Presidents Richard Nixon (1969–1974) and Ronald Reagan (1981–1989) appointed conservative justices to the Supreme Court and, as a result, the Court moved in a conservative direction. By the 1980s the majority of justices were less sympathetic to the rights of suspects, defendants, and prisoners. Nonetheless, despite the conservative direction of the Court, by 1990 it had not directly overturned any of the major Warren Court precedents, nor had it abandoned the basic principle that the Supreme Court should oversee the criminal process.

Conclusion

It is possible to draw several key conclusions about the constitutional protection of pretrial rights today. First, from a historical perspective, the expansion of pretrial rights is a relatively recent phenomenon, having occurred in just the last thirty years. Second, the status of pretrial rights continues to change. The Supreme Court may be expected to give more weight in the future to the needs of public safety rather than those of individual

substantial criminological research . . . indicated that very few criminals successfully "beat the system" because of technicalities

rights. Third, Supreme Court rulings are only one of several mechanisms by which pretrial rights may be protected. The powers of criminal justice officials are also defined and limited by codes of criminal procedure, administrative policies adopted by criminal justice agencies, and state bills of rights.

Cases

Mapp v. Ohio, 367 U.S. 643 (1961). The Supreme Court held that evidence obtained in violation of the Fourth Amendment's prohibition of unreasonable searches and seizures could not be used against a criminal suspect. This doctrine is referred to as the "exclusionary rule." Through the Fourteenth Amendment, the decision was applied to state and local proceedings.

Miranda v. Arizona, 384 U.S. 436 (1966). The Court held that in order to assure the privilege against self-incrimination, the police were required to advise a criminal suspect of his or her rights. The resulting "Miranda warning" included advice that the suspect had a right to remain silent, that anything he or she said could be used against the suspect, that the suspect had a right to an attorney, and that if he or she could not afford an attorney, one would be provided.

New York v. Quarles, 467 U.S. 649 (1984). The Court created a "public safety" exception to the Miranda ruling. In order to protect themselves against possible harm, police officers could ask a criminal suspect questions—in this instance about the location of a weapon—without first advising the suspect of his or her right to remain silent.

Tennessee v. Garner, 471 U.S. 1 (1985). The Court ruled unconstitutional a Tennessee law that allowed the police to use deadly force against "fleeing felons." The Court upheld that shooting a suspect was a "seizure" under the Fourth Amendment and that the shooting of unarmed suspects who pose no immediate danger to the community was unreasonable.

Suggested Readings

Liva Baker, *Miranda: Crime, Law and Politics* (New York: Atheneum, 1983). Lengthy, detailed account of the most controversial Supreme Court decision on the rights of suspects. Written for a general audience.

Archibald Cox, *The Warren Court* (Cambridge: Harvard University Press, 1968). A brief overview of the Warren Court's pathbreaking decisions. Places the major criminal procedure decisions in the context of the Court's decisions in the areas of civil rights and First Amendment rights. Very useful for the person not trained in constitutional law.

Lawrence M. Friedman and Robert V. Percival, *The Roots of Justice: Crime and Justice in Alameda County, California, 1870–1910* (Chapel Hill: University of North Carolina Press, 1981). An extremely detailed scholarly study of criminal justice in one community. In addition to statistics on the handling of cases, offers many anecdotes that recreate the feel of the criminal justice system.

Yale Kamisar, *Police Interrogations and Confessions* (Ann Arbor: University of Michigan Press, 1980). A collection of previously published articles by one of the leading experts on the rights of criminal suspects. Detailed analysis of legal doctrine, but also useful for putting *Miranda* and other controversial cases in historical context.

Leonard Levy, *Original Intent and the Framers' Constitution* (New York: Macmillan, 1988). A collection of previously published articles on constitutional law that contains the best criticism of the "original intent" argument. Extremely useful for the nonspecialist.

Anthony Lewis, *Gideon's Trumpet* (New York: Vintage Books, 1966). Although it does not deal with rights before trial specifically, it is the best account of a major Supreme Court decision on individual rights. A brief, extremely readable classic.

Richard E. Morgan, *Disabling America: The "Rights Industry" in Our Time* (New York: Basic Books, 1984). A conservative critique of the growth of judicially protected rights in recent decades. One chapter is devoted to criminal justice. Places criminal procedure issues in a broader context of individual rights.

Bernard Schwartz, ed., *The Roots of the Bill of Rights*, 5 vols. (New York: Chelsea House, 1980). An extremely useful collection of original documents on the origins of the Bill of Rights, beginning with the Magna Carta. Includes a useful commentary on each document by the editor.

James Stark and Howard W. Goldstein, *The Rights of Crime Victims* (New York: Bantam Books, 1985). A brief overview of the rights of crime victims. Written for a general audience in question-and-answer format.

Samuel Walker, *Popular Justice: A History of American Criminal Justice* (New York: Oxford University Press, 1980). A short history of American criminal justice. Places the development of constitutional rights during the Warren Court era in historical context.

VII

David J. Bodenhamer

TRIAL RIGHTS OF THE ACCUSED

The scene is familiar to television viewers. Two lawyers—one for the prosecution, one for the defense—engage in a battle of wits over the fate of a defendant charged with crime, all conducted in public before a dispassionate jury of peers and an impartial judge. The trial unfolds in stages: opening arguments, presentation of evidence, skilled examination of witnesses, eloquent summations. Defense attorneys are vigilant in protection of the accused's rights. Each element of the drama frames the question of guilt or innocence and assures us that the combat is fair. Tension builds until the judge issues carefully worded instructions and the jury retires for its decision. In the final act the defendant either stands acquitted or faces punishment. The outcome reaffirms cherished ideals: we are a people committed to law; the law is exacting but fair; defendants have rights upon trial; and justice results from strict adherence to legal procedures.

The reality of American criminal justice often falls short of these ideals. Most cases do not come to trial. Harried and overworked prosecutors and judges offer a reduced sentence to a defendant in exchange for a guilty plea. Most trials are not neat and well-ordered affairs. There is much confusion and delay; lawyers usually are not eloquent; judges may be inattentive; and juries are not always impartial or objective. Yet even with its flaws American trial law is unequaled in the protection it offers to the accused. Indeed, the rights of criminal defendants are central to our constitutional liberty. Why is this so, and how did rights of the accused become so important?

Theory of Rights for the Accused

"The history of American freedom is, in no small measure, the history of procedure."[1] Supreme Court Justice Felix Frankfurter's epigraph expresses a fundamental article of faith about our constitutional heritage: liberty and rights cannot exist without due process of law. Procedural fairness and consistency are essential elements of due process, the touchstone of Anglo-American jurisprudence.

In the criminal law of a free society, a proper concern for due process is crucial. Without it, individual liberty is especially vulnerable to arbitrary governmental power. And, as numerous scholars have noted, freedom from official capriciousness is essential to all other human rights. This ideal is an old one, and its significance in western culture can scarcely be overstated. Government holds such power that any criminal trial between the government and a citizen is inherently unequal. Our conception of justice demands that this inequality be removed. Anglo-American law balances the contest between government and the individual by restraining official power. It makes defendants' rights inviolable; in theory, failure to follow due process will result in acquittal.

Do the rights of criminal defendants limit too much government's ability to protect lives and property? Why should we make it difficult to arrest and convict wrongdoers? Our history suggests several answers. First, we have long believed that freedom is so precious that it is better, as an old English maxim says, for ninety-nine guilty persons to go free than for one innocent person to suffer punishment. Also, we have concluded that unrestrained power always destroys liberty. Finally, we accept the notion that truth emerges when impartial observers weigh the competing claims made by opposing sides in an equal contest.

Sources of Defendants' Rights

The Anglo-American conception of due process dates at least to the Magna Carta (1215), when feudal barons required King John of England to follow the law of the land in royal prosecutions. From this beginning developed a long tradition of limiting governmental power by granting certain protections to individuals charged with crimes. Today, this history remains important to understanding the meaning of these rights, but in American law the Bill of Rights is the most important source of due process guarantees.

The federal Bill of Rights devotes more attention to the requirements for a fair criminal process than it does to any other right or group of rights. The Fourth, Fifth, Sixth, and Eighth

procedural fairness and consistency are essential elements of due process, the touchstone of Anglo-American jurisprudence

DAVID J. BODENHAMER

amendments outline twelve provisions regarding arrest, trial, and punishment that constitute a miniature code of criminal procedure. The rights of defendants during and after trial include: protection against double jeopardy and self-incrimination (Fifth Amendment); speedy and public trial by an impartial jury, confrontation with prosecution witnesses, compulsory process for obtaining witnesses and evidence, and assistance of counsel (Sixth Amendment); and prohibition against cruel and unusual punishments (Eighth Amendment). Numerous other rights governing trials and appeals fall under "due process of law," the Fifth and Fourteenth Amendment clause which represents the community's pledge of fair play in prosecuting crime.

Code of criminal procedure

Double jeopardy

Not all rights important to criminal process are in the Bill of Rights. *Habeas corpus*, which requires a judge to release an unlawfully detained prisoner, is in Article I, Section 9, of the Constitution, as is an absolute prohibition of bills of attainder and *ex post facto* laws. Article III secures a jury trial in all federal criminal cases. State constitutions and statutes also contain rights that balance the contest between government and the accused.

Habeas corpus

Bills of Attainder
Ex post facto

History of Trial Rights

The framers of the Bill of Rights based trial rights of the accused on colonial practices and on their understanding of English history, especially the long tradition of restricting the power of government. Initially, the guarantees applied only to the central government. Under the federal system, states, not the national government, had primary responsibility for protecting these rights. Only since the 1930s has the Supreme Court protected defendants' rights in state courts by interpreting the Fourteenth Amendment's due process clause to include the Bill of Rights' definition of fair trial. Today most rights of criminal defendants have national application. Each of the constitutional safeguards has a long and complex history, but even a brief examination of these protections over time reveals a central theme: in Justice Frankfurter's words, rights of the accused have "gathered meaning from experience."[2] Even seemingly straightforward requirements such as trial by jury, not to mention more general concepts such as due process, have changed meaning considerably throughout our past.

The English Background

Anglo-Saxon criminal proceedings contained certain features which became hallmarks of English justice. There was a definite and known accuser who publicly confronted the accused, trials were open, and members of the community enforced the rules of fairness. The Norman Conquest (1066) introduced the grand jury

government holds such power that any criminal trial between the government and a citizen is inherently unequal

Grand jury

TRIAL RIGHTS OF THE ACCUSED

Petit jury

Prerogative courts

Common law

to inquire into matters of crime and the petit or trial jury of twelve local men to decide guilt or innocence. By the time of the Magna Carta, trial by jury was an established feature of the common law.

In the sixteenth and seventeenth centuries, the Tudor and Stuart monarchies created prerogative courts to strengthen royal control of justice. These courts, especially the notorious Star Chamber, used secret proceedings and torture to control dissent, including personal religious beliefs which differed from state policy. Prosecutions in these courts involved an examination under oath without the accused knowing the charges against him or her, the identity of prosecution witnesses, or the content of their testimony. Prerogative courts sat without juries, and very few defendants secured an acquittal. The existence of these tribunals clearly challenged the constitutional traditions of England and weakened the protection of trial by jury.

The English Civil War and Interregnum (1642–1660) ended prerogative courts, but it was still difficult for common law courts to protect the rights of the accused. Judges sat at the pleasure of the king and controlled the jury by fining or imprisoning jurors who returned verdicts against the judge's wishes. These measures stirred much controversy. Finally, in the Glorious Revolution the Parliament enacted a Bill of Rights (1688) and other measures which restated some traditional rights of Englishmen and established new liberties, including requirements for proper impaneling of jurors and prohibition of cruel punishments or excessive fines and bails.

Colonial Developments

Early English settlers in the New World desired to reform the common law and strengthen its protection of traditional rights. They sought especially to simplify the law and make it understandable. In this aim, they largely succeeded. They restated the law in plain English and published it for distribution. The colonists deviated from English law primarily to mitigate its harshness and remove its capriciousness. The number and definition of crimes diminished sharply, as did the severity of punishment.

Rights of the accused became an important part of colonial justice. Unlike the common law, colonial codes explained in plain terms what rights were and what purposes they served. For example, the Massachusetts Body of Liberties (1641) included formal requirements for speedy and equal justice, bail, right of counsel, trial by jury (mentioned in six sections), challenge of jurors, no double jeopardy, no cruel and unusual punishments, and prohibition of torture. These guarantees were not absolute, nor were the provisions new. Each of them had some precedent in common law, royal decree, or Parliamentary statute. Still, they were stated positively in a written code, a circumstance previously un-known in English experience.

These rights varied from colony to colony and were only em-bryonic forms of modern practices. The trial itself was a model of simplicity, often taking no more than an hour or two. Jury trials were relatively uncommon. Most cases resulted in summary judg-ment, administered by a judge who took an active role in the pro-ceedings. Even in colonies which granted a limited right to counsel, the accused faced the court alone. The judge protected a defendant's rights at trial, ensuring, for example, that a plea was not coerced or that an oath was not used to compel incriminat-ing testimony. Defendants could challenge prosecution witnesses, although they rarely knew in advance the evidence against them. Only in some colonies could the accused call witnesses in his or her own behalf. There was no cross-examination. Yet even with these restrictions, the colonial conception of due process was more extensive than its English counterpart and contrasted dra-matically with the developing procedures of European states.

The American Revolution and the Bill of Rights

By the eve of the Revolution safeguards for the accused had be-come part of the common language about the liberties of Englishmen in the New World. In their struggle against Great Britain, colonists firmly believed there could be no liberty with-out fixed and certain guards against arbitrary action. Central to their understanding of liberty was the right of jury trial and the guarantee of due process of law. Jury trial was especially impor-tant. Without it, all other rights would ultimately fail. Only a jury from the neighborhood, independent in its judgments, formed an impregnable shield against arbitrary government.

Parliamentary innovations of the 1760s and 1770s challenged the primacy of the local jury and made the Americans place a high value on its preservation. The Stamp Act of 1765 gave vice-admiralty courts jurisdiction over violations of law. These courts operated without juries. Upon protest, Parliament repealed the Stamp Act, but the colonists had been alerted to the threat to their liberties. They began to define their rights more carefully and to guard them jealously.

In the Declaration of Independence the revolutionaries listed those rights which they claimed the King had denied. Prominent among them were violations of safeguards for the accused, all of which mocked the guarantee of due process of law: dependent judges who served at the King's pleasure; feigned trials; changes of venue or location to avoid local control of justice; deprivation of trial by jury.

Ironically, the grievances that stirred such passions before 1776 reflected a more limited set of rights than those embodied in

Venue

even in colonies which granted a limited right to counsel, the accused faced the court alone

TRIAL RIGHTS OF THE ACCUSED

revolutionary state constitutions and later in the federal Bill of Rights. In the process of creating new state governments, Americans identified those rights important to their conception of ordered liberty. Their search was wide-ranging. They would seize the opportunity that history provided to participate in a great experiment to expand the meaning of liberty. Their recent experiences also persuaded them that these fundamental rights deserved formal protection in written constitutions.

Virginia, the oldest colony, led the movement toward a new constitutional order. Its Declaration of Rights, approved on June 12, 1776, reveals how powerful a consensus had developed among Americans on the extent of their fundamental rights. Much of the Declaration addressed procedural guarantees available to the criminally accused. Repeated from prior documents was an injunction against cruel and unusual punishments taken verbatim from the English Bill of Rights of 1688, a pledge of due process using language reminiscent of the Magna Carta, and the ancient right of trial by a local jury. New safeguards included security from general warrants and protection against self-incrimination. The document also mandated speedy trials, confrontation with accusers and witnesses, compulsory process, and unanimous verdicts.

Other states also placed rights beyond the reach of government. New Jersey extended the right of counsel to all criminal defendants. Pennsylvania guarded against corruption in the appointment of juries and made punishments proportionate to the crime. The Massachusetts Constitution of 1780 included an extensive compendium of trial rights, among them use of a local jury, unanimous verdicts, protection against self-incrimination, compulsory process, and access to counsel. Maryland prohibited bills of attainder.

Clearly, something was happening to expand previous conceptions of rights of the accused. Revolutionaries began to endorse guarantees that until 1776 had received scant notice or that went well beyond the common law. The right to counsel is a striking example of this advance in individual rights. Both in Great Britain and in the colonies a person charged with a felony had no right to the advice or representation of counsel. In theory, the judge was a neutral protector of an accused's rights. Not until 1836 did Parliament extend the right to counsel to all criminal defendants. Americans took this step in their new state constitutions.

The Constitution of 1787 included only a few of these rights, primarily requiring a jury in all federal criminal trials and prohibiting bills of attainder. Under the federal system states were responsible for protecting civil rights. But strong opposition to the new charter forced adoption of a Bill of Rights to safeguard the

the right to counsel is a striking example of this advance in individual rights

DAVID J. BODENHAMER

liberties of the people from intrusion by the central government. Rights of the accused received major emphasis in the amendments: four of the eight substantive articles concerned criminal procedure almost exclusively. The guarantees came directly from the colonial and revolutionary experience; the safeguard against double jeopardy was the only new one added to the canon of rights.

Nineteenth-Century Trial Rights

Concern for procedural fairness became more intense in the first half of the nineteenth century, although the focus was on the states, not the national government. In 1833, the Supreme Court held in *Barron* v. *Baltimore* that the Fifth Amendment, and by implication the entire Bill of Rights, restrained only Congress. Criminal matters fell almost exclusively within the states' jurisdiction. But the ideas and language of the first ten amendments were also found in state constitutions, and state legislatures and courts assumed responsibility for protecting rights of the accused.

Barron v. Baltimore, 1833

Primary emphasis was on the forms of justice, with jury selection and trial rules assuming much importance. Technical correctness served as a touchstone of due process. State supreme courts, in particular, elaborated more precise standards in matters of confessions and double jeopardy and defined more carefully the roles of judge and jury. Antebellum jurists also protected the integrity of due process against legislative interference. In 1854, for example, the Massachusetts Supreme Court declared unconstitutional a law which allowed proceedings without an indictment, omitted jury trial, and did not permit the defendant to face the accusers or to compel testimony. Constitutional guarantees of rights, the court explained, were "absolutely necessary to preserve the advantages of liberty, and maintain a free government."[3]

Some changes in criminal law itself gave new definition to the language of rights. The early republic witnessed numerous efforts to ban certain punishments, including the death penalty, as cruel and unusual. States created penitentiaries as a substitute for capital or corporal punishment for most felonies. By the 1840s Michigan and Wisconsin had abolished the death penalty entirely; other states sharply restricted its use and replaced public hangings with private executions.

Capital punishment
Corporal punishment

Jury trial acquired a different meaning during the nineteenth century as judges repudiated the notion that juries could determine the law in criminal cases. A new rule emerged: the judge decides law, the jury decides facts. Stringent rules for the admission of evidence, judicial authority to set aside verdicts contrary to the evidence, and the right of the state to appeal were important corollaries of this principle. Also, juries became less representative and trustworthy as economy-minded legislatures permitted by-standers at court to take the place of voters chosen at random for jury duty.

By the end of the nineteenth century, administrative efficiency, not rights, had become the watchword of criminal justice. Full-time judges and prosecutors adopted plea bargaining, bench trial, and indeterminate sentences to circumvent unpredictable jury trial and make punishment more certain. State appellate courts were uneasy about plea bargaining, but by the early twentieth century the practice had replaced jury trial in many jurisdictions. Defendants had a right to counsel, but few could afford it. The state had no obligation to appoint a defense lawyer. An ever-widening gap was emerging between due process ideals and court practices, especially for immigrants, blacks, and the poor.

The federal Bill of Rights had little impact on nineteenth-century criminal process because the U.S. Supreme Court consistently denied its protection to defendants in state courts. The Fourteenth Amendment's due process clause, the Court held in 1884, did not incorporate the guarantees of the first eight amendments and make them binding on the states. The Constitution left states free to experiment with criminal process, including traditional rights of defendants. Federal guarantees applied to federal courts alone. Here the Supreme Court protected trial rights of the accused, but increasingly these safeguards bore slight correspondence to the practice of criminal justice.

Twentieth-Century Nationalization of Trial Rights

Early in the twentieth century the Supreme Court incorporated the rights of speech and press under Fourteenth Amendment protection because the justices deemed them fundamental to liberty. But always the Court refused to apply the Bill of Rights to state criminal trials. Finally in the famous Scottsboro case, *Powell v. Alabama* (1932), the justices concluded that the Fourteenth Amendment's due process clause guaranteed assistance of counsel to defendants charged with capital crimes in state courts.

Several reasons account for the change. During the post–World War I years states failed to protect the most basic rights of defendants, especially ethnic and racial minorities. A major national investigation by the Wickersham Commission revealed the open contempt many police departments held for rights guaranteed by state and federal constitutions. By the 1930s numerous organizations, notably the American Civil Liberties Union and the National Association for the Advancement of Colored People, were ready to lead an effort to nationalize the Bill of Rights for criminal defendants.

Even so, the Supreme Court refused to apply federal rights wholesale to state criminal process. The Fourteenth Amendment, the justices held in *Palko v. Connecticut* (1937), imposed on

Plea bargaining
Bench trial
Indeterminate sentence

See Hurtado v. California, 1884

Powell v. Alabama, 1932

Palko v. Connecticut, 1937

DAVID J. BODENHAMER

the states only rights essential to a "scheme of ordered liberty."[4] In criminal matters, the guarantee of fair trial alone was fundamental to liberty. States could employ widely different procedures without denying fair treatment. Not even trial by jury was essential to fairness, even though the revolutionary generation considered it the bulwark of their liberties.

From the 1930s through the 1950s the Supreme Court grappled with the meaning of the Fourteenth Amendment phrase, due process of law. The fair-trial test meant that the Court decided case-by-case which rights enjoyed constitutional protection. This approach vastly expanded the catalog of nationalized rights, that is, provisions of the Bill of Rights binding on the states, especially given the previous absence of such guarantees. By 1960, fundamental trial rights included public trial, impartial jury, and counsel (Sixth Amendment), and prohibition of cruel and unusual punishments (Eighth Amendment). Yet other rights now considered essential were not included: protection from double jeopardy and self-incrimination, and the right to trial by jury, among others.

Even though states no longer had unlimited discretion to experiment with criminal procedures, not everyone was satisfied with the fair-trial interpretation of the Fourteenth Amendment. A divided Court defended the approach as necessary to protect the federal system's division of power, but critics claimed the case-by-case determination of rights had produced uncertain standards to guide law officers and trial courts. Even state officials had grown weary of learning long after trial that state procedures used to convict were unconstitutional.

In the 1960s an activist majority of liberal justices, led by Chief Justice Earl Warren, abruptly abandoned the fair-trial test of defendants' rights and incorporated the Fourth, Fifth, Sixth, and Eighth amendments into a national code of criminal procedure. *Gideon v. Wainwright* (1963), a landmark case in this due process revolution, mandated assistance of counsel in all serious criminal cases. Significantly, the states themselves urged the Court to nationalize this right because previous decisions left too much uncertainty in the law.

Other important decisions incorporated Fifth and Sixth amendment guarantees—protection against self-incrimination, compulsory process, speedy trial, and trial by jury—into the due process clause of the Fourteenth Amendment, thus creating new restraints on state criminal process. *In re Gault* (1967) extended certain due process requirements to juvenile courts. The Court continued to insist that poverty should be no impediment to justice by requiring the state to furnish transcripts to indigent defendants. And it maintained its long-established position that confessions be truly voluntary.

Within five years, the Warren Court had extended to the

See Incorporation doctrine

Gideon v. Wainwright, 1963

. . . critics claimed the case-by-case determination of rights had produced uncertain standards to guide law officers and trial courts

TRIAL RIGHTS OF THE ACCUSED

states all of the trial rights required by the Bill of Rights. These actions brought only scattered protest. Unlike the highly controversial decisions involving police procedures—*Mapp v. Ohio* (1961) and *Miranda v. Arizona* (1966), for example—most people accepted the Court's premise that trial rights of the accused were fundamental liberties and thus national in scope. No longer did the expression and application of rights depend so much on accidents of geography.

The due process revolution in trial and appeal rights slowed in the 1970s under a more conservative Court. The justices extended the right to counsel in all trials that could lead to imprisonment and guaranteed jury trial in all petty misdemeanors punishable by confinement of six months or longer. But the Court also allowed states to experiment with the size of juries and accepted nonunanimous verdicts in all but capital cases.

Primarily in cases involving capital punishment, the Burger Court moved beyond the Warren Court's conception of due process. *Furman v. Georgia* (1972) nullified state-imposed death penalties as arbitrary, capricious, and discriminatory against blacks, the poor, and other groups at the margin of society. Although the Court never decided that execution was necessarily cruel and unusual punishment, the justices outlawed mandatory death sentences and approved a two-stage process for capital cases, with guilt determined first and punishment fixed later by predetermined standards.

Furman v. Georgia, 1972

Contemporary Issues

The rights of defendants upon trial are not nearly so controversial today as are the pretrial guarantees which restrain police practices. Still, certain issues are subject to debate. For example, lawyers in highly visible cases have at times hired psychologists to conduct extensive pretrial screening of the list of potential jurors to eliminate individuals who may be predisposed to convict the defendant. Some commentators believe this technique threatens the concept of a jury of peers and, given its expense, the ideal of equal justice under law. There is frequent conflict in cases of great notoriety between the news media's right to free speech and free press in reporting on a case before trial and the defendant's right to an impartial jury. Also, the death penalty remains controversial. The Supreme Court in recent years has moved to reduce sharply the number of appeals available to defendants on death row and to expedite consideration of their cases. One result has been a dramatic increase in the number of executions during the late 1980s, with hundreds of condemned felons still waiting for their sentences to be carried out.

It is too early to know what modifications or new interpreta-

DAVID J. BODENHAMER

tions the Supreme Court in the 1990s will make in the trial rights of defendants. Under the leadership of Chief Justice William Rehnquist, who assumed his position in 1986, the Court has more often favored the prosecution than the defense. With the retirement of Justice William Brennan, a law-and-order majority will likely control the Court for the next decade. But to date, the justices have not reversed completely any of the more liberal decisions of the Warren Court. One development worth watching is the re-emergence of state supreme courts as primary defenders of rights of the accused. Recently some state courts have begun to go beyond minimum standards established by the U.S. Supreme Court. But many state supreme courts operate with elected judges, and voters may not support efforts to create more liberal trial rights.

Conclusion

By 1990 rights of the accused were truly national. Court decisions since the 1930s have enhanced trial rights and made the balance of power between the state and the defendant more equal than ever. No longer can courts deny counsel or engage in discriminatory jury selection, to mention but a few practices from previous decades. Constitutional safeguards upon trial have indeed gained meaning from experience; undoubtedly, they will continue to do so. There will always exist fundamental differences on the proper balance between order and liberty, on the role of courts in expanding trial rights, and on the definition of constitutional terms such as "equal protection" and "due process of law." What should be reassuring is the debate itself, which makes real the concept of popular democracy and revitalizes the American commitment to a society governed by law. This continuing attention to individual rights upon trial helps keep the Bill of Rights a vital document, a full two centuries after its adoption.

Notes

[1]*Malinski v. New York*, 324 U.S. 401, 414 (1945).

[2]*National Mutual Insurance Co. v. Tidewater Transfer Co., Inc.* 387 U.S. 582, 646 (1948).

[3]*Fisher v. McGirr*, 1 Gray (Mass.), 33, 40–41.

[4]*Palko v. Connecticut*, 302 U.S. 319, 325–26 (1937).

Cases

Barron v. Baltimore, 7 Peters 243 (1833). In one of Chief Justice John Marshall's last opinions, a unanimous Court held that the

Fifth Amendment, and by implication the Bill of Rights, restrained only the federal government and not the states. This decision meant that Americans of the nineteenth century had to look to state constitutions and state courts for protection of their trial rights.

Furman v. Georgia, 408 U.S. 238 (1972). The Court determined that capital punishment was arbitrarily administered, violating the Eighth Amendment's ban on cruel and unusual punishments. This case did not outlaw the death penalty, although in effect it nullified the capital punishment statutes of most states, forcing them to rewrite these statutes to provide a more rigorous scheme for imposing death sentences.

Gideon v. Wainwright, 372 U.S. 335 (1963). Upon the appeal of an indigent defendant, the Court ruled that the Sixth Amendment right to counsel applied to all persons charged with a serious crime and required states to provide one for defendants without the financial resources to hire a lawyer. This case was one of the first decisions of the Warren Court to incorporate trial rights guaranteed in the Bill of Rights into the due process clause of the Fourteenth Amendment.

Hurtado v. California, 110 U.S. 516 (1884). The Court refused to incorporate the Fifth Amendment requirement of grand jury indictment into the due process clause of the Fourteenth Amendment and thus apply it to the states. This decision reaffirmed the principle of Barron v. Baltimore (1833) that the Bill of Rights applied only to the central government.

Palko v. Connecticut, 302 U.S. 319 (1937). Another landmark decision that opened the door to incorporation of trial rights as part of the Fourteenth Amendment's due process clause, thus binding state as well as federal courts. If the right in question was essential to a "scheme of ordered liberty," that is, if one could not imagine a fair trial without the right, then it was guaranteed by the Fourteenth Amendment. This case established the "fair trial" test for determining on a case-by-case basis whether federally guaranteed trial rights had been violated.

Powell v. Alabama, 287 U.S. 45 (1932). Also known as the Scottsboro case, this decision guaranteed the right to counsel to all defendants charged with a capital crime, whether in state or federal court. It was one of the first times the Supreme Court established a minimum national standard of protection for defendants at trial.

Suggested Readings

Richard C. Cortner, *The Supreme Court and the Second Bill of Rights: The Fourteenth Amendment and the Nationalization of Civil*

DAVID J. BODENHAMER

Liberties (Madison, Wisc.: University of Wisconsin Press, 1981). A comprehensive and analytical narrative of the incorporation of the Bill of Rights into the due process clause of the Fourteenth Amendment, this book includes much detail on both case facts and arguments before the Court.

David Fellman, *The Defendant's Rights Today* (Madison, Wisc.: University of Wisconsin Press, 1975). A detailed, right-by-right survey of rights of the accused, this book is a dated but still valuable guide to the development of trial rights.

Lawrence M. Friedman and Robert V. Percival, *The Roots of Justice: Crime and Punishment in Alameda County, California, 1870–1910* (Chapel Hill, N.C.: University of North Carolina Press, 1981). This pathbreaking study of local criminal justice offers the most comprehensive portrait available of how trial rights operated in practice at the end of the nineteenth century.

Fred Graham, *The Due Process Revolution: The Warren Court's Impact on Criminal Law* (New York: Hayden, 1970). This assessment of the Warren Court's expansion of rights of the accused, written by a CBS News reporter, is a solid survey of the numerous decisions on defendants' rights during the 1960s. It offers a good, readable introduction to the most important period for trial rights of the accused in the Court's history.

Anthony Lewis, *Gideon's Trumpet* (New York: Random House, 1964). This bestselling book on *Gideon v. Wainwright* (1963) was written by the New York *Times'* prize-winning commentator on the U.S. Supreme Court. Filled with details about the case in state courts and on federal appeal, the book served as the basis for a popular made-for-TV movie of the 1980s.

Steven Phillips, *No Heroes, No Villains: The Story of a Murder Trial* (New York: Random House, 1972). Based on the true story of a policeman's murder, this book is a well-written, dramatically narrated account of a single murder trial in New York City. It serves as an excellent introduction to the modern criminal justice system and the trial rights of defendants as they actually occur in a typical felony case.

Bernard Schwartz, *The Great Rights of Mankind: A History of the Bill of Rights* (New York: Oxford University Press, 1977). An overview of the development and implementation of the Bill of Rights, this volume serves as a good, easy-to-understand introduction to a complex subject. Edited by the same scholar is *The Bill of Rights: A Documentary History* (2 vols., New York, 1971), a collection of important legal and political documents on the development of American rights, including trial rights of the accused.

VIII

Gordon Morris Bakken

PROPERTY RIGHTS

A hypothetical homeowner enjoying the American dream wants to build a covered patio to enhance the dream. The homeowner's pride of possession suffers a shock to find the building permit comes with strings attached. A condition of the permit from the building commissioner's office requires that the homeowner allow for public access through the backyard to an adjacent public facility. Further, this governmental claim to ongoing use of an important piece of the homeowner's property occurs without any compensation. Could this happen in America? Does not the homeowner have some protection against the governmental decision? What is the extent of that protection?

The collision of individual versus public interests in such matters as building permits or the space in which to build a freeway, sports complex, city industrial park, or city hall has generated the legislation and judicial decisions that constitute the history of the property clause of the Fifth Amendment.

Personal Property

What exactly is "property"? In addition to real estate interests, property also is personal property, the cars and clocks and other material things that we possess and use. Even more than things, property is ideas, inventions, music, and verse. Property can be something to be received in the future as well as something that exists in the present. Property can be a crop in the ground or cargo dispatched to a distant shore. Property is wealth in itself and a means of creating wealth. Conflicts generated by the various ways individuals, corporations, and governments have viewed their rights in property, their uses of property, and the Fifth Amendment's language resulted in the constitutional law and history that we will explore.

The History of Property Before the Bill of Rights

The American Revolution reflected concerns that traditional protections under the British Constitution were no longer viable. When Parliament attacked the protection of trial by jury in revenue matters and trial by jury in the local venue for certain crimes, colonists knew that the authority of custom, of ownership, and of inheritance of property rights was vulnerable. At the time of the Revolution, colonists knew that they had rights in property, whether real or personal, tangible or intangible. Of equal importance, eighteenth-century constitutional theorists saw that Americans had property in rights. Rights were incorporeal, but still property that (like the right to bring a legal action) could be transferred to another person. Property as authority for rights was positive, much like the authority of custom. Colonists inherited rights just as they inherited other forms of property, and the authority to make laws flowed from property, custom, and prescription as well as the sovereign's command. Parliament's attacks upon colonial property and property in rights made necessary a Revolution to secure constitutional rights and liberty.

Venue

See Intangible property

See Incorporeal rights

Actions of colonial legislatures and some equity courts advanced property interests for women. Under common law, upon marriage a woman lost her legal identity and ownership of property. During the eighteenth century, colonial legislatures and chancery courts changed the law to grant married women equitable separate estates, to facilitate the inheritance of property, and to authorize the use of property. Colonial lawmakers became increasingly aware that expanding the property rights of married women benefited society.

See Coverture

In the confederation period, stay laws and paper money schemes again threatened property in rights. State legislatures, influenced by debtor demands for relief, passed stay laws (statutes limiting the collection of debts) and statutes making depreciated paper money legal tender for preexisting debts. The former limited the creditor's ability to collect a debt in a timely fashion, and the latter forced creditors to accept paper money in payment for loans made in gold. In both cases the property in the right to collect a rightful debt was diminished in value. Both types of laws severely injured creditor interests and threatened future credit markets. The Federalists saw these acts as portents of democratic excesses impairing the gains of the Revolution and heralding the need for a written national constitution as a means of protecting the rights and liberties of Americans.

Our Constitution and Bill of Rights

The Constitution provided structural and procedural protections for our rights in property. The federal constitution established a republican form of government designed to balance the interests of creditors and debtors, propertied minorities and unpropertied majorities in a way that could protect property rights. The separation of powers was a cornerstone of such protection. In particular, the federal judiciary had the strongest potential to protect individual property rights against the excesses of democratic zeal. The Fifth Amendment in the Bill of Rights made specific the elements of that protection: "No person shall be . . . deprived of life, liberty, or property, without due process of law; nor shall private property be taken for public use, without just compensation."

Eminent domain

The taking of private property for a public use with just compensation flows from government's power of eminent domain. The limits of this power are defined by the language of the Fifth Amendment—private property may be taken only for a public use and only with the payment of just compensation. When a taking occurs, what constitutes a public use? what is just compensation? and when is it to be paid? were questions left to state legislatures and judges to resolve. The Fifth Amendment applied only to the federal government, and states were limited only by their constitutions as interpreted by legislatures and courts. In *Barron*

Barron v. Baltimore, 1833

v. Baltimore (1833) the U.S. Supreme Court declared that the Bill of Rights "demanded security against the apprehended encroachments of the General Government, not against those of the local governments." The states were free to act, within the confines of their constitutions.

The States Act

The states behaved much as they had in the confederation period, modifying judicial decisions and denying compensation to injured landowners. In 1795 the Connecticut legislature set aside the decree of a court and granted a new hearing in the same court. In *Calder* v. *Bull* (1798) Justice Chase wrote that laws that

Calder v. Bull, 1798

impaired lawful contracts or took the property of A and gave it to B violated the great first principle of the social compact, the protection of personal liberty and private property. Chase and others believed that Americans had rights in property that were vested and not subject to legislative alteration.

Other state legislatures in the 1790s began to invoke the eminent domain power. State statutes authorized entrepreneurs to build milldams that flooded the private property of others. These Milldam Acts designated such mills quasi-public businesses operating in the public interest because they milled grain produced in an agricultural community. By allowing mill owners to flood the lands of others, the legislatures overturned the English common-law rule that such a dam constituted a nuisance. Flooded owners usually had statutory recourse to sue, but only for specified damages. This practice limited the liability of entrepreneurs and made the risk of enterprise manageable.

Following the precedent of the Milldam Acts, state legislatures into the nineteenth century expanded the quasi-public business concept to include turnpike, canal, and, by the 1830s, railroad corporations. These special legislative charters put the power of eminent domain into corporate hands as an inducement to the private sector to invest in public transportation. The public received transportation facilities without public expense; corporations were able to take with compensation private property that promised the best future profits. The public retained authority to regulate these corporations but without having to raise taxes to build and maintain these vital transportation facilities. The goal of these legislative initiatives was to put property to productive, dynamic use.

See Future interest

The rapid expansion of the power of eminent domain before the Civil War generated numerous lawsuits, leaving state courts the job of sorting out the meaning of property rights. The courts told entrepreneurs that the creation of a railroad franchise corporation that would compete with a turnpike did not constitute a taking requiring compensation. State and federal courts also maintained that the legislative creation of a competing enterprise that destroyed the value of another enterprise was not unconstitutional because such "creative destruction" benefited the public through the resulting increased services and efficiency.

From Vested Rights to Substantive Due Process of Law

The federal court's reaction to perceived state excesses of social and economic engineering included the creation of a new doctrine based upon the Fifth Amendment. The earlier vested rights doctrine, as declared in the ruling by Justice Chase in *Calder* v. *Bull*, was grounded in a general philosophy of government. Substantive due process was derived from both this doctrine and the language of the amendment.

Vested rights

Substantive due process of law

Substantive due process of law was formulated in *Dred Scott* v. *Sandford* (1857). Relying upon a New York case and the vested rights theory, Chief Justice Taney declared that the federal government had no power to infringe upon any property rights held by a citizen under state law. In this case, the property was a slave (Dred Scott), and Taney ruled that the Fifth Amendment guaranteed that property to his owner, a citizen, along with the liberty

Dred Scott v. Sandford, 1857

to use that property free from any federal action if the owner had committed no offense against state law. Taney had linked vested rights and the Fifth Amendment to protect property in human beings. The Civil War and the Thirteenth Amendment would reverse the holding, but the formula of linkage would live on as substantive due process.

The Civil War also generated a controversy over the power of the Congress to confiscate the property of Confederates. In *Miller v. United States* (1871) the Supreme Court sustained Congress's confiscation of property as part of its war powers.

Miller v. United States, 1871

The U.S. Supreme Court, using the Fourteenth Amendment to selectively apply the Bill of Rights to the states, extended substantive due process protection to cases involving personal labor, livelihood, and avocation. In one of these cases, *Allgeyer v. Louisiana* (1897), the Court added liberty of contract to the due process protection afforded by the Fourteenth Amendment. In another, the Court struck down a New York law regulating working conditions and hours in the baking industry in *Lochner v. New York* (1905). Substantive due process doctrine had become a conservative constitutional law tool and afforded the Court a significant role in deciding the nature of reform in the work place. Conservative justices used the doctrine to strike down state regulations they personally disliked.

Allgeyer v. Louisiana, 1897

Lochner v. New York, 1905

The Expansion of Public Interest and Eminent Domain

With the industrial revolution and the railroad rapidly expanding the American economy, legislators found it easy to expand the concept of businesses having a public interest. In the West, legislators and Constitutional Convention delegates moved eminent domain powers into private hands, thereby redefining traditionally private interests as public ones. Miners, ranchers, and farmers all clamored for water and ways to bring it to their enterprises. Lawmakers easily recognized a public interest in providing a water supply to an expanding urban population. Private interest groups, like miners and ranchers, claimed aridity as the environmental justification for private eminent domain. Western lawmakers eventually gave cities as well as mining corporations the authority of eminent domain to reach miles beyond their boundaries to obtain water for enterprise.

Taney had linked vested rights and the Fifth Amendment to protect property in human beings

Aridity in the West was the reason another property law concept changed in the nineteenth century. Water was not plentiful, nor did it flow steadily. Miners needed water to operate their sluices just as much as farmers and ranchers needed water for crops and cattle. Western law accommodated the environment with the law of prior appropriation, which, for eminent domain

Prior appropriation

purposes, gave the first user of water the right to enter adjacent property to convey the water to the user's property. Even the digging of canals or the laying of water pipe over another's private property became commonplace in the developing West.

Lawmakers recognized that economic progress would be stalled if owners of land abutting water sources could refuse access to productive users. To promote productive use, legislators actually conceptualized eminent domain power in private hands for private benefit as having a public benefit. In the process the property rights of some were impaired although compensation was paid. How far states could go with this concept was again a matter for courts to decide.

In another area of expansion of property rights, women gained some legal rights in property and transactions in the late nineteenth century. Specifically, lawmakers extended *femme sole* (the rights of married women to conduct business independently of their husbands) legal status to women. This extension of all rights in property later contributed to the spread of woman's suffrage in several western states.

Femme sole

The Courts Review Change

In general, judges found expanded entrepreneurial authority constitutional. One court welcomed the expansion of women's property rights as part of the spirit "of a more enlightened age."[1] Courts tried to find a public benefit in private eminent domain provisions. Judges frequently cited aridity as sufficient cause for the legislative grants. But there were limits. For example, the U. S. Supreme Court held unconstitutional a legislative grant, without the reservation of state supervisory rights, to a private association, which authorized the taking of part of a railroad right-of-way to construct a grain elevator for the sole use of the association members. Similarly, when special districts created for road improvement, drainage, or other purposes taxed their membership, dissenting landowners had a right to a hearing to determine whether they would benefit. Justice Willis Van Devanter proclaimed in 1916 "that there is an inseparable union between the public good and due regard for private rights should not be forgotten."[2] The balance was not an easy one to maintain as America matured economically.

Political Reform

The granting of public eminent domain to corporations waned under political criticism and action. Populists and Progressives claimed that such corporate power was an abuse and that eminent domain belonged only in the hands of the people. In re-

to promote productive use, legislators . . . conceptualized eminent domain power in private hands for private benefit as having a public benefit

sponse, lawmakers tightened statutory authority and gave juries more latitude in finding the amount of compensation.

The New Deal brought a revival of the use of quasi-public entities to accomplish public goals. The Tennessee Valley Authority (TVA), part of the first New Deal, proposed goals far beyond the scale of milldam entrepreneurs or irrigation developers of prior centuries. TVA was to build multipurpose dams for flood control and hydroelectric power purposes. In addition, the Authority would manufacture fertilizer, improve navigation, foster soil conservation, engage in reforestation, and perform social work in local communities. The Authority had the power of eminent domain, and in the process of building dams and flooding lands, that power was challenged in court.

Ashwander v. TVA, 1936

In *Ashwander* v. *TVA* (1936) the U.S. Supreme Court found the TVA to be constitutionally within the national defense and navigational improvement powers. The declared purposes of the statute creating the TVA, production of explosives for military purposes, and navigational improvements put the TVA within the scope of federal power. The TVA's exercise of eminent domain, both in acquiring and flooding property, also fell within the traditional scope of governmental power. The Supreme Court emphasized that a legislative determination of public need gave the power to take property. What the TVA was doing was within the government's traditional and active role in the improvement of navigation and flood control. The latter function had become manifest in the early twentieth century in the West where irrigation activity had shifted from private development to massive federal reclamation projects. In TVA litigation these two historical developments converged in the context of the New Deal's social and economic goals.

Eminent Domain in the Age of Aquarius

In the 1960s cities vastly expanded the use of municipal development authorities to build sports stadiums, create industrial parks, and expand recreational facilities. But municipal schemes to attract business and improve the community's environment were hardly new. Rather post-Depression quests for growth stimulated renewed enthusiasm for action by public authorities promoting some public purpose or benefit. Challenged on the private use—public purpose question, courts usually affirmed the government's use of the municipal authority to advance the interests of the community through private hands upon land or facilities acquired with public capital and with public powers. However, some state courts started to question the actions. The Washington Supreme Court voided a port authority's taking of property in order to provide industrial development sites for private firms.

The judges wanted the authority to prove that the taking was for a 'really public use' rather than a government declaration that the port authority had a plan to put the property to a higher and better economic use than that of its current owner. Another court struck down a zoning ordinance that prohibited the use of property for a shopping center based on evidence that the zoning was intended to prevent competition with an existing nearby shopping center. Again, courts freely inquired into the nature of the public benefit.

No Property and New Property

After the famous "court-packing fight" with President Franklin D. Roosevelt in 1937, the U.S. Supreme Court abandoned the practice of applying substantive due process analysis to economic regulations. After a long series of cases, the Court finally openly acknowledged its changed position in *Ferguson v. Skrupa* (1963) upholding a Kansas statute that put all debt collection agencies out of business and gave that business to the state's lawyers. The Court simply refused to sit as a "superlegislature to weigh the wisdom of legislation." The fact that all debt collectors except lawyers lost their livelihood was not a matter of judicial concern. A person did not necessarily have a property right to any occupation. Also emerging in the 1960s was the concept of "new property."[3] Some legal commentators wondered whether a kind of entitlement to governmental largess under the rapidly expanding federal welfare and regulatory system actually constituted a new form of property.

Ferguson v. Skrupa, 1963

Paying for Regulation's Impact

In the 1970s America rediscovered a concern for the welfare of the environment, and by the 1980s the reach of state and federal regulations regarding the use of property had expanded. Generally, regulations for environmental protection, like historic preservation, received favorable judicial treatment. However, when a public regulatory entity's action failed to demonstrate that the regulation served a public purpose, the Supreme Court struck it down. The California Coastal Commission made a building permit conditional upon the granting of an uncompensated, permanent, public-access easement to the beach. The Commission acted upon the belief that such action protected the public's ability to see the beach, assisted the public in overcoming the psychological barrier to use of the beach, and relieved beach congestion. In *Nollan v. California Coastal Commission* (1987), the U.S. Supreme Court found that the reasons advanced by the Commission were mere expressions of belief that the public

Nollan v. California Coastal Commission, 1987

would best be served by a continuous strip of publicly accessible beach rather than evidence of a public purpose. The state remained free to use its power of eminent domain by paying just compensation for the easement.

Similarly, when Los Angeles County passed an ordinance prohibiting the construction or reconstruction of buildings in a flood protection area, the Supreme Court approved the taking with a requirement for compensation. The Court looked at the extent of use denied and, finding it complete, ruled that the just compensation required by the Fifth Amendment be paid.

Conclusion

Transient necessities

The hypothetical homeowner who begins our essay would be considerably reassured by such cases as *Nollan v. California Coastal Commission*. Even though new facts, public interests, or transient necessities may push constitutional doctrine to other positions, we know the due process and just compensation protections of the Fifth Amendment are available to property owners. We know that legislatures responding to the demands of changing constituencies have made extensive use of quasi-public entities to advance general social and economic interests. We see a two-hundred-year history of government on all levels using the power of eminent domain to advance the public interest, and we see citizens going to the judiciary for compensation when they believe their property interests have been impaired. The structure of government devised at the founding of the nation to adjust the claims to property made by its citizens and their government remains in place to hear and determine the meaning of the property clause of the Fifth Amendment.

Notes

[1] *Ray v. Ray*, 1 Idaho 566, 578 (1874).

[2] *Embree v. Kansas City Road District*, 240 U.S. 242, 248 (1916).

[3] Charles A. Reich, "The New Property," 73 *Yale Law Journal* (1964), 733–87.

Cases

Allgeyer v. Louisiana, 165 U.S. 578 (1897) added liberty of contract to the due process protection afforded by the Fourteenth Amendment.

Ashwander v. TVA, 297 U.S. 288 (1936) upheld the New Deal's Tennessee Valley Authority legislation as within the national defense and navigational improvement powers.

Barron v. Baltimore, 7 Pet. 243 (1833) held that the Bill of Rights applied only to the federal government.

Calder v. Bull, 3 Dallas 386(1798) was the case in which Justice Chase announced the vested rights doctrine declaring that laws impairing contracts or taking property from A and giving it to B violated the first principles of the social compact and were void.

Dred Scott v. Sandford, 19 How. 393 (1857) linked vested rights and the Fifth Amendment to protect property. This substantive due process doctrine would flower in the late nineteenth century.

Ferguson v. Skrupa, 372 U.S. 726 (1963) upheld a Kansas statute outlawing debt collection by any person not admitted to the state bar of Kansas. The case signaled the Court's disinterest in the impact of state economic regulation of occupations.

Lochner v. New York, 198 U.S. 45 (1905) used substantive due process doctrine to void a New York statute regulating the working conditions and hours of bakers.

Miller v. United States, 11 Wallace 268 (1871) upheld Congress's power to confiscate Confederate property under the war powers clause of the Constitution.

Nollan v. California Coastal Commission, 483 U.S. 825 (1987) struck down an order of the California Coastal Commission which made conditional a building permit on the grant of public access to a beach, reasoning that the order was a taking without compensation.

Suggested Readings

Richard A. Epstein, *Takings: Private Property and the Power of Eminent Domain* (Cambridge, Mass.: Harvard University Press, 1985). A strongly worded condemnation of departures from the original understanding of the Fifth Amendment and the practices of government in satisfying transient welfare state interests at the expense of property owners. This book calls for a rethinking of the constitutional doctrines that enabled the welfare mentality of the 1980s.

Kermit L. Hall, *The Magic Mirror: Law in American History* (New York: Oxford University Press, 1989). A significant contribution to the interrelations of public and private law, this book puts eminent domain issues in the general context of social and economic change.

James Willard Hurst, *Law and Economic Growth* (Cambridge, Mass.: Harvard University Press, 1964). A thoroughly documented history of the Wisconsin lumber industry demonstrating the interplay of economic and social interests and legal institutions, this book explains how legislatures, courts, and private interests worked to release the energy of private property in trees.

Charles A. Reich, "The New Property," 73 *Yale Law Journal* (1964), 733–87. A significant contribution to our understanding of the impact of the New Deal legislation beginning the process of centralization in the federal government of regulatory agencies and welfare institutions, this article calls for the protection of individual interests and personal dignity from concentrations of power.

John Phillip Reid, *Constitutional History of the American Revolution: The Authority of Rights* (Madison, Wisc.: University of Wisconsin Press, 1986). A thoroughly documented and argued analysis of the intellectual and cultural basis for constitutional rights, this book is critical to an understanding of eighteenth-century constitutionalism.

Marylynn Salmon, *Women and the Law of Property in Early America* (Chapel Hill: University of North Carolina Press, 1986). An analysis of contracts, property transactions, divorces, estates, and provisions for widows, this book demonstrates the diversity of colonial law and how some legislatures and courts worked to liberate women from some of the constraints of the English common law.

Harry N. Scheiber, "Property Law, Expropriation, and Resource Allocation by Government, 1879–1910," 33 *Journal of Economic History* (March, 1973), 232–51. An important article for understanding the changes of the nineteenth century. Professor Scheiber explains how the power of eminent domain was used to take land away from private owners for important social and economic purposes.

Melvin I. Urofsky, *A March of Liberty: A Constitutional History of the United States* (New York: Alfred A. Knopf, 1988). A thorough and comprehensible survey of American constitutional history.

IX

Sandra F. VanBurkleo

THE RIGHT TO PRIVACY

Privacy is a multifaceted, elusive concept. It calls to mind a cluster of human values and interests, many of them incompatible with the information-gathering and policing functions of modern governments. In a lay sense, the term "privacy" implies secrecy, solitude, or withdrawal from the company of others. One can speak meaningfully of a *right* to privacy, however, only when individuals decide to defend these values and interests within organized society. Privacy claims spring from tension between an individual's conscious struggle for autonomy, and community demands for proximity, disclosure, or conformity. Legal philosopher Charles Fried puts it this way: to talk about the "privacy of a lonely man on a desert island would be to engage in irony." A person enjoying the right to privacy must consciously "grant or deny access to others."[1] In Robinson Crusoe's case, talk about a right to privacy would be relevant only if he chose to object, for example, to questions posed by a census taker. Without some kind of intrusion and subsequent protest, he would be merely *alone*.

In 1928, Associate Justice Louis D. Brandeis (using an expression coined earlier by Judge Thomas Cooley of the Michigan Supreme Court) characterized the right to privacy as "the right to be let alone—the most comprehensive of rights and the right most valued by civilized men." Yet Brandeis and Cooley probably had in mind relatively narrow zones of legal protection. For Brandeis, the right to be let alone was a right "not to be dragged into publicity"; it did not encompass the many areas of life and thought associated nowadays with the constitutional right to privacy.[2]

In a broader and much older sense, the right to privacy signifies the general condition of being withdrawn lawfully from public interest or scrutiny. In the late eighteenth century, British subjects on both sides of the Atlantic assumed the existence of personal sanctuaries into which government could not decently intrude. A good many specific rights rooted in the ancient English constitution (such as the right to be free from unwarranted searches, or liberty of conscience) addressed key elements of this general right to autonomy in relations with government. There is a strong suggestion of this umbrella-like conception of privacy in Brandeis's definition of the "right to be let alone" as the "most comprehensive of rights." More recently, the right to privacy—with certain important exceptions—seems to have reacquired the broad sense of limits to be placed upon both public disclosure and governmental control of personal affairs.

This chapter describes the process by which the right to privacy came to be embodied in American law—first as a general constraint upon arbitrary government, then as a limited action in tort, and finally as a judicially recognized, highly controversial fundamental liberty.

Foundations

When James Madison presented a Bill of Rights to Congress in 1789, privacy was nowhere mentioned; neither the British nor their discontented American colonists imagined a constitutional right to privacy *per se*. They did clearly recognize a right to be free of arbitrary government, to be secure in the exercise of personal liberty, and to be guaranteed a legal remedy whenever government, in its zeal to keep public order, ignored time-honored rules of law and procedure. Eighteenth-century British lawyers sometimes called this version of the right to be let alone the "security of liberty"[3]—the assurance that ministers and magistrates would not deprive subjects of rights or invade private sanctuaries (such as homes and minds) without due process of law. The sheriff could not break down one's door without a warrant; public officials could not intrude upon or force public disclosure of an individual's spiritual or political convictions without compelling reasons and strict adherence to established procedure.

Maintenance of the rule of law, in fact, was taken to be the *essence* of civil liberty and autonomy, not its opposite. On the eve of the American Revolution, an English parliamentarian might have said that the real enemy of liberty was licentiousness (or anarchy), not law. British colonists in Boston or Philadelphia entirely agreed. Even in revolutionary America, good government was synonymous with predictable, law-abiding government; good public officials were those who followed the rules and respected

Tort

Due process

in the late eighteenth century, British subjects on both sides of the Atlantic assumed the existence of personal sanctuaries into which government could not decently intrude

SANDRA F. VANBURKLEO

the privileges and immunities of citizens. When Anglo-Americans thought about freedom, negative liberties sprang to mind first: government was expected *not* to deprive freemen of life, personal security, or property arbitrarily. Britons also claimed positive liberties. The Crown was expected, for instance, to protect the public welfare, to guard freedom of expression within limits set by Parliament, and to police the realm. Yet, in the main, the British concept of liberty consisted of a long list of "thou-shalt-nots" designed to preserve human dignity in relations with government; and Anglo-Americans were proudly *British*.

Privileges and immunities clause

This attachment to the security of liberty (and related fear of tyrannical invasions of private spaces or thoughts) propelled Americans toward revolution after Parliamentary adoption of the seemingly lawless Intolerable Acts. By 1787, similar anxieties about the tendency of *all* centralized governments to weaken or destroy civil liberties prompted Federalists to construct a tiered federation and delicately branched general government as safeguards against tyranny. Much the same impulse underlay the ferocious debate after 1789 over the merits of a written Bill of Rights. While the right to privacy was not named in the amendments ratified by the states in 1791, the First Federal Congress took pains to protect critical elements of the right to be let alone. Procedural guarantees such as the right to be free of unreasonable searches and the privilege against self-incrimination were itemized in the Fourth and Fifth amendments. The Third Amendment banned the quartering of soldiers in homes, and a web of First Amendment guarantees affirmed the sanctity of minds—the citizens' right to harbor or express unpopular political and religious opinions without fear of punishment.

Although members of the First Federal Congress disagreed as to which arm of government posed the greatest threat to personal security, James Madison viewed the Bill of Rights as a potentially useful tool against the poor judgment and passions supposedly inseparable from the legislative process. In his view, popularly elected assemblies were the most powerful of all republican institutions and therefore the "most likely to be abused." To the extent that a written declaration of rights might prevent exercises of "undue power" by legislative majorities, he said, "it cannot be doubted but such declaration is proper."[4]

Beyond these fond hopes, though, Madison was ambivalent about the merits of an enumerated list of rights. On the one hand, he feared that a poorly constructed federal bill might amount to little more than a "parchment barrier"—like the underenforced Bills of Rights attached to state constitutions after 1775—against the powers of the general government. On the other hand, Madison feared extreme libertarianism. He agreed to sponsor the bill in Congress partly to control its content. The

on the eve of the American Revolution, an English parliamentarian might have said that the real enemy of liberty was licentiousness, . . . not law

THE RIGHT TO PRIVACY

Antifederalist George Mason remarked in 1789 that Madison viewed the proposed amendments as a "tub to the whales"—that is, as a device tossed overboard to distract opponents of the Constitution while Federalists guided the Ship of State safely into harbor.[5]

Others were less equivocal than Madison. Antifederalists hailed the Bill as the sovereign people's main hedge against the loss of personal security in dealings with the federal government. A pamphleteer calling himself "An Old Whig" implored fellow Pennsylvanians in October 1787 to insist upon an explicit itemization of rights. "Before we establish a government, whose acts will be the SUPREME LAW OF THE LAND," he wrote, "we ought carefully to guard ourselves...against the invasion of those liberties which it is essential for us to retain, which it is of no real use to government to strip us of; but which in the course of human events have been too often insulted."[6] Alexander Hamilton was equally fervent in his opposition to a written bill—not because he was opposed to rights, but because enumeration seemed to him to jeopardize the security of persons and property. Hamilton and other High Federalists argued, in strikingly traditional British terms, that the Constitution itself was a Bill of Rights reserving for the people all powers and freedoms not expressly delegated to the federal government. They thought, too, that "codes" harshly circumscribed the zone of liberty available to republicans, wrongly implied that rights not listed were nonexistent, and (by introducing the subject of rights into constitutional texts) invited government to stick its foot in liberty's door.

James Madison responded to the Federalist complaint—and, somewhat later, to Antifederalist misgivings about the watered-down quality of key amendments—with the Ninth Amendment and related Tenth Amendment. In recent years, philosophical skeptics and constitutional fundamentalists have castigated the Ninth Amendment as an unfathomable "ink blot" (to borrow Judge Robert Bork's term), notable mainly for its obscurity:[7]

The enumeration in the Constitution, of certain rights, shall not be construed to deny or disparage others retained by the people.

Impatience is understandable: at first reading, the amendment seems to be little more than a slightly paranoid constitutional shield designed to deflect unspecified attacks upon individual or state liberties by the federal government. Yet the vaguely worded Ninth Amendment, no less than the more particularized Fourth or Fifth, probably was intended to be rights-bearing in the sense that it stood for and legitimized rights not otherwise enumerated in the federal bill.

skeptics and constitutional fundamentalists have castigated the Ninth Amendment as an unfathomable "ink blot"... notable mainly for its obscurity

SANDRA F. VANBURKLEO

Madison's object was simple enough: if federal officials could be expected to misbehave, then (and within important limits) the list of rights had to be elastic. Who could predict exactly what public officials might try to do in future decades, or what republican citizens might require to defend themselves? While presenting possible amendments to the House of Representatives in 1789, Madison suggested in section four of his draft of a Bill of Rights that the

exceptions here or elsewhere in the constitution, made in favor of particular rights, shall not be so construed as to diminish the just importance of other rights retained by the people, or as to enlarge the powers delegated by the constitution; but either as actual limitations of such powers, or as inserted merely for greater caution.

The inclusion of an amendment "merely for greater caution" suggests overkill, which is exactly what Madison intended. His references to "actual limitations of...powers" and "other rights retained by the people," however, were more complicated, and in some ways more interesting. Madison probably did *not* mean to entrust state legislatures with basic rights; by 1789, his fear of majoritarianism was well developed. Time and again, he warned that, in republics, the "real power" lay with "the majority of the Community." Future invasions of liberty would come, said Madison, not from "acts of Government contrary to the sense of its constituents, but from acts in which the Government is the mere instrument of the major number of the Constituents."[8]

Majoritarianism

Nor did Madison's Ninth Amendment invite elected officials to decide which rights beyond those enumerated in the Bill were possessed by citizens. Like Hamilton, Madison assumed that judges would review acts of legislatures for constitutionality, in the process neutralizing the influence of self-interested legislators (or "demagogues") and their constituents. The Ninth Amendment, in other words, carries with it the presumption that judges would accept responsibility for preserving the right to be let alone when and if federal lawmakers overstepped their bounds. And, when read in light of the Tenth Amendment (which reserves unspecified "powers" to the states or to the people), it seems clear that the judges in question would be local rather than federal. In the end, Madison hoped to refer ultimate responsibility for unenumerated liberties to small-scale republican communities. While he meant not to entrust legislators with basic rights, he also did intend to buttress local governments—to achieve what he called "a salutary effect against the abuse of power" in the several states.[9]

future invasions of liberty would come..."from acts in which the Government is the mere instrument of the major number of the Constituents"

THE RIGHT TO PRIVACY

Privacy in the Nineteenth Century

As a young lawyer in Boston in 1890, Louis Brandeis published (with his former partner Samuel Warren as co-author) the first sustained argument for legal protection of "The Right of Privacy" as an action in tort, not as a constitutional claim. Brandeis and Warren defined the right to privacy narrowly. It included only the individual's right to control disclosures of information about "thoughts, emotions, and sensations" properly belonging to the domain of private life. This article, published in the *Harvard Law Review*, has been called "the most influential law review article ever written." Dean Roscoe Pound of the Harvard Law School said it had done "nothing less than add a chapter to our law."[10]

In a literal sense, Pound was right. But the resulting impression of a major watershed in the law after 1890 also fosters the unfortunate notion that privacy is a modern legal construct that mysteriously popped up at the end of the nineteenth century. Recent scholarship confirms that privacy, in the narrow sense of control over the extent to which one's thoughts or emotions are accessible to others, was fairly well protected before 1890. The technologies available to Victorian Americans pale when compared to modern computers and satellites; but nineteenth-century legislators and judges often proscribed invasive uses of ears, eyes, and hands.

In the constitutional arena, the federal Bill of Rights, while addressed infrequently by the Supreme Court after 1791, proved to be more than a "parchment barrier." Judges and commentators often pointed to the laudatory influence of the several amendments containing the elements of a general right to be let alone. They also significantly advanced the career of the narrow informational conception of the right to privacy. The First Amendment, said Justice Joseph Story in 1833, secured rights of "private sentiment" and "private judgment" by setting a high standard. Except when seized lawfully for use in criminal trials, the public mails were taken to be inviolate: a postmaster said confidently in 1855 that American law amply protected "the privacy of... thoughts" conveyed by letter. In Story's opinion, the Third Amendment secured "perfect enjoyment of that great right... that a man's house shall be his own castle." The Fifth Amendment put dampers on forced confessions during trials; and in 1868 Judge Cooley applauded the "very great particularity" required in search warrants before police officers could violate "the privacy of a man's premises."[11]

Assemblymen and judges elaborated upon constitutional and legal protections, fashioning an impressive defense of privacy in the sense of control over personal information. As early as 1811, a Louisiana court ruled in the case of *Dennis v. Leclerc* that

Dennis v. Leclerc, 1811

Brandeis and Warren defined the right to privacy narrowly

SANDRA F. VANBURKLEO

letters could not be published without consent. Lawyers and litigants also made good use of the law of trespass to defend the householder's sacred "right of shutting his door."[12] California, like many other states, passed a statute in 1872 making it a crime for individuals to open, read, or publish sealed letters addressed to others. Courts and legislatures outlawed religious tests for public officials, the disclosure of census information by federal agents after the information had reached Washington, and, somewhat later, the tapping of telegraph lines.

African Americans held in bondage constituted an important exception to these generalizations; as "property," they enjoyed privacy only at the behest of masters. Similarly, white women's right to be let alone was partial and tenuous. Yet privacy always had been a gender-specific right, denied especially to married women. Female privacy claims—among them, demands for access to abortion, birth control information, or certain procedural liberties—usually ran afoul of customary and legal imputations of "dependency" and "diminished capacity." As with children, women's minds and personalities were taken to be unformed and susceptible to both irrationality and external control. The very idea of a wifely "sanctuary," moreover, violated the common law doctrine of coverture, by which the ideas and interests of spouses were assumed to be identical. When married women enjoyed reproductive or procedural freedom, they usually did so in the absence of law to the contrary or by virtue of community forbearance.

Coverture
See also Marital unity

See Procedural rights

After 1850, women's already precarious privacy rights shrank appreciably. The notorious Comstock Act—named for Anthony Comstock, the head of the New York Society for the Suppression of Vice—passed Congress in 1873. The act made it a federal offense to "sell, or offer to sell, or...give away, or offer to give away, or...[possess]...an obscene or indecent book...or any article or medicine...for causing abortion." Even opponents of abortion and "lewd" literature sometimes denounced the law as an unprecedented invasion of personal liberty by government.[13]

In the states, pregnant or sexually active women increasingly were subjected to "mini-Comstock laws" which, for the first time in American history, outlawed abortion, abortion-related drugs, and birth control devices. Between 1860 and 1880, an antiabortion drive led by doctors and several religious groups contributed to passage of about forty such statutes. During these years, thirteen states enacted the first anti-abortion laws in their history; more than twenty states tightened old statutes. Lawmakers also codified the novel idea that interruption of gestation at any point in a pregnancy should be criminal. In the process, they jettisoned the ancient common law "quickening" doctrine, which permitted abortion during the first three months of preg-

nancy. Legislators decided, too, that state police powers should be brought to bear upon over-the-counter abortion medications, on the generally accurate ground that the drugs were unreliable and dangerous. Illinois passed the first antidrug law in 1871; other states soon followed.

Legislators often were motivated by the precepts of Victorian protectionism. In Connecticut, for instance, the assembly punished abortionists much more severely than their patients. This decision, state judges explained in 1904, was "based largely on protection due to the woman"—the need to afford "protection against her own weakness," against the "criminal lust and greed of others," and against the "moral turpitude" that supposedly inhered in women seeking abortion or birth control.[14]

Still, for middle- and upper-class white men, the legal system in the nineteenth century generally respected what Story termed "the implied or necessary intention and duty of privacy and secrecy."[15] Courts had not yet located a constitutional right to privacy in the federal Bill of Rights. Yet by 1890 an elaborate network of amendments, statutes, common law rules, and customs protected Americans from invasions of privacy much more extensively than twentieth-century lawyers have recognized.

The Privacy Tort

After 1890, a number of developments made possible by new technology—the telephone, wiretaps, Kodak cameras, microphones, and mass-distribution newspapers—led to new, sometimes frightening invasions of privacy. In their path-breaking article, Warren and Brandeis had emphasized the threat posed by newspapers "overstepping...the obvious bounds of propriety and decency," filling entire pages with "idle gossip, which can only be procured by intrusion upon the domestic circle." They sought to prove that "existing law affords a principle which can properly be invoked to protect the privacy of the individual" against "popular curiosity" and suggested that earlier judicial statements (such as English cases recognizing that private letters could not be published without consent) exemplified "a general right to privacy" securing to an individual the "right of determining, ordinarily, to what extent his thoughts, sentiments, and emotions shall be communicated to others."[16]

Over the years, the Warren and Brandeis article has spawned much commentary and new law. In the 1990s, some form of a right to privacy is recognized in most American states, either by judicial decision or statute. The privacy label, moreover, often is applied to situations well beyond the instances of unwanted public disclosure of private facts envisioned by Warren and Brandeis. Legal scholars distinguish three other kinds of cases that seem to involve the right to privacy: those involving direct intrusion into

the privacy label...applied to situations well beyond the instances of unwanted public disclosure of private facts

SANDRA F. VANBURKLEO

private places or affairs through regulation or eavesdropping; publicity which, through distortion or misrepresentation, places someone in a "false light in the public eye"; and unauthorized use of a person's name or picture for commercial purposes.[17]

The first cases recognizing a right to privacy involved the use of advertising photographs without the consent of the person whose picture had been taken. On the eve of publication of the Warren-Brandeis article, judges did not seem to be particularly impressed with privacy claims occasioned by widespread abuse of new-fangled Kodak cameras. By 1903, the tide had turned. In that year, New York legislators passed a law permitting suit for the use of one's "name, portrait or picture" for advertising purposes without written permission. Two years later, in the case of *Pavesich v. New England Life Insurance Co.*, the Georgia Supreme Court relied on Warren and Brandeis to grant relief to a man whose photograph had been used without his consent in a newspaper advertisement. Very quickly, *Pavesich* became the leading case on the right to privacy. By 1905, in other words, Warren and Brandeis had managed to establish the concept of privacy as an organizing category in American tort law.

Pavesich v. New England Life Insurance Co., 1905

Yet the aspect of privacy that most concerned them—the right to keep private activities out of newspapers—is one in which courts generally have been most reluctant to intervene, mainly because of obvious conflicts with principles of free speech and press. Warren and Brandeis conceded that the right to privacy could not be used "to prohibit any publication of matter which is of public or general interest," but never explicitly said how the line should be drawn. Brandeis himself was ambivalent about the whole project. He once said that he wanted to write a companion piece—"one that would really interest me more"—to be called "The Duty of Publicity," arguing that, if the "broad light of day could be let in upon men's actions, it would purify them as the sun disinfects."[18]

Constitutionalizing the Right to Privacy

Warren and Brandeis noted in their 1890 article that myriad "mechanical devices threaten to make good the prediction that 'what is whispered in the closet shall be proclaimed from the housetops.' "[19] Despite state laws prohibiting wiretaps, federal agents found them useful tools for gathering otherwise unavailable evidence, especially in dealings with bootleggers. In the 1928 case of *Olmstead v. United States*, Chief Justice William Taft, speaking for a divided Supreme Court, ruled that wiretaps by federal agents, although undertaken against state law, were permissible searches and seizures because electronic surveillance did not involve forcible trespass.

Olmstead v. United States, 1928

In *Olmstead*, Justice Brandeis filed an eloquent dissent. He argued, first, that the Fourth and Fifth Amendments conferred "against the government" a *constitutional* right to informational privacy (the constitutional equivalent of the privacy tort); and, second, that the Fourth Amendment did not require trespass but rather covered "every unjustifiable intrusion on the privacy of the individual, whatever the means employed." Common decency and a healthy regard for liberty, he thought, demanded that "government officials shall be subjected to the same rules of conduct that are commands to the citizen."[20]

Katz v. United States, 1967

In the 1967 case of *Katz* v. *United States*, the Supreme Court embraced this view and overruled *Olmstead*. In *Katz*, the Court responded to mounting concern about the preservation of privacy in the face of threats from new techniques of electronic and video surveillance. Americans had come to fear resemblances between their governments and George Orwell's "Big Brother." While this concern has not abated, attention gradually has shifted to the problem of preventing reckless dissemination of the vast quantities of information about individuals accumulated both by government and private agencies and readily accessible in computer data banks. While a series of federal statutes running from the Freedom of Information Act of 1966, through the Privacy Act of 1974, to the Video Privacy Protection Act of 1988 do not restrict the kinds of information governments may gather, they do place limits upon the uses to which information might be put. They also give individuals access to their own files and a right to correct inaccuracies.

Poe v. Ullman, 1961

The *Katz* decision was foreshadowed by two Supreme Court cases involving challenges to an old Connecticut statute banning the use of contraceptive devices. In *Poe* v. *Ullman* in 1961, the Supreme Court on procedural grounds dismissed a suit that had been brought by a married couple with several congenitally abnormal children; but in one of the *Poe* dissents, Associate Justice John Marshall Harlan concluded that the law was an "intolerable and unjustifiable invasion of privacy in the conduct of the most intimate concerns of an individual's personal life." In passing, Harlan noted that, for purposes of the Fourth Amendment, a distinction between "intrusion into the home" and into "the life which characteristically has its place in the home" was "so insubstantial as to be captious."[21]

Griswold v. Connecticut, 1965

Four years later, the dissents lodged by Harlan and his colleague, William O. Douglas, finally bore fruit. In the 1965 case of *Griswold* v. *Connecticut*, a Supreme Court majority held the state's anticontraception statute unconstitutional. The Court's ruling in *Griswold* clearly marks the beginning of the transition from privacy as an action in tort, to the modern constitutional right to privacy. In *Griswold*, operators of a Planned Parenthood clinic successfully provoked a test of the Connecticut law by openly providing advice about birth control and contraceptive devices to married couples. Justice Douglas declared that the idea of allowing police to enforce a ban on birth control devices by searching a marital bedroom was "repulsive to the notion of privacy surrounding the marriage relationship"[22]—language which provided a link to the old idea of privacy as immunity from governmental surveillance.

But the sanctity of bedrooms was not really threatened in *Griswold*. The issue was not one of the privacy of a particular space so much as one of intrusion into the intimacies of the marital relationship and personal choice. Indeed, Douglas's opinion in *Griswold* assumed that the Connecticut law did *not* violate the express language of any of the first ten amendments. Rather, he was prepared to say that it denigrated the *spirit* of parts of the Bill. Past decisions had shown, said Douglas, that the "specific guarantees in the Bill of Rights have penumbras (haloes), formed by emanations from those guarantees that help give them life and substance." These emanations created "zones of privacy"; one such zone included the right of association which, although absent from the First Amendment, had been inferred from the spirit of the text. In Douglas's judgment, similar emanations from the Third, Fourth, and Fifth amendments together created a "zone of privacy" at least broad enough to encompass the marital relationship.[23]

In *Eisenstadt* v. *Baird* (1972), the right to use birth control devices was extended to unmarried couples; the idea of marital privacy recognized in *Griswold* was transmuted into "the right of the *individual*, married or single, to be free from unwarranted governmental intrusion into matters so fundamentally affecting the person as the decision whether to bear or beget a child." A year later, the Court concluded in *Roe* v. *Wade* that the right of personal privacy recognized in earlier decisions was "broad enough to encompass a woman's decision whether or not to terminate her pregnancy" through abortion, at least during the first trimester.[24] In *Roe*, Associate Justice Harry Blackmun effectively revived the traditional common law "quickening" doctrine: after the third month of pregnancy, lawmakers (acting from the state's interest in preserving life) were free to impose reasonable restrictions upon women's access to abortion facilities.

Eisenstadt v. Baird, 1972

Roe v. Wade, 1973

New Directions

The Supreme Court continues to speak of a constitutional right to privacy, although there is considerable controversy about where this right should be located in the Constitution. A prime candidate just might be James Madison's Ninth Amendment. For the most part, Justice Douglas's talk about "emanations" and

the Court's ruling in Griswold *clearly marks the beginning of the transition from privacy as an action in tort, to the modern constitutional right to privacy*

"penumbras" has been abandoned. Justice Blackmun's *Roe* v. *Wade* opinion suggested that the right to privacy was part of the "liberty" protected by the Due Process Clause of the Fourteenth Amendment. But he also noted that it might be derived, as the lower court had held, from the Ninth Amendment.

In *Griswold*, Douglas had studiously avoided relying on the Due Process Clause out of aversion to the idea of "substantive due process," which had been used by the Court before 1936 to strike down economic and social legislation. Associate Justice Arthur Goldberg's concurring opinion in *Griswold* (written for himself, Chief Justice Warren, and Justice Brennan) underscored the Ninth Amendment as an additional ground for holding the Connecticut statute unconstitutional. Although Goldberg insisted that the Ninth did not constitute "an independent source of rights," he was certain that the amendment had been added in 1789 so that rights enumerated in the Bill of Rights might "not be deemed exhaustive." Douglas agreed: his concurring opinion in *Doe* v. *Bolton* (which applied as well to *Roe* v. *Wade*) relied heavily on the Ninth Amendment. In his view, Madison's amendment encompassed a broad range of unenumerated rights such as

Doe v. Bolton, 1973

autonomous control over the development and expression of one's intellect, interests, tastes, and personality, . . .

freedom of choice in the basic decisions of one's life respecting marriage, divorce, procreation, contraception, and the . . . upbringing of children, [and]

freedom to care for one's health and person, freedom from bodily restraint or compulsion, freedom to walk, stroll, or loaf.[25]

Yet, despite frequent references to the Ninth by litigants, judges, and scholars, no majority Supreme Court decision has been squarely based on it. The considerable vitality and scope of the present-day law of privacy flows instead from an ongoing, dramatic reorientation of First, Fourth, Fifth, and Fourteenth amendment cases. In the 1990s, the concept of privacy encompasses much more than the right to control information envisioned by Louis Brandeis. Cases like *Griswold* and *Roe* concern privacy, after all, not in the restricted sense of immunity from uninvited observation and disclosure of personal information, but in the general sense of immunity from governmental control over minds, bodies, and homes.

Doctrinal reorientation has been swift and sweeping. Numerous old court rulings, originally decided on other grounds, have been redescribed and reconceptualized in terms of privacy. Thus, the law of privacy has emerged as an organizing category capable of absorbing and redirecting traditional legal classifications. A few examples make the point. First Amendment rulings on the right of association or anonymity (such as the 1962 decision in *NAACP* v. *Button*) have been reclassified as disputes having to do with "associational privacy" or "political privacy." The right of parents to direct children's education and upbringing recognized in cases like *Meyer* v. *Nebraska* (1923) and *Pierce* v. *Society of Sisters* (1925) have been recast in terms of "familial privacy." The 1942 case of *Skinner* v. *Oklahoma*, in which the Court ruled on vague grounds that a man accused of the relatively minor crime of chicken-stealing and then sentenced to sterilization could not be subjected to such a cruel and unusual medical procedure, appears in law texts as a privacy case. Current debates about the constitutionality of drug testing, which once might have been described as search, self-incrimination, or due process problems, are termed privacy disputes.

NAACP v. Button, 1962

Meyer v. Nebraska, 1923
Pierce v. Society of Sisters, 1925
Skinner v. Oklahoma, 1942

Yet expansion and reorientation can be overemphasized: in at least two important areas, the law of privacy may well be contracting. As courts confront cases involving drug use, for instance, Fourth and Fifth amendment informational privacy—the kind of privacy which Louis Brandeis *and* American revolutionaries particularly venerated—seems to be losing ground. In several recent decisions, such as the 1989 cases of *Skinner* v. *Railway Labor Executives Association* and *National Treasury Employees Union* v. *Von Raab*, the Supreme Court weighed public safety against Fourth Amendment guarantees of freedom from unreasonable searches, and concluded that drug testing of railroad and customs workers, even without warrants or individualized suspicion, were reasonable exercises of Congressional regulatory power.

Skinner v. Railway Labor
Executives Association, 1989

National Treasury Employees
Union v. Von Raab, 1989

Reproductive freedom also has contracted. While the privacy umbrella now encompasses women's intellectual, economic, and procedural liberty—aspects of the right to be let alone which James Madison's generation rarely contemplated—the Supreme Court has exhibited a notable reluctance in the years since *Roe* v. *Wade* to expand or defend the contours of the constitutional right to privacy in cases involving reproductive freedom. In its July 1989 decision in *Webster* v. *Reproductive Health Services*, the Court had little trouble affirming the constitutionality of one section of a Missouri statute that disallowed the use of public facilities and public funds for poor women seeking abortions. The majority also declined comment on the statute's preamble, which declared (contrary to the quickening doctrine at the heart of *Roe*) that human life exists at conception.

Webster v. Reproductive Health
Services, 1989

More recently, the Court approved limited state regulation of abortion among teenagers. A 1988 Minnesota law mandated notification of both parents in advance of abortion unless young women could prove parental abuse or neglect; in such cases, teen-

Jane Hodgson v. Minnesota, 1990

Ohio v. Akron Center for Reproductive Health, 1990

recent attempts to say precisely what privacy means have transformed the concept into an accessible, fathomable legal tool

agers could petition local courts for suspension of the rule. A 1985 Ohio statute imposed criminal penalties upon physicians who refused to notify one parent on behalf of a teenager contemplating abortion; as in Minnesota, the law included a so-called judicial bypass. On June 25, 1990, amidst sharp division on the bench, a slim Supreme Court majority decided in *Jane Hodgson v. Minnesota* that, while Minnesota's two-parent rule did not serve a compelling state interest and violated teenagers' privacy rights, the judicial bypass portion of the law *was* constitutional. On the same day, in *Ohio v. Akron Center for Reproductive Health*, the Court held that Ohio's one-parent provision was constitutionally permissible, given the immaturity of teenagers and the state's interest in promoting family cohesion. The Court also accepted the burdens placed upon physicians by the Ohio law, on the ground that doctors expected to have to intervene in family life. Additional tests of anti-abortion legislation (such as the stringent laws prevailing in Guam and Pennsylvania) probably will appear on the Supreme Court docket as early as 1991–92.

Conclusion

Recent developments in the constitutional law of privacy have been controversial. Since privacy claims typically challenge government's right to compromise individual autonomy in the name of community well-being, controversy is unsurprising. More to the point, disagreements about how to ensure "the security of liberty" in relations with government are at least as old as the republic. If Americans are concerned in the 1990s about erosions of a general right to be let alone, so were Federalists and Antifederalists in 1789. Elements of this umbrella-like right to autonomy appear in the Bill of Rights—in the First, Fourth, Fifth, and Ninth amendments, for example, and perhaps in the spirit of the entire Bill. But the right to privacy itself was either too fundamental or too vague for explicit mention. Indeed, privacy *per se* has acquired legitimacy and constitutional standing only since the 1890s—first as an extra-constitutional action in tort, then as a constitutional right limited to informational privacy, and finally as a multifaceted constitutional liberty.

To some extent, the modern right to privacy recaptures eighteenth-century understandings of the "security of liberty"; in other respects, the concept of privacy has been radically altered. African Americans no longer fall between constitutional cracks; and while reproductive freedom is still contested, female autonomy in less controversial areas has been drawn securely beneath the privacy umbrella. Most lawyers would say, moreover, that the old, nonspecific right to be let alone was too vague to be useful. Recent attempts to say precisely what privacy means have transformed the concept into an accessible, fathomable legal tool with reasonably well-specified boundaries.

This obsession with particularity might have alarmed James Madison. On the other hand, his fondest hope was that Americans would squabble endlessly about proper relations between authority and liberty. To the extent that zones of privacy tend to expand as a result of lawsuits and demonstrations on the steps of the Supreme Court, Madison would have been immensely gratified.

Notes

[1] Charles Fried, "Privacy: A Moral Analysis," in Ferdinand D. Schoeman, ed., *Philosophical Dimensions of Privacy: An Anthology* (New York: Cambridge University Press, 1984), 209–210.

[2] *Olmstead v. United States*, 277 U.S. Reports 438, 478 (1928); Thomas M. Cooley, *Treatise on the Law of Torts*, Students' Edition (Chicago: Callaghan and Co., 1907), 195.

[3] John Philip Reid, *Concept of Liberty in the Age of the American Revolution* (Chicago: University of Chicago Press, 1988), 68; for an American example, Alexander Hamilton, *Federalist* No. 83 (Modern Library Edition 1937), 553.

[4] James Madison, "Speech to the House Explaining His Proposed Amendments and His Notes for the Amendment Speech," reprinted in Randy E. Barnett, *Rights Retained By the People: The History and Meaning of the Ninth Amendment* (Fairfax, Vir.: George Mason University Press, 1989), 58.

[5] James Madison to Thomas Jefferson, October 17, 1788, quoted in Barnett, *Rights Retained By The People*, 22 ("parchment barriers"); George Mason to John Mason, July 31, 1789, quoted in Kenneth R. Bowling, " 'A Tub to the Whales': The Founding Fathers and Adoption of the Federal Bill of Rights," *Journal of the Early Republic* 8, No. 3 (Fall 1988), 233.

[6] "An Old Whig IV," Philadelphia *Independent Gazetteer*, October 27, 1787, in John Kaminski and Richard Leffler, eds., *Federalists and Antifederalists: The Debate Over the Ratification of the Constitution* (Madison, Wisc.: Madison House, 1989), 158–59.

[7] Robert Bork, testimony before Congress, quoted in Barnett, *Rights Retained By the People*, 1.

[8] Madison, "Speech to the House...," in Barnett, *Rights Retained By the People*, 55; Madison to Thomas Jefferson, October 17, 1788, quoted in Barnett, *Rights Retained By the People*, 21.

[9] Madison, "Speech to the House...," in Barnett, *Rights Retained By the People*, 60.

[10]Samuel Warren and Louis Brandeis, "The Right to Privacy," *Harvard Law Review*, IV, No. 5 (December 1890), 193–220, at 195; Roscoe Pound quoted in James H. Barron, "Warren and Brandeis, *The Right to Privacy*, 4 Harv. L. Rev. 193 (1890): Demystifying a Landmark Citation," *Suffolk University Law Review*, XIII, No. 4 (Summer 1979), 876; Alan Westin, *Privacy and Freedom* (New York: Atheneum, 1968), 337.

[11]Westin, *Privacy and Freedom*, 330–338.

[12]*Dennis v. Leclerc*, 1 Mart. (La.) 297 (1811); for "shutting his own door," *State v. Armfield*, 9 N.C. 246, 247 (1822), discussed in Note, "The Right to Privacy in Nineteenth Century America," *Harvard Law Review*, 94 (1981), 1985.

[13]James Mohr, *Abortion in America: The Origins and Evolution of National Policy* (New York: Oxford University Press, 1978), 196.

[14]Ibid., 196, 201.

[15]Quoted in Westin, *Privacy and Freedom*, 337.

[16]Warren and Brandeis, "The Right of Privacy," 196–98.

[17]Barron, "Warren and Brandeis," 879.

[18]Quoted in Barron, "Warren and Brandeis," 912.

[19]Warren and Brandeis, "The Right to Privacy," 195.

[20]*Olmstead v. United States*, 277 U.S. Reports 438, 478, 485 (1928).

[21]*Poe v. Ullman*, 367 U.S. Reports 497, 539, 551 (1961).

[22]*Griswold v. Connecticut*, 381 U.S. Reports 479, 486 (1965).

[23]Ibid., 484.

[24]*Eisenstadt v. Baird*, 405 U.S. Reports 438, 453 (1972); *Roe v. Wade*, 410 U.S. Reports 113, 153 (1973).

[25]*Griswold*, 492; *Doe v. Bolton*, 410 U.S. Reports 179, 211, 213 (1973).

Cases

Dennis v. Leclerc, 1 Mart. (O.S.) 297 (La., 1811). An editor in Louisiana claimed a First Amendment right to publish a letter without the author's consent. A state court rejected his claim, contending that publication violated the author's expectation of confidentiality and privacy.

Doe v. Bolton, 410 U.S. 179 (1973). In this companion case to *Roe v. Wade*, the Court invalidated a Georgia law modeled after the American Law Institute's recommended abortion statute, on the ground that the statute abrogated the privacy right described in *Roe*.

Eisenstadt v. Baird, 405 U.S. 438 (1972). The Court extended the privacy right identified in *Griswold* (which applied only to married couples) to all individuals.

Griswold v. Connecticut, 381 U.S. 479 (1965). The Supreme Court ruled that a Connecticut anti–birth control law, while not a violation of the express language of any of the first ten amendments, impinged upon a general constitutional right to privacy found in the "penumbras" of the Fourth, Fifth, Fourteenth, and Ninth amendments.

Jane Hodgson v. Minnesota, 110 S. Ct. 2926 (1990). The Minnesota legislature passed a statute requiring teenagers who sought abortions to notify both parents, or in cases of abuse or neglect, to seek permission from a judge. The Supreme Court ruled that while the two-parent rule did not serve a compelling state interest and violated young women's right to privacy the judicial bypass was a constitutionally permissible alternative to parental notification.

Katz v. United States, 389 U.S. 347 (1967). The Supreme Court put an end to the notion, set forth in *Olmstead*, that electronic surveillance should be exempted from Fourth and Fifth amendment prohibitions against unreasonable searches and self-incrimination.

Meyer v. Nebraska, 262 U.S. 390 (1923). The Court reversed the conviction of a German teacher who had taught a modern foreign language (German) despite a Nebraska statute outlawing such a practice. The justices found that the liberty protected by the Fourteenth Amendment included "the right to enjoy those privileges long recognized at common law as essential to the orderly pursuit of happiness by free men." Among those privileges was the "right to acquire useful knowledge."

NAACP v. Button, 371 U.S. 42 (1962). A Virginia statute made it illegal for organizations (in this case, the NAACP) to offer advice about legal rights or to refer individuals to specific lawyers for help in civil rights disputes. The Court ruled that opinions expressed by the NAACP, as well as any resulting associations, were protected fully by the First and Fourteenth amendments.

National Treasury Employees Union v. Von Raab, 109 S. Ct. 1384 (1989). The Supreme Court held that drug testing of customs workers was subject to the reasonableness requirement of Fourth Amendment searches and that testing as conducted by the Customs Service met that standard.

Ohio v. Akron Center for Reproductive Health, 110 S. Ct. 2972 (1990). An Ohio law required physicians to notify at least one parent when teenagers sought abortions; whenever young women were reluctant for good reason to notify parents, physicians were allowed to seek permission from a state court. The Supreme Court judged the law constitutionally permissible, given the woman's age and the state's ongoing interest in promoting family cohesion.

Olmstead v. United States, 277 U.S. 438 (1928). Before *Olmstead*, the Supreme Court had decided that the Fourth Amendment prohibition against unlawful searches and seizures meant searches involving forcible trespass. Because wiretaps undertaken by federal agents did not involve forcible trespass, the Court found them constitutionally permissible.

Pavesich v. New England Life Insurance Co, 122 Ga. 190 (1905). In this early state case recognizing a right of privacy in tort law, the Georgia Court of Appeals decided that unauthorized use of a man's photograph for advertising purposes constituted a violation of his right to privacy.

Pierce v. Society of Sisters, 268 U.S. 510 (1925). The Supreme Court unanimously invalidated an Oregon compulsory public school law when it was challenged by a private religious and military school. Because *Pierce* involved a religious institution, it sometimes is cited as a religious freedom case; in recent years, it also has been characterized as a case involving familial privacy.

Poe v. Ullman, 367 U.S. 497 (1961). A married couple and their doctor sued for a declaratory judgment against the constitutionality of Connecticut's anti–birth control law, which made it a crime to use contraceptives or to be an accessory in their use. A Supreme Court majority ruled that the case was not a justiciable controversy because there was no actual threat of prosecution in Connecticut.

Roe v. Wade, 410 U.S. 113 (1973). The Supreme Court struck down a Texas law banning abortions except when pregnancy threatened a woman's life. Associate Justice Harry Blackmun ruled that the right of privacy described in *Griswold* v. *Connecticut* was broad enough to encompass a woman's right during the first trimester to decide whether or not to end a pregnancy; thereafter, the state's interest in preserving life would support restriction.

Skinner v. Oklahoma, 315 U.S. 535 (1942). A state court issued a sterilization order when a man previously convicted of robbery stole some chickens. The court argued that criminal tendencies might be inheritable. The U.S. Supreme Court reversed the order on equal protection grounds; recently, *Skinner* has been cited in defense of a right of procreation.

Skinner v. Railway Labor Executives Association, 109 S. Ct. 1402 (1989). The Court held that while the Fourth Amendment applied to drug testing, the tests required by the Federal Railroad Administration were reasonable, given the federal government's interest in protecting travelers.

Webster v. Reproductive Health Services, 109 S. Ct. 3040 (1989). In defiance of portions of *Roe v. Wade*, Missouri had enacted a statute imposing restrictions upon abortion and declaring in the preamble that life begins at conception. Among other restrictions, the law ruled out the use of public facilities or public money for abortions on the ground that the existence of privacy rights did not oblige states to accept financial burdens incurred when such rights were exercised.

Suggested Readings

Randy Barnett, ed. *The Rights Retained By the People: The History and Meaning of the Ninth Amendment* (Fairfax, Vir.: George Mason University Press, 1989). The best available introduction to the history of the Ninth Amendment.

David H. Flaherty. *Privacy in Colonial America* (Charlottesville: University Press of Virginia, 1972). A fascinating study of early American ambivalence about privacy rights.

David H. Flaherty. *Protecting Privacy in Surveillance Societies: The Federal Republic of Germany, Sweden, France, Canada, and the United States* (Chapel Hill: University of North Carolina Press, 1989). A comparative study of the impact of information-gathering technology in the modern world.

Michael Kammen. *Sovereignty and Liberty: Constitutional Discourse in American Culture,* chapter 3, "Personal Liberty and American Constitutionalism" (Madison: University of Wisconsin Press, 1988). Skillfully identifies changing conceptions of what the right of privacy means within the broader context of American liberty.

James C. Mohr. *Abortion in America* (New York: Oxford University Press, 1978). A good general history of abortion that illuminates social and cultural underpinnings.

John Philip Reid. *The Concept of Liberty in the Age of the American Revolution* (Chicago: University of Chicago Press, 1988). A useful, controversial study of early understandings of liberty within the British empire.

John H. F. Shattuck, ed. *Rights of Privacy* (Skokie, Ill: National Textbook Company, 1977). A handbook, written for lay audiences, that provides a readable, detailed summary of privacy law.

Laurence H. Tribe. *American Constitutional Law*, 2nd Edition, chapter 15, "Rights of Privacy and Personhood" (Mineola, N.Y.: Foundation Press, 1988). A noted constitutional lawyer defends the constitutionalization of privacy rights.

Alan F. Westin. *Privacy and Freedom* (New York: Atheneum Press, 1967). A militant discussion of relations between privacy and liberty since American independence.

SANDRA F. VANBURKLEO

X

Paula Petrik

WOMEN AND THE BILL OF RIGHTS

During the deliberations of the Continental Congress in 1776, Abigail Adams cautioned her husband, John, future ambassador and president:

Remember the Ladies, and be more generous and favorable to them than your ancestors. Do not put such unlimited power into the hands of the Husbands. Remember all Men would be tyrants if they could. If particular care and attention is not paid to the Ladies we are determined to foment a Rebellion, and will not hold ourselves bound by any Laws in which we have no voice, or Representation. [1]

John and Abigail Adams were accustomed to each other's banter and, perhaps, John understood his wife's remark in that context. In any case, neither he nor the other framers responded then or later during constitutional debates to Abigail Adams's challenge. With few exceptions, the idea of specifically including women in the body of the Constitution or in the Bill of Rights stood outside the framers' experience and philosophical ken. As a result, the Bill of Rights did not apply in significant ways to women.

Both traditional views of women's place and legal prohibitions conspired to exclude women from the rights enumerated in the first ten amendments. For a woman the legacy of the Revolutionary War was ambiguous. While the First Amendment guaranteed freedom of speech, cultural conceptualizations of womanhood severely circumscribed women's rights in this re-

the Bill of Rights did not apply in significant ways to women

gard. Except in church, women, for example, could not generally speak in public before mixed audiences of men and women. Not until women's participation in the reform movements of the early nineteenth century did their appearance in public forums become acceptable. And even then there were restrictions. Similarly, legal checks undermined women's right to an impartial jury of peers, a right sustained by the Sixth Amendment. Until the early twentieth century, for example, a contested divorce was tried before a jury. Since women brought roughly two-thirds of the divorce suits, an all-male jury imposed a considerable disadvantage for a woman attempting to leave an unhappy marriage. Due process rights outlined in the Fifth Amendment were largely irrelevant to women. Their property transferred to their husband's control at marriage. Most obviously, neither the Constitution nor the Bill of Rights specified who was eligible to vote.

Due process

After the Revolution

Neither before nor after the Revolution did anyone in the new republic dispute that women were citizens, nor did the federal constitution limit national citizenship to men. But Americans believed that the power to define citizenship resided with the states, and the states limited suffrage to those with the capacity for reason and sound judgment, those qualities associated at the time mainly with adult white males. While the federal constitution originally may have implied a more comprehensive right to vote in presidential elections, the framers in 1787 advocated local control of who should and should not vote. States, in consequence, supported an array of customs and statutes barring whole classes of persons from the polling places. Lack of the franchise also prevented the same groups from exercising the obligations and privileges arising from the vote such as office holding and jury service. After 1776, moreover, states adopted statutory language that routinely excluded aliens, indigents, African Americans, felons, idiots, children, and women from holding the franchise. There were exceptions, most notably New Jersey. Until 1807, when New Jersey lawmakers altered the statute to include gender-specific language, effectively barring women, African Americans, and aliens, women had voted and been cheered on in their endeavor.

...the states limited suffrage to those with the capacity for reason and sound judgment, those qualities associated at the time mainly with adult white males

In addition to the narrowly defined nature of women's citizenship was the common law doctrine of *coverture* and the closely related concept of marital unity. The British legal commentator William Blackstone wrote, in so many words, that the very being of woman was suspended during marriage or at least incorporated into that of her husband, under whose wing she maintained her legal existence. The common law rendered a married

Coverture
Marital unity

woman (*femme covert*) civilly dead, and defined her as incapable of exercising a citizen's most basic rights, including the right to convey property and enter into contracts. A husband acted for his wife, contracting for her and bringing suits in her name. All property, both real and personal, became the husband's when a woman married. Except for dower (the setting aside of one-third of a husband's estate for his widow), a woman's capacity to arrange a pre-nuptial agreement, and a woman's right to establish a trust for the protection of her children, wives were wholly dependent on their spouses. Divorce under coverture not only meant the loss of a woman's property but also of her children. An unmarried woman (*femme sole*) or a widow (*relict*) fared much better in this arrangement, retaining economic and legal rights on a par with men.

Femme covert

Real property
Personal Property
Dower

Femme sole
Relict

Responding to their new role in post-revolutionary America, women embraced the idea of "republican motherhood" as a means to exercise citizenship and political influence. By educating sons for the republic and providing secure homes for its citizens, so the ideology went, women would possess political power. In other words, women would exercise their citizenship privately through their traditional roles of mother and wife instead of publicly as persons with legal identities and as voting citizens.

The First Phase, 1848—1890: Early Setbacks

In the early nineteenth century, however, women's participation in public political endeavors increased, chiefly because of their role as rank and file in the abolition movement and as captains of benevolent and reform organizations. In 1848 at the Seneca Falls Convention on women's rights, participants set forth the Declaration of Sentiments, modeled on the Declaration of Independence. In the document, Elizabeth Cady Stanton addressed three major areas of concern: coverture and its associated legal disabilities, occupational opportunity, and woman suffrage. While the declaration as a whole was generally conservative and while many sentiments summarized familiar grievances, the demand for the franchise seemed the most extreme and provoked the greatest public response. Even some members of the Seneca Falls leadership considered the issue too radical—"so advanced that Mrs. [Lucretia] Mott feared its inclusion would hurt the infant movement."[2]

After the Seneca Falls meeting, women's rights supporters shared platforms with antislavery groups and continued to raise the issue of woman suffrage, but the debates firmly centered on slavery during the years before the Civil War. The conflict between North and South absorbed women's energies, and it was only after the Civil War that women had their first opportunity to achieve their political objective. In the campaigns for the ratification of the Fourteenth Amendment, which inserted the word "male" into the Constitution for the first time, and the Fifteenth Amendment, which afforded African Americans the right to vote but omitted any reference to gender, women developed further their rationalizations for suffrage. Generally, the early suffragists united behind an argument grounded in natural rights; a smaller group justified its claim by referring to women's peculiar nature—namely, that women would bring their superior moral judgment into the political arena to counter society's baser influences if given the vote. The results of these early campaigns were two: political defeat and the division of the woman suffrage organization into two competing factions—one of which was willing to defer to African American interests and another which adamantly refused to yield to the "negroes' hour."

After the ratification of the two amendments, woman suffrage advocates attempted to test the new constitutional provisions, specifically the Privileges and Immunities Clause of the Fourteenth Amendment ("No state shall make or enforce any law which shall abridge the privileges or immunities of citizens of the United States"), more directly by voting at the polls. On November 5, 1872, in Rochester, New York, Susan B. Anthony and thirteen like-minded women voted. Two weeks later, authorities arrested the women and charged them with the federal criminal offense of having voted without the lawful right to vote. At the conclusion of the *United States of America v. Susan B. Anthony* (1873), the judge ruled that the Privileges and Immunities Clause did not apply to women and directed the all-male jury to bring in a guilty verdict. The following day when the judge asked if the prisoner had any words before he pronounced sentence, Anthony, rehearsing the basic inequities of women's position, challenged the judge's view. Sentence could not be pronounced, Anthony argued, because his action was a "denial of [her] citizen's right to vote, the denial of [her] right of consent as one of the governed, the denial of [her] right of representation as one of the taxed, the denial of [her] right to a trial by a jury of [her] peers as an offender against the law, therefore the denial of [her] sacred right to life, liberty, property and—"[3] The judge interrupted this remark and several others by ordering Anthony to be still and sit or stand, in a kind of courtroom vaudeville, but in the end he imposed the statutory fine. Because of her lawyer's gracious but misguided payment of her $1000 bail and the judge's refusal to imprison Anthony until payment of the fine, Anthony's case did not reach the Supreme Court, unlike Virginia Minor's, which did.

Coincidentally with Susan B. Anthony's voting in New

Privileges and immunities clause

**United States v.
Susan B. Anthony, 1873**

York, Virginia Minor with her husband, Francis, filed suit in 1872 against a St. Louis registrar. Abiding by a Missouri statute expressly denying women the right to vote, the bureaucrat had refused to register Virginia Minor. In *Minor* v. *Happersett* (1875), the Minors invoked a broad range of constitutional provisions in their arguments but concentrated on the Privileges and Immunities Clause, arguing that voting was a privilege tied to citizenship. From the outset, the Minors faced difficult problems. In the first place, all the states denied women the right to vote; therefore, practice was against them. Second, although they argued that the Fourteenth Amendment conferred suffrage on African Americans, the existence of the Fifteenth Amendment undermined their interpretation of the Privileges and Immunities Clause. Third, the Constitution explicitly allocated to the states the power to define voter qualifications.

Minor v. Happersett, 1875

The Minors confronted these problems in several different ways with varying degrees of skill. As to the Fifteenth Amendment, the Minors frankly brushed aside the straightforward language of the Amendment, claiming that the provision had only tangential bearing on the case. Concerning the states' right to set voter qualifications, the Minors distinguished between the power to set qualifications for voting, which the states admittedly possessed, and the power to restrict or limit suffrage, which they argued exceeded state authority. The Minors did not persuade the Supreme Court. Finding support both in and beyond the Constitution, the Court ruled:

The Constitution does not define the privileges and immunities of citizens. For that definition we must look elsewhere. In this case we need not determine what they are but only whether suffrage is necessarily one of them. . . . The amendment did not add to the privileges and immunities of a citizen. It simply furnished an additional guaranty for the protection of such as he already had. No new voters were necessarily made by it. . . . In this condition of the law in respect to suffrage in the several States it cannot for a moment be doubted that if it had been intended to make all citizens of the United States voters, the framers of the constitution would not have left it to implication.[4]

In both *Anthony* and *Minor*, the courts braved the problem of interpreting the Privileges and Immunities Clause of the Fourteenth Amendment. Clearly, Congress had not intended to enfranchise women by the passage of the Fourteenth Amendment. Yet, it was difficult to deal with the broad language of the amendment in such a way as to articulate a reasonable and consistent understanding of the amendment's meaning. After all, African Americans and women were groups "similarly situated," to use a

Similarly situated group

descriptive twentieth-century term. To limit the application of the language to one group created theoretical problems.

For the time being, the political setbacks in the ratification process and the related decisions rendered in *Minor* and *Anthony* stymied women's efforts to secure the franchise, so they turned to another issue raised in the Seneca Falls Declaration of Sentiments: occupational opportunity. Myra Bradwell, the successful publisher of the *Chicago Legal News*, had applied for admission to the Illinois Bar in 1869. Although she had successfully passed the bar examination, the Illinois Bar denied her admission solely because of her sex.

Bradwell v. Illinois, 1873

In *Bradwell* v. *Illinois* (1873), women's claims again rested on the Privileges and Immunities Clause. Bradwell's attorney argued:

> . . . the profession of the law . . . is an avocation open to every citizen of the United States. And while the Legislature may prescribe qualifications for entering upon this pursuit, they cannot, under the guise of fixing qualifications, exclude a class of citizens from the bar. . . . [A] qualification to which a whole class of citizens never can attain, is not a regulation of admission to the bar, but is, as to such citizens a prohibition.[5]

As happened in *Minor* v. *Happersett*, the court denied that admission to practice law (and any other occupation governed by state licensing) was among the privileges and immunities belonging to citizens; such vocations were, in fact, within the power of the states to regulate. Besides reference to constitutional issues, several concurring justices asserted other, culturally biased rationales. The weight of history, nature, and divine creation, the justices claimed, reinforced their constitutional interpretation:

> It certainly cannot be affirmed, as an historical fact, that [occupational choice] has ever been established as one of the fundamental privileges and immunities of the sex. . . . The natural and proper timidity and delicacy which belongs to the female sex evidently unfits it for many of the occupations of civil life. The constitution of the family organization, which is founded in the divine ordinance as well as in the nature of things, indicates the domestic sphere as that which properly belongs to the domain and function of womanhood. . . . The paramount destiny and mission of woman are to fulfill the noble and benign offices of wife and mother. This is the law of the Creator. And the rules of civil society must be adapted to the general constitution of things, and cannot be based upon exceptional cases.[6]

the weight of history, nature, and divine creation, the justices claimed, reinforced their constitutional interpretation

With *Minor* and *Bradwell*, women's initial efforts to secure the franchise and open various occupations by federal fiat via the

Privileges and Immunities Clause failed, showing that the clause did not represent the best strategy for realizing women's claim to the vote.

Women were able to effect changes, however, regarding the third item on the Seneca Falls' agenda: the disabilities of coverture. In 1848, New York's Married Women's Property Act allowed women to own property apart from their husbands. Still a conservative measure, the act retained the elements of coverture. By 1855, Massachusetts allowed women the right to keep their earnings. During the 1860s and 1870s several states and territories allowed women to carry on businesses in their own right under sole tradership declarations. Such declarations implied the right to contract and sue, although states placed limitations on the amount of capital a woman could invest. Following Connecticut's lead, other states granted married women reasonable contractual rights. One by one, states fell into line so that by 1895, married women could convey in various ways their separate property, contract, and bring suit.

With the establishment of land grant institutions, woman's occupational options increased too, and individual women gained admission to the professions. Women such as Elizabeth Blackwell became doctors; Arabella Mansfield of Iowa and others gained admission to state bars; and still others such as Ella B. Knowles of Montana, who became Assistant Attorney General, parlayed their law degrees into successful political careers. Still, women could not vote, and the range of their vocational options remained restricted and reserved for exceptional women.

The Second Phase, 1890–1960: The Problems of Victory

With the unification of the formerly rival suffrage groups into the National American Woman Suffrage Association in 1890, the woman suffrage movement took on new energy and displayed heightened political awareness. Even limited experience in politics suggested to the women that they needed to employ more expedient political tactics, and they increasingly linked their political arguments to the notion of "woman's special qualities" rather than "natural rights." Because of women's superior moral sensibility, the argument went, voting rights for women would result in the general improvement of society and good government. Allying themselves with the Populists and later the Progressives and increasing their membership through alliances with other women's reform and cultural groups, suffragists made piecemeal progress in individual states. The costs in time and money in combination with successive defeats soon convinced the suffrage leadership of the necessity for a constitutional amendment.

even limited experience in politics suggested to the women that they needed to employ more expedient political tactics

Adroitly turning women's support of war work during World War I into a political bargaining chip with President Woodrow Wilson, suffragists expected presidential support. When it was not immediately forthcoming, Alice Paul, leader of the Women's Party, the radical wing of the woman suffrage movement, used civil disobedience to remind the president of his promise to see the legislation through Congress. Her maneuver also galvanized public opinion in support of women. Once approved by the Congress, the Nineteenth Amendment went to the states for ratification, a process successfully completed in 1920. Many western states had already granted suffrage to women, and Montana, taking the political process one step further, had elected Jeanette Rankin to the House of Representatives in 1916.

Politicians looked forward to women's voting with some trepidation and early on courted their favor with platforms that included women's concerns. Soon, however, the party bosses discovered that women did not vote as a bloc. Except for the passage of Prohibition in several states, women tended to vote like their male counterparts. National political parties soon dispensed with their earlier concern for women's issues and returned to business as usual.

What difference, then, did the Nineteenth Amendment make? The answer is unclear. Whether woman suffrage failed to garner the political power and societal influence that the suffrage leadership had envisioned is still subject to debate. Women did not gain the power that the leadership expected to fall to women with the vote, but they did influence public policy by winning political offices across the nation fitted to "women's nature" in the fields of public health, education, and culture. Nonetheless, the Nineteenth Amendment endowed women with the *political badge* of citizenship, bringing them closer to actual citizenship in the fullest sense and guaranteeing them political parity.

Women's "politics of expediency" left a legacy to the twentieth century in the form of "protective" labor laws. During the campaign for woman suffrage, advocates had argued that women had special qualities. Social reformers applied the argument to the work place, maintaining that women workers needed "special" protection because there was something inherently "different" about them. That major "difference" turned out to be women's "female functions:" their childbearing capacity and child-rearing responsibilities. Concomitant with this thinking was the very real plight of women industrial workers who labored long hours in wretched conditions for a fraction of the wages paid to their male counterparts.

Both perceptions influenced *Muller* v. *Oregon* (1908), a case involving an Oregon laundry operator's violation of a state statute mandating a ten-hour day for women, and *Adkins* v. *The*

Muller v. Oregon, 1908

Adkins v. The Children's Hospital of the District of Columbia, 1923

Children's Hospital of the District of Columbia (1923), a case centering on establishing a minimum wage for women workers. Convinced by a long brief characterized by quasi-scientific evidence of women's biological differences, the court upheld Oregon's law in *Muller*, pointing to the "common sense" correlation between women's ill health and overwork. In *Adkins*, despite similar sociological evidence outlining the impact of substandard wages on women and children, the Court remained unconvinced. According to the Court, the relationship between health and hours on the job was direct, while the connection between health and wages was not.

The Court's decision in *Muller* had the immediate effect, among others, of prohibiting women's night work, defining heavy work, and limiting women's access to various occupations. With its "invocation of the allegedly many and fundamental differences between the sexes, the decision crystallized the prejudices of the age and thus achieved a far greater impact on constitutional history than its holding warranted."[7] *Muller* v. *Oregon*, in sum, effectively blocked future bids for women's equality in the work place. While protective legislation tempered the worst exploitative aspects of the work place for women in the early part of the century, it increasingly hindered women's aspirations as technology obviated certain job requirements. Because opponents of protective legislation counted *Adkins* a victory, the high court's decision confirmed yet again the widening split in the women's movement into two antagonistic groups. On the one side stood women like those in the National Consumers' League who promoted "protective" legislation rationalized by women's biological differences; on the other stood women like those on the roster of the National Women's Party who championed full equality rooted in women's right to contract their labor freely.

Both women's groups generally made little progress in the years immediately following *Adkins*. Further attempts at protective legislation, the centerpiece of the "protectionist" organizations' program, and congressional passage of the Equal Rights Amendment, the central plank in the National Women's Party's platform, languished. The Great Depression frustrated both groups' plans. New Dealers enacted a raft of minimum wage measures and, at the same time, local agencies campaigned to remove women from the work force. World War II further distracted citizens from women's issues, and postwar recovery diverted them into a frenzy of consumption.

By the 1960s, women's equality still appeared illusory, even in the criminal justice system. *Hoyt* v. *Florida* (1961) showed the Court's unwillingness to provide the same rights to women as they did to other groups. Florida law provided that no woman

with its "invocation of the allegedly many and fundamental differences between the sexes [Muller] crystallized the prejudices of the age"

Hoyt v. Florida, 1961

could serve on a jury unless she journeyed to the district court house and enrolled for jury duty. Because men faced no such requirement, Florida jury lists were disproportionately male, resulting in many all-male juries. Hoyt, convicted of murdering her husband with a baseball bat, claimed that this statute denied her equal protection because female jurors would have been more sympathetic to the circumstances of her case (her husband's adultery, her willingness to forgive him, and her "insanity" defense). The Supreme Court upheld the Florida statute.

The Third Phase, 1964–Present: Unfinished Business

But beginning in the mid-1950s with the civil rights movement and continuing through the subsequent decades with the appearance of various feminist groups, women's issues increasingly came onto the political stage, forming the basis for the third women's movement. In 1964, Congress enacted the Civil Rights Act. In an attempt to defeat the measure, a southern opponent managed to insert the word "sex" into the proposed law. What was essentially a joke intended to kill the legislation actually provided a potentially powerful tool for women's rights, but even including the word "sex" in the act apparently did not guarantee that women would benefit from the Equal Protection Clause. ("No state shall deny to any person within its jurisdiction the equal protection of the laws.") Although some observers anticipated that the Supreme Court might subject *both* race and gender to "strict scrutiny" and thereby expand the definition of equal protection, the prospect seemed doubtful. In the years following 1964, the Court tinkered with the idea that women, like African Americans, comprised a "suspect class" and that states had to provide a "compelling rationale" as opposed to a "reasonable rationale" when they formulated legislation that made gender distinctions. While the Court came close to defining women as a "suspect class," the justices retreated from full endorsement of the principle.

In *Reed v. Reed* (1971), for example, the Court ruled that an Idaho law prohibiting women from assuming the role of estate administrators was arbitrary and impermissible under the equal protection clause. *Frontiero v. Richardson* (1973), a case involving differential benefit rules for male and female members of the military, challenged sweeping generalizations about men's role as breadwinners and women's role as homemakers. The assumption underlying the benefit statutes was that female spouses of servicemen would normally be dependent on their husbands. In Sharron Frontiero's case, her husband was dependent on her and she, accordingly, applied for dependent benefits for her husband. The

Strict scrutiny

Suspect class

Reed v. Reed, 1971

Frontiero v. Richardson, 1973

Court again concluded that sex could not be made the basis for special disadvantages but went further in pronouncing women a "suspect class." *Kahn* v. *Shevin* (1974) demonstrated the difficulties in dealing with gender. In considering a Florida law that granted a special tax exemption to women, the Court seemed, on the one hand, to be helping widows because cultural perceptions of womanhood had prevented them from holding decent jobs. Widows, in short, did not possess the economic means equal to those of widowers. On the other hand, *Kahn* seemed to discriminate against men. Equally poor widowers were subject to the tax. In essence, *Kahn* not only rendered unclear what kinds of discrimination might be permitted but also abandoned the women-as-a-suspect-class position taken by the Court in *Frontiero. Kahn*, in short, jeopardized the usefulness of the Equal Protection Clause as a legal tool. Such inconsistencies renewed the conviction of legal theorists and feminist groups alike that an amendment was still necessary to resolve these ambiguities. In 1972, when equal rights champions reintroduced the Equal Rights Amendment in Congress, as they had done each year since its introduction in 1923, they finally gained the required two-thirds majority and began the arduous journey of ratification through the states.

Kahn v. Shevin, 1974

Equal protection clause

From the 1960s and 1970s, the Court also entertained cases concerning procreative freedom. Basing its decisions on the Right to Privacy—a concept nowhere expressly mentioned in the Bill of Rights but associated with a number of amendments—the Court declared void the law that prohibited the distribution of birth control information and the dispensation of birth control devices to both married and unmarried persons, including minors. Such decisions, along with the general climate of social change and the activism of feminist groups, paved the way for *Roe* v. *Wade* (1973) in which the Court held that a woman's right to an abortion fell under the Right to Privacy. Other decisions, both further defining and restricting the holding in *Roe*, followed throughout the succeeding two decades.

Roe v. Wade, 1973

Conclusion: In the Good Times A'Comin'

Largely because of the political maneuvering of conservative groups and miscalculations on the part of ERA leadership, the ERA ratification effort fell four states short and failed in 1982. Decisions following *Roe* v. *Wade*, too, signaled a partial retreat from the decision. The demise of the ERA and litigation in both the nineteenth and twentieth centuries expose the central elements of the continuing ambiguity for women of guarantees provided by the Bill of Rights. On the one side of the dilemma is the irrefutable fact of women's biological capacity to bear children and all the considerations flowing from that fact; on the other

side is the dream of gender-neutral legal equality and its possibilities. To reconcile or to balance the goals of these two, often conflicting perceptions still lies at the heart of judicial interpretation of the Bill of Rights in regard to women.

Courts aggravate this dilemma by continuing to employ rationalizations amicable to discriminatory legislation. Chief among them has been "an express reliance on a mythology of male supremacy, which confines women to a subordinate social role and then patronizingly 'protects' them against even their own attempt to change that role."[8]

Such an attitude is not confined to judges but is common to both men and women in all strata of society. This fundamental perception of women's inferiority frustrated women's rights supporters in the nineteenth century and continues to slow women's advancement today.

As the historical record suggests, judicial interpretation of the Constitution has been persistently equivocal as far as women are concerned. Reliance on the stratagems of the Privileges and Immunities and the Equal Protection clauses have largely proved useless and inconclusive, respectively. Women's social and legal equality still requires an Equal Rights Amendment, if only to settle such matters as "suspect class" and "strict scrutiny" when it is applied to gender-related concerns. If Abigail Adams could comment on the contemporary situation, she would most likely bemoan women's laggardly progress. She would have to exhort lawmakers, yet again, to "remember the ladies."

Notes

[1] Quoted in Edward T. James, ed., *Notable American Women, A Biographical Dictionary*, Vol. 1 (Cambridge: Harvard University Press, 1971), 7.

[2] Aileen Kraditor, *Ideas of the Woman Suffrage Movement, 1890–1920* (New York: Anchor Books, 1971), 1.

[3] Quoted in Barbara Allen Babcock, et al., *Sex Discrimination and the Law, Cases and Remedies* (Boston: Little, Brown, 1975), 9.

[4] Ibid, 14.

[5] Ibid, 5.

[6] Ibid, 6.

[7] Ibid, 37.

[8] Ibid, 105.

Cases

Adkins v. The Children's Hospital of the District of Columbia, 261 U.S. 525 (1923). At the core of *Adkins* were two competing issues: Did women have the right to contract their labor freely, or did their gender differences argue for special treatment? Despite another Brandeis study, the Court struck down the District of Columbia statute, resulting in the disappearance of minimum-wage measures until the economic calamity of the Depression forced enactment of minimum-wage measures for both sexes.

Bradwell v. Illinois, 16 Wall. 131 (1873). In an effort to expand women's occupational choices, Bradwell unsuccessfully relied on the Privileges and Immunities Clause to substantiate her claim that citizenship authorized occupational choice and that a state could not exclude whole classes of people.

Frontiero v. Richardson, 411 U.S. 677 (1973). Although *Frontiero* bases its successful claim for discrimination on violation of the Due Process Clause of the Fifth Amendment, the most important holding was the Court's determination of sex as a suspect classification. Such a determination implied that the Court would apply "strict scrutiny" to subsequent cases involving gender.

Hoyt v. Florida, 368 U.S. 57 (1961). Although the Court reviewed other cases involving the racial and ethnic balance of jury composition, oddly, it viewed the all-male jury in *Hoyt* as carrying "no constitutional significance." Subsequently, most states enacted nondiscriminatory jury service statutes.

Kahn v. Shevin, 416 U.S. 351 (1974). At issue in *Kahn* was the application of the Equal Protection Clause to the question of whether widowers were entitled to the same tax exemption as widows. While the Court, via several different arguments, upheld Florida law, *Kahn* halted the Court's progress toward developing sex as a "suspect classification." The decision also posed a new danger. "Remedying" past discrimination might well replace "protecting" women as a judicial rationale, resulting in yet another species of discrimination.

Minor v. Happersett, 21 Wall. 163 (1875). In 1869, the National Woman Suffrage Association endorsed the use of the Privileges and Immunities Clause as a short-cut to woman suffrage. Minor, like Anthony, attempted to use the clause to extend the franchise to women by arguing (unsuccessfully) that suffrage was coextensive with citizenship.

Muller v. Oregon, 208 U.S. 412 (1908). At issue in *Muller* was the relationship between women's health, particularly their reproductive health, and hours on the job. Influenced by Louis Brandeis's massive sociological brief that set out in detail the alleged differences between the sexes, the Court upheld the Oregon statute and, at the same time, placed a judicial stamp of approval on culturally influenced definitions of gender.

Reed v. Reed, 404 U.S. 71 (1971). Using the Equal Protection Clause, the Court ruled that Idaho's statute giving preference to male estate administrators was not in tune with the constitutional mandate of equal protection and was, moreover, arbitrary. *Reed* also planted the seeds for interpretations of women as a "suspect class" in subsequent decisions.

Roe v. Wade, 410 U.S. 113 (1973). Texas law, like most other state statutes, forbade abortion except "for the purpose of saving the life of the mother." *Roe* and a parallel case, *Doe v. Bolton*, had successfully challenged abortion laws on the district level by arguing on the basis of Right to Privacy. The court agreed and struck down statutes prohibiting abortion.

United States of America v. Susan B. Anthony, 24 F. Cas. (No. 14459) 829 (1873). Although only one of several cases resulting from women's suffrage actions, the Anthony case is the best articulation of nineteenth-century woman suffrage ideology. Arrested under a provision of the Civil Rights Act of 1870, Anthony requested her defense arguments in federal court on the Privileges and Immunities Clause. At stake was whether citizenship implied suffrage; the Court decided it did not.

Suggested Readings

Charles W. Akers, *Abigail Adams: An American Woman.* (Boston: Little, Brown and Company, 1980). In a readable biography suited to secondary students, the author links the events of Adams's personal life to her ideas of government and citizenship.

Lois W. Banner, *Elizabeth Cady Stanton: A Radical for Women's Rights* (Boston: Little, Brown and Company, 1980). Like *Abigail Adams*, this volume is short, readable, and suited to secondary students. The author draws heavily on Stanton's own writings to achieve an "inside" narrative of the progress of woman suffrage.

Jane DeHart-Mathews and Linda K. Kerber, eds., *Women's America: Refocusing the Past* (Oxford: Oxford University Press, 1987). One of the more successful of the introductory women's history texts, Mathews's and Kerber's book contains both scholarly articles and short selections of primary sources, including snippets specifically devoted to women and the law.

Ellen Carol DuBois, *Feminism and Suffrage: The Emergence of an Independent Women's Movement in America, 1848–1869* (Ithaca, NY: Cornell University Press, 1978). DuBois explores the difference between the two women's organizations both before and after the Civil War and provides an account of the split between the groups and its effect on women's progress toward the vote.

Sara Evans, *Personal Politics: The Roots of Women's Liberation in the Civil Rights Movement and the New Left* (New York: Alfred A. Knopf, 1979). One of the few volumes that describes and explains the second feminist movement of the twentieth century, Evans's book locates the origins of the movement within both the civil rights and antiwar movements.

Eleanor Flexner, *Century of Struggle: The Woman's Rights Movement of the United States* (Cambridge, Mass.: Harvard University Press, 1975). Flexner's account is the standard work on the woman suffrage movement. Less analytical than *Feminism and Suffrage*; for example, Flexner furnishes a chronological and biographical account of the course of the movement.

Linda Gordon, *Woman's Body, Woman's Right: Birth Control in America* (New York: Penguin Books, 1976). A primarily Marxist analysis of women's concerns with reproductive rights. Gordon provides an overview of the problems women encountered when they challenged prevailing legal and cultural restraints on birth control.

Robert L. Griswold, *Family and Divorce in California, 1850–1890: Victorian Illusions and Everyday Realities* (Albany, NY: State University of New York Press, 1982). In this study of divorce behavior among Californians, Griswold uses court cases to discover how litigants' interpretation of divorce law altered over time. Although the text is *not* primarily a legal study, the introduction provides the most comprehensive overview of the issues and basic arguments in family and women's history.

Michael Grossberg, *Governing the Hearth: Law and the Family in Nineteenth-Century America* (Chapel Hill, NC: The University of North Carolina Press, 1985). Covering such topics as courtship, marriage, divorce, and child custody, Grossberg provides the most readable account of the development of domestic law. His discussions of marriage and courtship are especially engaging and provoke interesting discussion.

Linda K. Kerber, *Women of the Republic: Intellect and Ideology in Revolutionary America* (Chapel Hill, NC: University of North Carolina Press, 1980). Examining several topics, Kerber gauges the effect of the Revolutionary War on women. Especially appropriate for any discussion on the ideological backdrop to the question of woman suffrage and divorce law, the book argues the development of "republican motherhood" as women's avenue into politics and citizenship.

James C. Mohr, *Abortion in America: The Origins and Evolution of National Policy, 1800–1900* (Oxford: Oxford University Press, 1978). The standard work on the history of abortion legislation, Mohr's volume successfully argues that anti-abortion legislation is a relatively new invention. Locating the origins of legislative change in the increasing influence of the American Medical Association, among others, he provides a background to *Roe* v. *Wade* and allied cases.

PAULA PETRIK

XI

Paul Finkelman

RACE AND THE CONSTITUTION

Each morning thousands of children board school buses, bound for schools far from their homes. They are being "bused" to create racially integrated schools. Often this busing is the result of court orders issued by federal judges. Why is this happening? Why have the courts, which are removed from the people and often remote, become "super school boards" for many towns and cities in America?

This question may never be fully answered. The details of court-ordered busing involve complex legal arguments and facts that are often unique to each school district. Starting with *Swann v. Charlotte-Mecklenburg Board of Education* (1971), the Supreme Court has often upheld busing plans mandated to create integrated schools. In the last two decades busing has been a hot political issue in cities as diverse as Boston, Los Angeles, Detroit, Denver, and Charlotte. Yet, today busing is a fact of life for tens of thousands of school children. Moreover it is no longer particularly controversial. Many Americans at least understand, even if they don't always agree with, the rationale behind busing: that it is a remedy designed to eliminate vestiges of racial segregation and provide educational equality for all Americans.

School busing is just one of many important current issues involving race relations. This essay provides a general background to the problem of race and the Constitution that can help put this and other current issues in perspective.

Swann v. Charlotte-Mecklenburg Board of Education, 1971

Race and the Constitution: The Historical Overview

Race has profoundly affected constitutional development. Slave-holding interests won out in the debates of 1787; the new Constitution protected slavery, helping to perpetuate bondage for millions of African Americans. The national compact defined most Indians as members of foreign nations, thus putting them beyond the pale of constitutional protection. Not until passage of what are called the Civil War Amendments (the Thirteenth, Fourteenth, and Fifteenth) were constitutional liberty, equality, and political rights established for nonwhites. And it took the Twenty-fourth Amendment to prohibit poll taxes, which had been used to disfranchise nonwhites.

Many Americans have faced discrimination. National policies of expulsion and removal combined with their anomalous constitutional status give American Indians a unique constitutional history. At various times Catholics, Jews, immigrants and their descendants from Ireland, Germany, Italy, Latin America, and Asia have faced violence and discrimination. In the American South and West, Asian Americans and Hispanics were segregated, along with blacks. During World War II nearly 120,000 Japanese Americans, most of whom were citizens, were interned, under armed guard, in what were euphemistically called "relocation camps."

Despite the diverse history of discrimination against minorities, this essay concentrates on African Americans and the Constitution because most of the cases and statutory developments on race and law have resulted from slavery and segregation, and their legacy, racial inequality. Today questions about racial discrimination, school integration, and affirmative action deeply trouble jurists, politicians, and the public. Most Americans now find racial discrimination both morally wrong and constitutionally impermissible; less agreement exists on the proper remedies to end racial inequality.

Slavery and the Constitution: 1787

most of the cases and statutory developments on race and law have resulted from slavery and segregation, and their legacy, racial inequality

Delegates at the Philadelphia Convention heatedly debated the place of slavery in the new constitutional order. Despite the traditional historical emphasis on the division between the large states and small states, James Madison told the Convention "that the States were divided...not by their difference in size, but...principally from their having or not having slaves." This created the "great division of interests" in the nation. Speaking for his state, in one debate a South Carolinian insisted "that their negroes may not be taken from them....."[1]

PAUL FINKELMAN

The Constitution protected slavery in many ways, including allowing the African slave trade to continue until at least 1808; counting slaves for purposes of representation in Congress and in determining the electoral votes of the states; guaranteeing federal troops to suppress slave rebellions; and guaranteeing masters the right to recover their runaway slaves.[2] Most important of all, the Constitution did not give the national government power to interfere with slavery where it already existed. South Carolina's Charles Cotesworth Pinckney bragged, "We have a security that the general government can never emancipate them, for no such authority is granted; and. . .all rights not expressed were reserved by the several states."[3]

Two slavery-related clauses are commonly misunderstood. The Constitution did not end the African slave trade in 1808; it only prohibited Congress from stopping the trade before 1808. The three-fifths clause did not declare that blacks were to be counted as three-fifths of a person for purposes of representation. The clause only applied to slaves, and not to the nation's growing free black population. Nor was the clause a form of racial discrimination. Opponents of slavery actually did not want to count slaves at all for representation, while the slaveowners wanted to count slaves fully for representation. The clause was a political compromise which led to increased southern representation in Congress and enhanced southern power in the electoral college. Only as an afterthought, quite late in the Convention, was this clause linked to direct taxation.

Slavery and Constitutional Politics: 1787–1861

Debates over slavery often dominated antebellum constitutional discourse. The Northwest Ordinance (1787) prohibited slavery north of the Ohio River. The Compromise of 1820, passed after acrimonious debate, brought Missouri into the Union as a slave state but prohibited slavery in the vast territory north and west of Missouri. Debates over the Wilmot Proviso (1846), the adoption of the Compromise of 1850, and the Kansas-Nebraska Act (1854) renewed the controversy over slavery in the territories. In *Dred Scott* v. *Sandford* (1857) Chief Justice Roger B. Taney, speaking for the Supreme Court, declared that the Missouri Compromise violated the Bill of Rights because the Fifth Amendment's due process clause protected the property of slaveowners. Taney also held that blacks could not be citizens of the United States, even if they were free citizens in the state where they lived. In a controversial and historically inaccurate analysis, Taney concluded that at the nation's founding blacks "had no rights which the white man was bound to respect."[4] Thus the protections of

Dred Scott v. Sandford, 1857

the Constitution and the Bill of Rights did not apply to either free blacks or slaves.

The fugitive slave laws of 1793 and 1850 denied alleged fugitive slaves many of the due process protections found in the Fourth, Fifth, Sixth, Seventh, and Eighth amendments. The law of 1850 even prohibited alleged fugitives from testifying in their own defense. In *Prigg* v. *Pennsylvania* (1842) and *Ableman* v. *Booth* (1859) the Supreme Court upheld these laws, thus protecting the property claims of masters rather than the liberty or due process rights of blacks and their northern white allies.

Prigg v. Pennsylvania, 1842
Ableman v. Booth, 1859

The Civil War Amendments: 1865–1870

The Civil War radically changed the legal rights of all Americans. The Thirteenth Amendment (1865) ended slavery and empowered Congress to enforce its provisions with "appropriate legislation." The antislavery Republicans who wrote the amendment thought it would both end slavery and force the South to enfranchise black men and give all blacks basic legal rights and protections. Most Republicans agreed the amendment abolished "all badges and incidents of slavery,"[5] but few could agree on what constituted a "badge of slavery." Thus Congress's powers under the amendment's enforcement clause remained in dispute.

To the shock of most Republicans, the South responded to the Thirteenth Amendment by virtually re-enslaving African Americans with harsh laws, collectively known as black codes, which severely limited the legal and economic rights of the former slaves. The black codes regulated how former slaves could buy property, what kind of labor contracts they could sign, and even where they could move or live. Congress quickly passed, over President Andrew Johnson's veto, the Civil Rights Act of 1866 to protect the civil rights and civil liberties of the freedmen. This law declared that the former slaves were citizens of the United States and protected their rights to "make and enforce contracts," to sue in courts, to own property, and to have the "full and equal benefit of all laws and proceedings for the security of person and property, as is enjoyed by white citizens."[6] The bill's major sponsor, Senator Lyman Trumbull of Illinois, argued that Congress could adopt such sweeping legislation under the Thirteenth Amendment.

Black codes

Some members of Congress believed the Civil Rights Act of 1866 exceeded the powers authorized by the Thirteenth Amendment. This prompted Congressman John Bingham of Ohio to introduce, in 1866, what became the Fourteenth Amendment. When ratified in 1868 this amendment nullified the holding in *Dred Scott* by making all persons born in the United States citizens of the nation and of their state of residence. The Fourteenth Amendment also prohibited any state from abridging "the privi-

the Supreme Court upheld these laws, thus protecting the property claims of masters rather than the liberty or due process rights of blacks and their northern white allies

Privileges and immunities clause

Due process

leges and immunities of citizens of the United States," or denying its citizens "due process of law" or "equal protection of the laws."

Scholars, jurists, and lawyers disagree about what the drafters of the Fourteenth Amendment intended with such open-ended phrases. Most historians agree that at minimum they expected the "privileges and immunities" and "due process" clauses to apply most of the Bill of Rights to the states, insuring that the freedmen would have First Amendment rights to participate in politics and would be protected by fair trials and other criminal due process rights. Republicans supporting the amendment argued that it would guarantee southern blacks the Second Amendment right to form militia companies for purposes of self-defense. The meaning of the "equal protection" clause is less certain. Some scholars argue that it was not meant to prohibit segregation but only banned blatantly unequal treatment. Others argue that because segregation is blatantly unequal, the amendment prohibited such practices. They agree with Senator Jacob Howard, a supporter of the amendment who asserted that it was designed to "destroy all caste and class in the United States." In 1870 the nation adopted the third Civil War amendment, prohibiting discrimination in voting on the basis of "race, color, or previous condition of servitude." Like the Thirteenth and Fourteenth Amendments, the Fifteenth also had an enforcement clause. These were the first amendments to the Constitution which specifically gave Congress enforcement power. Five subsequent amendments have contained an enforcement clause.

During Reconstruction, Congress used these amendments to protect the freedom of blacks. After the adoption of the Fourteenth Amendment Congress re-enacted the Civil Rights Act of 1866, removing any doubts about its constitutionality. Three Enforcement Acts of 1870–71 guaranteed black suffrage, provided fines and imprisonment for persons who prevented the freedmen from voting, gave Congress the power to regulate elections in the South, and empowered the president to use federal troops to crush the Ku Klux Klan and other southern terrorist organizations. Finally the Civil Rights Act of 1875 prohibited private discrimination in accommodations, public conveyances, and public places of amusement, like theaters and restaurants. Had these laws been vigorously enforced, racial equality might have been achieved in the nineteenth century. But by 1875 the Supreme Court had begun to undermine the civil rights of the freedmen.

Liberty and Equality in the Age of Segregation: 1873–1915

The history of the Civil War amendments is one of uncertain application and mixed enforcement. The amendments' promise of equality was dashed by southern intransigence, northern impa-

had these rights been vigorously enforced, racial equality might have been achieved in the nineteenth century

tience with the continuing need for federal protection of blacks, and a Supreme Court incapable of accepting the dramatic constitutional changes brought about by the Civil War. Underlying these factors was the nation's pervasive racism. In the South intimidation, lynchings, and mob assaults undermined black freedom while discouraging northern intervention in southern affairs. In the North a growing ideology of social Darwinism made racism respectable and provided a justification for northern abandonment of blacks. From 1873 until 1915 African Americans steadily lost civil and political rights and economic opportunity as segregation and disfranchisement became the norm throughout the South and parts of the North. While not the harbinger of change, the Supreme Court ratified most of these developments through its decisions.

Slaughter House Cases, 1873

In the *Slaughter House Cases* (1873) the Court held that the "privileges and immunities" clause of the Fourteenth Amendment did not make the bill of rights applicable to the states. With strained logic the Court ruled that Americans had to turn to their states for protection of basic civil liberties. This doomed the freedmen to seek protection from their former masters who were already gaining control of southern state legislatures.

United States v. Reese, 1876

The protection of blacks evaporated after 1875. In *United States v. Reese* (1876) the Supreme Court struck down a federal statute designed to protect black suffrage on the grounds that the Fifteenth Amendment did not "confer the right of suffrage upon any one." In the *Civil Rights Cases* (1883) the Court gutted the Civil Rights Act of 1875, asserting that the Fourteenth Amendment did not allow Congress to legislate against private acts of discrimination. The Court also voided federal laws, known as the Ku Klux Klan Acts, adopted to protect blacks from Ku Klux Klan terrorism.

Civil Rights Cases, 1883

While failing to uphold federal laws protecting blacks, the Court usually supported state laws requiring discrimination. *Plessy v. Ferguson* (1896) was the capstone of this trend. Here the Court upheld a Louisiana law requiring segregation on railroad cars. Conceding that the Fourteenth Amendment was adopted "to enforce the absolute equality of the two races before the law," the Court quickly added that "it could not have been intended to abolish distinctions based upon color, or to enforce social, as distinguished from political equality, or a commingling of the two races...." The Court declared that "laws permitting, and even requiring, their separation in places where they are liable to be brought into contact do not necessarily imply the inferiority of either race to the other...." As long as segregated facilities were "equal" they were permissible. Segregation had now received the sanction if not the blessing of the Supreme Court.

PAUL FINKELMAN

In dissent, Justice John Marshall Harlan, a former slave-owner, protested that this decision "will not only stimulate aggressions, more or less brutal and irritating, upon the admitted rights of colored citizens, but will encourage the belief that it is possible, by means of state enactments, to defeat the beneficent purposes which the people of the United States had in view when they adopted the recent amendments to the Constitution.... The thin disguise of 'equal' accommodations for passengers in railroad coaches will not mislead any one, nor atone for the wrong this day done...."[7]

By the beginning of World War I, blacks, 90 percent of whom lived in the South, faced an almost entirely segregated world. Starting in the 1880s the South segregated its schools, hospitals, cemeteries, theaters, residential neighborhoods, railroads, elevators, and work places. In parts of the South blacks could not participate in sports with whites, fish on the same lakes, or even use the same telephone booths. Through a variety of restrictions and subterfuges, most blacks were denied the ballot. Many blacks were afraid to vote as racial violence and intimidation swept the South. In the last two decades of the nineteenth century more than 2,500 blacks were lynched in the South. Another thousand or so were murdered in this way in the first decade and a half of the new century. In addition to lynchings, violent race riots, such as the 1906 Atlanta riot, left scores of blacks dead. While predominant in the South, lynchings and riots were not confined to that region. In 1908 a two-day riot against African Americans in Springfield, Illinois—ironically the home and final resting place of Abraham Lincoln—left two blacks dead and dozens injured.

Between 1875 and 1915 the federal government, including the Supreme Court, abdicated responsibility for protecting the rights of racial and ethnic minorities from state action. Prevailing concepts of federalism allowed the states to regulate the rights of anyone within their jurisdiction. Then, in *Guinn v. United States* (1915) the Supreme Court finally enforced the Fifteenth Amendment against an Oklahoma "grandfather clause," which discriminated against all people whose grandparents were not able to vote—which meant blacks. Furthermore, in *Gitlow v. New York* (1925) the Supreme Court ruled that the Due Process Clause of the Fourteenth Amendment prohibited the states from denying their citizens fundamental liberties, including those protected by the First Amendment. These two cases mark the beginning of a revolution in federalism that would shift the focus of race relations from one of local control to one of national politics and Supreme Court litigation. At the same time, black and white activists began to agitate for what Abraham Lincoln had called "a new birth of freedom."

Guinn v. United States, 1915

RACE AND THE CONSTITUTION

Fighting Segregation, 1909–1970

In 1909 the black scholar W.E.B. DuBois joined with white reformers, including Joel Spingarn, Jane Addams, Oswald Garrison Villard (grandson of the abolitionist William Lloyd Garrison), and Moorfield Story, to organize the National Association for the Advancement of Colored People (NAACP).

For the next sixty years the NAACP provided attorneys in civil rights cases. By the end of World War II, blacks had won significant victories on issues involving voting, police brutality, criminal justice procedure, and graduate and professional education. Most of these cases were argued by the NAACP, although some successful arguments were made by the International Labor Defense (ILD), an organization with strong ties to the Communist Party. In the *Scottsboro Cases* (1932) the ILD won rulings guaranteeing effective counsel for indigent capital defendants and requiring that blacks be called for jury duty in the South. These cases did not save the Scottsboro boys from incarceration, but they did set precedents that would later be useful in expanding civil liberties and civil rights.

Black soldiers returned from World War II determined to fight racism at home as they had fought it abroad. Litigation by the NAACP and other groups, increased political participation by black Americans (made possible by Supreme Court victories in the 1940s), and a more enlightened justice department led to legal changes. With the stroke of a pen, President Truman ended segregation in the Army. An overnight change in administration policy ended federal support for segregation on interstate trains. In *Sweatt v. Painter* (1950) the Supreme Court held that a separate law school for blacks could never be equal to the University of Texas Law School. This undermined segregation in all state-funded professional and graduate schools and set the stage for *Brown v. Board of Education* (1954).

In *Brown* the Court held that "in the field of public education the doctrine of 'separate but equal' has no place. Separate educational facilities are inherently unequal." *Brown* stimulated a revolution in civil rights on three levels: through litigation, demonstrations, and legislation. In the Courts the NAACP and other organizations sued to end discrimination in education, public facilities, and other facets of life. Litigation was slow and expensive, but usually successful. By the end of the decade the *Brown* doctrine had been applied to most statutory segregation.

Declaring laws unconstitutional did not end segregation or discrimination. Nor did it immediately change life for most blacks. In the South, Martin Luther King and others led thousands of blacks, and a good many whites, in marches, demonstrations, and acts of civil disobedience to break down segregation. In this second level of the civil rights revolution, segregationists

---

Scottsboro Cases (1931–)

Sweatt v. Painter, 1950

Brown v. Board of Education, 1954

by the end of World War II, blacks had won significant victories on issues involving voting, police brutality, criminal justice procedure, and graduate and professional education

PAUL FINKELMAN

murdered more than a dozen civil rights activists, black and white. Thousands of demonstrators were beaten or jailed. In Birmingham, Alabama, a bombing at a church Sunday School killed four black children. Invoking their liberties under the Bill of Rights, demonstrators assembled, spoke, and petitioned. They relied on federal courts and constitutional requirements of due process to protect them from southern sheriffs and biased state courts. Civil rights marchers exercised First Amendment rights in order to help gain the voting rights promised blacks under the Fifteenth Amendment. From 1955 to 1970 the nation witnessed the Bill of Rights raised as a shield to protect people striving for their civil and political rights. The incorporation of the First Amendment to the states through the Fourteenth Amendment allowed civil rights demonstrators to claim protection of their right to free speech under the federal Constitution as they sought an end to segregation. The Rev. King and other activists also used the due process clause of the Fourteenth Amendment to fight for their rights under the equal protection clause of the same amendment.

The third level of the civil rights movement was political. In the 1930s northern blacks began to abandon the party of Lincoln for the Democratic Party of Franklin D. Roosevelt. Harry S. Truman won the 1948 presidential election with a strong civil rights plank, despite the exodus of "Dixiecrat" segregationists led by Strom Thurmond of South Carolina. In 1960 black votes in northern cities helped secure John F. Kennedy's victory. Presidential decrees by Truman, Kennedy, and Johnson ended segregation at the federal level and provided U.S. marshals to protect civil rights demonstrators. Although unsympathetic to integration, President Dwight D. Eisenhower sent troops to Little Rock to enforce a school desegregation order. President Kennedy later used military force to desegregate the University of Mississippi. In the 1950s and 1960s constitutional law took an ironic turn. Clauses in the Constitution designed to quell slave rebellions bolstered federal intervention on behalf of integration. *Ableman v. Booth* (1859), a case that upheld the fugitive slave law of 1850, became a precedent for enforcing court ordered school desegregation. Legislation at the federal level, including the Civil Rights Acts of 1957, 1960, and 1964, the Voting Rights Act of 1965, and the Open Housing Act of 1968, changed the legal landscape. Symbolic of this change was the 1967 appointment of Supreme Court Justice Thurgood Marshall, the black attorney who had successfully argued the *Brown* case a decade earlier.

Beyond Integration, 1970 to the Present

By 1970 the civil rights movement, Supreme Court decisions, presidential decrees, and Congressional action had destroyed

legislation at the federal level . . . changed the legal landscape

RACE AND THE CONSTITUTION

De jure segregation

De facto segregation

San Antonio Independent School
District v. Rodriguez, 1973

Plyer v. Doe, 1982

Regents of the University of
California v. Bakke, 1978

statutory, "de jure," segregation. Equality was the law of the land, but not yet the reality. Furthermore, the assassinations of Medgar Evers (1963), Malcolm X (1965), Martin Luther King (1968), and Robert F. Kennedy (1968) eroded the national civil rights leadership. Richard Nixon's election (1968) indicated a national mood that no longer supported massive changes in the social landscape. Nixon's vice-president, Spiro Agnew, expressed the more callous attitude toward civil rights with the statement, "If you've seen one ghetto, you've seen them all."

As the nation turned from civil rights toward what a Nixon administration cabinet member called "benign neglect," blacks found that their court and legislative victories were somewhat hollow. *De jure* segregation ended only to be replaced by *de facto* segregation caused by "white flight" from urban centers and the growth of private, segregated schools in the South. Public schools were no longer legally segregated, but few classrooms were truly integrated. Equally important, Americans discovered that striking down segregation statutes did not end minority poverty or isolation. In *San Antonio Independent School District v. Rodriguez* (1973) the Supreme Court allowed discrimination in the quality of schools based on the available tax monies from local districts. This decision, which had a terrible impact on Hispanics, blacks, and recent immigrants from Southeast Asia, indicates that an end to formal segregation does not necessarily guarantee equality of education or equality of opportunity. A decade later, in *Plyer v. Doe* (1982), the Court upheld the right of all children, even those illegally in the country, to attend public schools. These two cases, involving Hispanic Americans, indicate the growing complexity of American race relations and the continuing importance of the Fourteenth Amendment for all Americans.

In the 1970s and 1980s the civil rights groups demanded "affirmative action" to guarantee minorities access to higher education, civil service positions, union jobs, and government contracts. Some whites viewed this as a demand for quotas or "reverse discrimination." In *Regents of University of California v. Bakke* (1978) the Supreme Court upheld flexible college admissions programs that took race into account, but struck down strict racial quotas in admissions. In states where past discrimination had been legally required, courts mandated hiring quotas in police and fire departments and other municipal services in order to guarantee minority access to these jobs. In the late 1980s the Supreme Court upheld the principle of affirmative action but increasingly narrowed its scope. Similarly, the Court stepped away from other protections of civil rights such as allowing minorities to sue employers for racist remarks or other forms of prejudice that fall just short of discrimination in hiring.

As of the bicentennial of the Bill of Rights no responsible

PAUL FINKELMAN

leaders call for a return to segregation. But there is enormous disagreement on how to achieve realistic integration in a society still plagued by prejudice, fear, residential segregation, and poverty among minorities. The fact that an adult living in New York's Harlem has a shorter life expectancy than an adult in the poverty-stricken nation of Bangladesh suggests that formal equality has not eradicated the legacy of slavery and racism that has been with America since the founding. Ultimately, the achievement of equality for all Americans depends on how we use and implement the guarantees of the Bill of Rights. As James Madison argued, our liberties will be best protected "by the vigilant. . . spirit" of the American people.[8]

Notes

[1] Max Farrand, ed., *Records of the Federal Convention of 1787* (New Haven: Yale University Press, 1966) 1:486, 603–04.

[2] These protections are found in the following clauses of the Constitution: Art. I, Sec. 9, Cl. 1 and Art. V; Art. I, Sec. 2, Cl. 3 and Art II, Sec. 1, Cl. 2; Art I, Sec. 8, Cl. 15 and Art IV, Sec. 4; and Art IV, Sec. 2, Cl. 3.

[3] Jonathan Elliot, ed., *The Debates in the Several State Conventions on the Adoption of the Federal Constitution* (Washington, D.C.: 1836) 4:286.

[4] *Dred Scott* v. *Sandford*, 60 U.S. (19 Howard) 393, at 407 (1857).

[5] This term was used in *Civil Rights Cases*, 109 U.S. 3 at 20 (1883) to describe the scope of the amendment.

[6] "An Act to protect all Persons in the United States in their Civil Rights, and furnish the Means of their Vindication," Act of April 9, 1866, *U.S. Statutes at Large* Vol. 14, p. 27ff.

[7] *Plessy* v. *Ferguson*, 163 U.S. 537, Justice Brown, at 544; Justice Harlan at 560, 561 (1896).

[8] *Federalist* 57, Robert Rutland, ed., *The Papers of James Madison* (Chicago: University of Chicago Press, 1977) 10:523.

Cases

Ableman v. Booth, 21 Howard (U.S.) 506 (1859). Court upheld the 1850 fugitive slave act and asserted that the states could not interfere with federal law.

Brown v. Board of Education of Topeka, Kansas, 347 U.S. 483 (1954). Case in which the Supreme Court ruled that segregated public schools violated the equal protection clause of the Fourteenth Amendment. In this decision, the Court held that "separate educational facilities are inherently unequal."

Civil Rights Cases, 109 U.S. 3 (1883). Court struck down most of the Civil Rights Act of 1875 on the grounds that the Fourteenth Amendment could not be used to prohibit private acts of discrimination. Thus, the federal law banning discrimination in hotels, restaurants, and theatres was unconstitutional. In the 1960s similar legislation would be adopted, not under the enforcement clause of the Fourteenth Amendment, but under the Commerce Clause of Article I.

Dred Scott v. Sandford, 19 Howard (U.S) 593 (1857). Court declared that blacks, even free blacks with full civil and political rights living in the North, could not sue in the federal courts as "citizens" of a state. Court also held that the Missouri Compromise of 1820 was unconstitutional because under the Fifth Amendment Congress did not have the power to prohibit slaveowners from taking their property into the federal territories. This was the first use of substantive due process by the Supreme Court.

Guinn v. United States, 238 U.S. 347 (1915). Court struck down Oklahoma's "grandfather clause" which exempted from onerous registration requirements those people whose grandfathers could vote in 1866. This effectively disfranchised blacks in the state.

Hirabayashi v. United States, 320 U.S. 81 (1943) and **Korematsu v. United States,** 323 U.S. 214 (1944). In both cases the Supreme Court, ignoring the due process protections of the Fifth Amendment, sanctioned the internment of Japanese-American citizens in "relocation camps."

Plyer v. Doe, 457 U.S. 202 (1982). Court held that the children of illegal aliens in Texas cannot be banned from the public schools. The decision was based on the "equal protection clause" of the Fourteenth Amendment, which prohibits discrimination against all persons, regardless of their citizenship.

Prigg v. Pennsylvania, 16 Peters (U.S.) 539 (1842). Court upheld the constitutionality of the federal fugitive slave law of 1793 and struck down Pennsylvania's personal liberty law, which had been designed to protect free blacks from being claimed as fugitive slaves, but which could also be used to thwart the return of actual runaways.

Regents of the University of California v. Bakke, 438 U.S. 265 (1978). The Supreme Court ruled that the affirmative action admissions program at the University of California at Davis Medical School violated the equal protection clause of the Fourteenth Amendment because it contained a rigid quota. However, the Court also ruled that a university could take race and ethnicity into account when developing its admissions procedures.

San Antonio Independent School District v. Rodriguez, 411 U.S. 1 (1973). Court upheld the right of Texas to base its financing of schools on property taxes and other local taxes. This had the dual effect of allowing more state money to flow to the wealthier school districts and at the same time preventing equal educational opportunity for the mostly minority residents of the poorest district.

Scottsboro Cases. A famous case involving a nineteen-year struggle to free nine young African Americans falsely accused of rape. Seven of the trials occurred in the years 1931–1936 alone. Two of the most famous were **Powell v. Alabama** (see page 12) and **Patterson v. Alabama,** 287 U.S. 45 (1932).

Slaughter House Cases. 16 Wallace 36 (1873). See page 12.

Swann v. Charlotte-Mecklenburg Board of Education, 402 U.S. 1 (1971). Court upheld busing between urban and rural schools where the state (in this case North Carolina) had purposely drawn district lines to perpetuate segregation.

Sweatt v. Painter, 339 U.S. 629 (1950). Case in which the Supreme Court ordered the University of Texas School of Law to admit a black student, even though the state had recently set up a segregated law school for black students. The Court ruled that in the case of a law school the separate facility could never be equal.

United States v. Reese, 92 U.S. 214 (1876). The Court overturned the conviction of a Kentucky official who had been charged under the Enforcement Act of 1870 when he failed to count the vote of a black man. The Court asserted that the Fifteenth Amendment did not actually confer the right to vote on anyone, but only prohibited racial discrimination in voting. Since the Enforcement Act was not limited to racially motivated interference with voting, the Court found the act to be unconstitutional.

Suggested Readings

Paul Finkelman, "Slavery and the Constitutional Convention: Making a Covenant with Death," in Richard Beeman, ed., *Beyond Confederation* (Chapel Hill: University of North Carolina Press, 1987), 188–225. This article discusses the debates over slavery at the Constitutional Convention and the many ways in which the Constitution protected slavery.

John Hope Franklin and Alfred A. Moss, Jr., *From Slavery to Freedom*, 6th ed. (New York: A. A. Knopf, 1988). The basic introductory history of blacks in America and the place to begin reading about African-American history.

Richard Kluger, *Simple Justice* (New York: Random House, 1975). A long but highly readable history of race relations in America. Focusing mostly on the *Brown* case, it also touches on all issues of race and constitutional law from the founding to the mid-1970s.

August Meier and Elliott Rudwick, *From Plantation to Ghetto* (New York: Hill and Wang, 1966). A short survey of African-American history.

The Constitution of the United States

We the people of the United States, in Order to form a more perfect Union, establish Justice, insure domestic Tranquility, provide for the common defence, promote the general Welfare, and secure the Blessings of Liberty to ourselves and our Posterity, do ordain and establish This CONSTITUTION for the United States of America.

Article I

Section 1. All legislative Powers herein granted shall be vested in a Congress of the United States, which shall consist of a Senate and House of Representatives.

Section 2. The House of Representatives shall be composed of Members chosen every second Year by the People of the several States, and the Electors in each State shall have the Qualifications requisite for Electors of the most numerous Branch of the State Legislature.

No Person shall be a Representative who shall not have attained to the Age of twenty-five Years, and been seven Years a Citizen of the United States, and who shall not, when elected, be an Inhabitant of that State in which he shall be chosen.

Representatives and direct Taxes shall be apportioned among the several States which may be included within this Union, according to their respective Numbers, which shall be determined by adding to the whole Number of free Persons, including those bound to Service for a Term of Years, and excluding Indians not taxed, three fifths of all other Persons. The actual Enumeration shall be made within three Years after the first Meeting of the Congress of the United States, and within every subsequent Term of ten Years, in such Manner as they shall by Law direct. The Number of Representatives shall not exceed one for every thirty Thousand, but each State shall have at Least one Representative; and until such enumeration shall be made, the State of New Hampshire shall be entitled to chuse three, Massachusetts eight, Rhode-Island and Providence Plantations one, Connecticut five, New-York six, New Jersey four, Pennsylvania eight, Delaware one, Maryland six, Virginia ten, North Carolina five, South Carolina five, and Georgia three.

When vacancies happen in the Representation from any State, the Executive Authority thereof shall issue Writs of Election to fill such Vacancies.

The House of Representatives shall chuse their Speaker and other Officers; and shall have the sole Power of Impeachment.

Section 3. The Senate of the United States shall be composed of two Senators from each State, chosen by the Legislature thereof, for six Years; and each Senator shall have one Vote.

Immediately after they shall be assembled in Consequence of the first Election, they shall be divided as equally as may be into three Classes. The Seats of the Senators of the first Class shall be vacated at the Expiration of the second Year, of the second Class at the Expiration of the fourth Year, and of the third Class at the Expiration of the sixth Year, so that one-third may be chosen every second Year; and if Vacancies happen by resignation, or otherwise, during the Recess of the Legislature of any State, the Executive thereof may make temporary Appointments until the next Meeting of the Legislature, which shall then fill such Vacancies.

No Person shall be a Senator who shall not have attained to the Age of thirty Years, and been nine Years a Citizen of the United States, and who shall not, when elected, be an Inhabitant of that State in which he shall be chosen.

The Vice President of the United States shall be President of the Senate, but shall have no vote, unless they be equally divided.

The Senate shall chuse their other Officers, and also a President pro tempore, in the absence of the Vice President, or when he shall exercise the Office of the President of the United States.

The Senate shall have the sole Power to try all Impeachments. When sitting for that purpose, they shall be on Oath or Affirmation. When the President of the United States is tried, the Chief Justice shall preside: And no person shall be convicted without the Concurrence of two thirds of the Members present.

Judgment in Cases of Impeachment shall not extend further than to removal from Office, and disqualification to hold and enjoy any Office of honor, Trust, or Profit under the United States: but the Party convicted shall nevertheless be liable and subject to Indictment, Trial, Judgment, and Punishment, according to Law.

Section 4. The Times, Places and Manner of holding Elections for Senators and Representatives, shall be prescribed in each state by the Legislature thereof; but the Congress may at any time by Law make or alter such Regulations, except as to the Places of Chusing Senators.

The Congress shall assemble at least once in every Year, and such Meeting shall be on the first Monday in December, unless they shall by Law appoint a different Day.

Section 5. Each House shall be the Judge of the Elections, Returns and Qualifications of its own Members, and a Majority of each shall constitute a Quorum to do Business; but a smaller number may adjourn from day to day, and may be authorized to compel the Attendance of absent Members, in such Manner, and under such Penalties, as each House may provide.

Each House may determine the Rules of its Proceedings, punish its Members for disorderly Behavior, and, with the Concurrence of two thirds, expel a Member.

Each House shall keep a Journal of its Proceedings, and from time to time publish the same, excepting such Parts as may in their Judgment require Secrecy; and the Yeas and Nays of the Members of either House on any question shall, at the Desire of one fifth of those Present, be entered on the Journal.

Neither House, during the Session of Congress, shall, without the Consent of the other, adjourn for more than three days, nor to any other Place than that in which the two Houses shall be sitting.

Section 6. The Senators and Representatives shall receive a Compensation for their Services, to be ascertained by Law, and paid out of the Treasury of the United States. They shall in all Cases, except Treason, Felony, and Breach of the Peace, be privileged from Arrest during their Attendance at the Session of their respective Houses, and in going to and returning from the same; and for any Speech or Debate in either House, they shall not be questioned in any other Place.

No Senator or Representative shall, during the Time for which he was elected, be appointed to any civil Office under the Authority of the United States, which shall have been created, or the Emoluments whereof shall have been increased, during such time; and no Person holding any Office under the United States shall be a Member of either House during his continuance in Office.

Section 7. All Bills for raising Revenue shall originate in the House of Representatives; but the Senate may propose or concur with Amendments as on other bills.

Every Bill which shall have passed the House of Representatives and the Senate, shall, before it become a Law, be presented to the President of the United States; If he approve he shall sign it, but if not he shall return it, with his Objections, to that House in which it shall have originated, who shall enter the Objections at large on their Journal, and proceed to reconsider it. If after such Reconsideration two thirds of that House shall agree to pass the bill, it shall be sent, together with the objections, to the other House, by which it shall likewise be reconsidered, and if approved by two thirds of that House, it shall become a Law. But in all such Cases the Votes of both Houses shall be determined by Yeas and Nays, and the Names of the Persons voting for and against the Bill shall be entered on the Journal of each House respectively. If any Bill shall not be returned by the President within ten Days (Sundays excepted) after it shall have been presented to him, the Same shall be a Law, in like Manner as if he had signed it, unless the Congress by their Adjournment prevent its Return, in which Case it shall not be a Law.

Every Order, Resolution, or Vote to which the Concurrence of the Senate and House of Representatives may be necessary (except on a question of Adjournment) shall be presented to the President of the United States; and before the Same shall take Effect, shall be approved by him, or being disapproved by him, shall be repassed by two thirds of the Senate and House of Representatives, according to the Rules and Limitations prescribed in the Case of a Bill.

Section 8. The Congress shall have Power To lay and collect Taxes, Duties, Imposts and Excises, to pay the Debts and provide for the common Defence and general Welfare of the United States; but all Duties, Imposts and Excises shall be uniform throughout the United States;

To borrow money on the credit of the United States;

To regulate Commerce with foreign Nations, and among the several States, and with the Indian Tribes;

To establish a uniform Rule of Naturalization, and uniform Laws on the subject of Bankruptcies throughout the United States;

To coin Money, regulate the Value thereof, and of foreign Coin, and fix the Standard of Weights and Measures;

To provide for the Punishment of counterfeiting the Securities and current Coin of the United States;

To establish Post Offices and post Roads;

To promote the Progress of Science and useful Arts, by securing for limited Times to Authors and Inventors the exclusive Right to their respective Writings and Discoveries;

To constitute Tribunals inferior to the Supreme Court;

To define and punish Piracies and Felonies committed on the high Seas, and Offenses against the Law of Nations;

To declare War, grant Letters of Marque and Reprisal, and make Rules concerning Captures on Land and Water;

To raise and support Armies, but no Appropriation of Money to that Use shall be for a longer Term than two Years;

To provide and maintain a Navy;

To make Rules for the Government and Regulation of the land and naval forces;

To provide for calling forth the Militia to execute the Laws of the Union, suppress Insurrections and repel Invasions;

To provide for organizing, arming, and disciplining the Militia, and for governing such Part of them as may be employed in the Service of the United States, reserving to the States respectively, the Appointment of the Officers, and the Authority of training the Militia according to the discipline prescribed by Congress;

To exercise exclusive Legislation in all Cases whatsoever, over such District (not exceeding ten Miles square) as may, by Cession of particular States, and the acceptance of Congress, become the Seat of Government of the United States, and to exercise like Authority over all Places purchased by the Consent of the Legislature of the State in which the Same shall be, for the Erection of Forts, Magazines, Arsenals, dock-Yards, and other needful Buildings;—And

To make all Laws which shall be necessary and proper for carrying into Execution the foregoing Powers, and all other Powers vested by this Constitution in the Government of the United States, or in any Department or Officer thereof.

Section 9. The Migration or Importation of such Persons as any of the States now existing shall think proper to admit, shall not be prohibited by the Congress prior to the Year one thousand eight hundred and eight, but a tax or duty may be imposed on such Importation, not exceeding ten dollars for each Person.

The privilege of the Writ of Habeus Corpus shall not be suspended, unless when in Cases of Rebellion or Invasion the public Safety may require it.

No Bill of Attainder or ex post facto Law shall be passed.

No capitation, or other direct, Tax shall be laid unless in Proportion to the Census or Enumeration herein before directed to be taken.

No Tax or Duty shall be laid on Articles exported from any State.

No Preference shall be given by any Regulation of Revenue to the Ports of one State over those of another: nor shall Vessels bound to, or from, one State, be obliged to enter, clear, or pay Duties in another.

No Money shall be drawn from the Treasury, but in Consequence of Appropriations made by Law; and a regular Statement and Account of the Receipts and Expenditures of all public Money shall be published from time to time.

No Title of Nobility shall be granted by the United States: And no Person holding any Office of Profit or Trust under them, shall, without the Consent of the Congress, accept of any present, Emolument, Office, or Title, of any kind whatever, from any King, Prince, or foreign State.

Section 10. No State shall enter into any Treaty, Alliance, or Confederation; grant Letters of Marque and Reprisal; coin Money; emit Bills of Credit; make any Thing but gold and silver Coin a Tender in Payment of Debts; pass any Bill of Attainder, ex post facto Law, or Law impairing the Obligation of Contracts, or grant any Title of Nobility.

No State shall, without the Consent of the Congress, lay any Imposts or Duties on Imports or Exports, except what may be absolutely necessary for executing its inspection Laws: and the net Produce of all Duties and Imposts, laid by any State on Imports or Exports, shall be for the Use of the Treasury of the United States; and all such Laws shall be subject to the Revision and Control of the Congress.

No State shall, without the Consent of Congress, lay any duty of Tonnage, keep Troops, or Ships of War in time of Peace, enter into any Agreement or Compact with another State, or with a foreign Power, or engage in War, unless actually invaded, or in such imminent Danger as will not admit of delay.

Article II

Section 1. The executive Power shall be vested in a President of the United States of America. He shall hold his Office during the Term of four years, and, together with the Vice-President, chosen for the same Term, be elected, as follows:

Each state shall appoint, in such Manner as the Legislature thereof may direct, a Number of Electors, equal to the whole Number of Senators and Representatives to which the State may be entitled in the Congress: but no Senator or Representative, or Person holding an Office of Trust or Profit under the United States, shall be appointed an Elector.

The Electors shall meet in their respective States, and vote by Ballot for two persons, of whom one at least shall not be an Inhabitant of the same State with themselves. And they shall make a List of all the Persons voted for, and of the Number of Votes for each; which List they shall sign and certify, and transmit sealed to the Seat of the Government of the United States, directed to the President of the Senate. The President of the Senate shall, in the Presence of the Senate and House of Representatives, open all the Certificates, and the Votes shall then be counted. The Person having the greatest Number of Votes shall be the President, if such Number be a Majority of the whole Number of Electors appointed; and if there be more than one who have such Majority, and have an equal Number of Votes, then the House of Representatives shall immediately chuse by Ballot one of them for President; and if no Person have a Majority, then from the five highest on the List the said House shall in like Manner chuse the President. But in chusing the President, the Votes shall be taken by States, the Representation from each State having one Vote; a quorum for this Purpose shall consist of a Member or Members from two-thirds of the States, and a Majority of all the States shall be necessary to a Choice. In every Case, after the Choice of the President, the Person having the greatest Number of Votes of the Electors shall be the Vice President. But if there should remain two or more who have equal votes, the Senate shall chuse from them by Ballot the Vice-President.

The Congress may determine the Time of chusing the Electors, and the Day on which they shall give their Votes; which Day shall be the same throughout the United States.

No person except a natural-born Citizen, or a Citizen of the United States, at the time of the Adoption of this Constitution, shall be eligible to the Office of President; neither shall any Person be eligible to that Office who shall not have attained to the Age of thirty-five years, and been fourteen Years a Resident within the United States.

In Case of the Removal of the President from Office, or of his Death, Resignation, or Inability to discharge the Powers and Duties of the said Office, the same shall devolve on the Vice President, and the Congress may by Law provide for the Case of Removal, Death, Resignation, or Inability, both of the President and Vice President, declaring what Officer shall then act as President, and such Officer shall act accordingly, until the disability be removed, or a President shall be elected.

The President shall, at stated Times, receive for his Services a Compensation, which shall neither be increased nor diminished during the Period for which he shall have been elected, and he shall not receive within that Period any other Emolument from the United States, or any of them.

Before he enter on the execution of his Office, he shall take the following Oath or Affirmation:—"I do solemnly swear (or affirm) that I will faithfully execute the Office of the President of the United States, and will, to the best of my Ability, preserve, protect, and defend the Constitution of the United States."

Section 2. The President shall be Commander in Chief of the Army and Navy of the United States, and of the Militia of the several States, when called into the actual Service of the United States; he may require the Opinion, in writing, of the principal Officer in each of the executive Departments, upon any subject relating to the Duties of their respective Offices, and he shall have Power to Grant Reprieves and Pardons for Offenses against the United States, except in Cases of Impeachment.

He shall have Power, by and with the Advice and Consent of the Senate, to make Treaties, provided two thirds of the Senators present concur; and he shall nominate, and by and with the Advice and Consent of the Senate, shall appoint Ambassadors, other public Ministers and Consuls, Judges of the supreme Court, and all other Officers of the United States, whose Appointments are not herein otherwise provided for, and which shall be established by Law: but the Congress may by Law vest the Appointment of such inferior Officers, as they think proper, in the President alone, in the Courts of Law, or in the Heads of Departments.

The President shall have Power to fill up all Vacancies that may happen during the Recess of the Senate, by granting Commissions which shall expire at the End of their next Session.

Section 3. He shall from time to time give to the Congress Information of the State of the Union, and recommend to their Consideration such Measures as he shall judge necessary and expedient; he may, on extraordinary occasions, convene both Houses, or either of them, and in Case of Disagreement between them, with respect to the Time of Adjournment, he may adjourn them to such Time as he shall think proper; he shall receive Ambassadors and other public Ministers; he shall take Care that the Laws be faithfully executed, and shall Commission all the Officers of the United States.

Section 4. The President, Vice President and all civil Officers of the United States, shall be removed from Office on Impeachment for, and Conviction of, Treason, Bribery, or other high Crimes and Misdemeanors.

Article III

Section 1. The judicial Power of the United States, shall be vested in one supreme Court, and in such inferior Courts as the Congress may from time to time ordain and establish. The Judges, both of the supreme and inferior Courts, shall hold their Offices during good Behaviour, and shall, at stated Times, receive for their Services, a Compensation, which shall not be diminished during their Continuance in Office.

Section 2. The judicial Power shall extend to all Cases, in Law and Equity, arising under this Constitution, the Laws of the United States, and treaties made, or which shall be made, under their Authority;—to all Cases affecting ambassadors, other public ministers and consuls;—to all cases of admiralty and maritime Jurisdiction;—to Controversies to which the United States shall be a Party;—to Controversies between two or more States;—between a State and Citizens of another State;—between Citizens of different States;—between Citizens of the same State claiming Lands under Grants of different States, and between a State, or the Citizens thereof, and foreign States, Citizens or Subjects.

In all Cases affecting Ambassadors, other public Ministers and Consuls, and those in which a State shall be Party, the supreme Court shall have original Jurisdiction. In all the other Cases before mentioned, the supreme Court shall have appellate Jurisdiction, both as to Law and Fact, with such Exceptions, and under such Regulations as the Congress shall make.

The trial of all Crimes, except in Cases of Impeachment, shall be by Jury; and such Trial shall be held in the State where the said Crimes shall have been committed; but when not committed within any State, the Trial shall be at such Place or Places as the Congress may by Law have directed.

Section 3. Treason against the United States, shall consist only in levying War against them, or in adhering to their Enemies, giving them Aid and Comfort. No Person shall be convicted of Treason unless on the Testimony of two Witnesses to the same overt Act, or on Confession in open Court.

The Congress shall have power to declare the Punishment of Treason, but no Attainder of Treason shall work Corruption of Blood, or Forfeiture except during the Life of the Person attainted.

Article IV

Section 1. Full Faith and Credit shall be given in each State to the public Acts, Records, and judicial Proceedings of every other State. And the Congress may by general Laws prescribe the Manner in which such Acts, Records and Proceedings shall be proved, and the Effect thereof.

Section 2. The Citizens of each State shall be entitled to all Privileges and Immunities of Citizens in the several States.

A Person charged in any State with Treason, Felony, or other Crime, who shall flee from Justice, and be found in another State, shall on demand of the executive Authority of the State from which he fled, be delivered up, to be removed to the State having Jurisdiction of the crime.

No Person held to Service or Labour in one State, under the Laws thereof, escaping into another, shall, in Consequence of Law or Regulation therein, be discharged from such Service or Labour, but shall be delivered up on Claim of the Party to whom such Service or Labour may be due.

Section 3. New States may be admitted by Congress into this Union; but no new State shall be formed or erected within the Jurisdiction of any other State; nor any State be formed by the Junction of two or more States, or parts of States, without the Consent of the Legislatures of the States concerned as well as of the Congress.

The Congress shall have the Power to dispose of and make all needful Rules and Regulations respecting the Territory or other Property belonging to the United States; and nothing in this Constitution shall be so construed as to Prejudice any Claims of the United States, or of any particular State.

Section 4. The United States shall guarantee to every State in this Union a Republican Form of Government, and shall protect each of them against Invasion; and on Application of the Legislature, or of the Executive (when the Legislature cannot be convened) against domestic Violence.

Article V

The Congress, whenever two-thirds of both Houses shall deem it necessary, shall propose Amendments to this Constitution, or, on the Application of the Legislatures of two-thirds of the several States, shall call a Convention for proposing Amendments, which, in either Case, shall be valid to all Intents and Purposes, as part of this Constitution, when ratified by the Legislatures of three-fourths of the several States, or by Conventions in three-fourths thereof, as the one or the other Mode of Ratification may be proposed by the Congress; Provided that no Amendment which may be made prior to the Year One thousand eight hundred and eight shall in any Manner affect the first and fourth Clauses in the Ninth Section of the first Article; and that no State, without its Consent, shall be deprived of its equal Suffrage in the Senate.

Article VI

All Debts contracted and Engagements entered into, before the Adoption of this Constitution, shall be as valid against the United States under this Constitution, as under the Confederation.

This Constitution, and the Laws of the United States which shall be made in Pursuance thereof; and all Treaties made, or which shall be made, under the Authority of the United States, shall be the supreme Law of the Land; and the Judges in every State shall be bound thereby, any Thing in the Constitution or Laws of any State to the Contrary notwithstanding.

The Senators and Representatives before mentioned, and the members of the several State Legislatures, and all executive and judicial Officers, both of the United States and of the several States, shall be bound by Oath or Affirmation to support this Constitution; but no religious Test shall ever be required as a qualification to any Office or public Trust under the United States.

Article VII

The Ratification of the Conventions of nine States shall be sufficient for the Establishment of this Constitution between the States so ratifying the same.

Done in Convention by the Unanimous Consent of the States present the Seventeenth Day of September in the Year of our Lord one thousand seven hundred and Eighty-seven, and of the Independence of the United States of America the Twelfth. In Witness whereof We have hereunto subscribed our Names.

Articles in Addition to, and Amendment of, the Constitution of the United States of America, Proposed by Congress, and Ratified by the Legislatures of the Several States, Pursuant to the Fifth Article of the Original Constitution.

Amendment I [1791]

Congress shall make no law respecting an establishment of religion, or prohibiting the free exercise thereof; or abridging the freedom of speech, or of the press; or the right of the people peaceably to assemble, and to petition the Government for a redress of grievances.

THE CONSTITUTION OF THE UNITED STATES

Amendment II [1791]

A well regulated Militia, being necessary to the security of a free State, the right of the people to keep and bear Arms shall not be infringed.

Amendment III [1791]

No Soldier shall, in time of peace, be quartered in any house, without the consent of the Owner, nor in time of war, but in a manner to be prescribed by law.

Amendment IV [1791]

The right of the people to be secure in their persons, houses, papers, and effects, against unreasonable searches and seizures, shall not be violated, and no Warrants shall issue, but upon probable cause, supported by Oath or affirmation, and particularly describing the place to be searched, and the persons or things to be seized.

Amendment V [1791]

No Person shall be held to answer for a capital or otherwise infamous crime, unless on a presentment or indictment of a Grand Jury, except in cases arising in the land or naval forces, or in the Militia, when in actual service in time of War or public danger; nor shall any person be subject for the same offence to be twice put in jeopardy of life or limb; nor shall be compelled in any criminal case to be a witness against himself, nor be deprived of life, liberty, or property, without due process of law; nor shall private property be taken for public use, without just compensation.

Amendment VI [1791]

In all criminal prosecutions, the accused shall enjoy the right to a speedy and public trial, by an impartial jury of the State and district wherein the crime shall have been committed, which district shall have been previously ascertained by law, and to be informed of the nature and cause of the accusation; to be confronted with the witnesses against him; to have compulsory process for obtaining witnesses in his favor, and to have the Assistance of Counsel for his defence.

Amendment VII [1791]

In suits at common law, where the value in controversy shall exceed twenty dollars, the right of trial by jury shall be preserved, and no fact tried by a jury, shall be otherwise reexamined in any Court of the United States, than according to the rules of the common law.

Amendment VIII [1791]

Excessive bail shall not be required, nor excessive fines imposed, nor cruel and unusual punishments inflicted.

Amendment IX [1791]

The enumeration in the Constitution, of certain rights, shall not be construed to deny or disparage others retained by the people.

Amendment X [1791]

The powers not delegated to the United States by the Constitution, nor prohibited by it to the States, are reserved to the States respectively, or to the people.

Amendment XI [1798]

The Judicial power of the United States shall not be construed to extend to any suit in law or equity, commenced or prosecuted against one of the United States by Citizens of another State, or by Citizens or Subjects of any Foreign State.

Amendment XII [1804]

The Electors shall meet in their respective States and vote by ballot for President and Vice-President, one of whom, at least, shall not be an inhabitant of the same State with themselves; they shall name in their ballots the persons voted for as President, and in distinct ballots the person voted for as Vice- President, and they shall make distinct lists of all persons voted for as President, and of all persons voted for as Vice-President, and of the number of votes for each, which lists they shall sign and certify, and transmit sealed to the seat of the government of the United States, directed to the President of the Senate;—The President of the Senate shall, in the presence of the Senate and House of Representatives, open all the certificates and the votes shall then be counted;—The person having the greatest number of votes for President, shall be the President, if such number be a majority of the whole number of Electors appointed; and if no person have such majority, then from the persons having the highest numbers not exceeding three on the list of those voted for as President, the House of Representatives shall choose immediately, by ballot, the President. But in choosing the President, the votes shall be taken by states, the representation from each state having one vote; a quorum for this purpose shall consist of a member or members from two-thirds of the states, and a majority of all the states shall be necessary to a choice. And if the House of Representatives shall not choose a President whenever the right of choice shall devolve upon them, before the fourth day of March next following, then the Vice-President shall act as President, as in the case of the death or other constitutional disability of the President.—The person having the greatest number of votes as Vice-President, shall be Vice-President, if such number be a majority of the whole number of Electors appointed, and if no person have a majority, then from the two highest numbers on the list, the Senate shall choose the Vice-President; a quorum for the purpose shall consist of two-thirds of the whole number of Senators, and a majority of the whole number shall be necessary to a choice. But no person constitutionally ineligible to the office of President shall be eligible to that of Vice-President of the United States.

Amendment XIII [1865]

Section 1. Neither slavery nor involuntary servitude, except as a punishment for crime whereof the party shall have been duly convicted, shall exist within the United States, or any place subject to their jurisdiction.

Section 2. Congress shall have power to enforce this article by appropriate legislation.

Amendment XIV [1868]

Section 1. All persons born or naturalized in the United States, and subject to the jurisdiction thereof, are citizens of the United States and of the State wherein they reside. No State shall make or enforce any law which shall abridge the privileges and immunities of citizens of the United States; nor shall any State deprive any person of life, liberty, or property, without due process of law; nor deny to any person within its jurisdiction the equal protection of the laws.

Section 2. Representatives shall be apportioned among the several States according to their respective numbers, counting the whole number of persons in each State, excluding Indians not taxed. But when the right to vote at any election for the choice of electors for President and Vice-President of the United States, Representatives in Congress, the Executive and Judicial officers of a State, or the members of the Legislature thereof, is denied to any of the male inhabitants of such State, being twenty-one years of age, and citizens of the United States, or in any way abridged, except for participation in rebellion, or other crime, the basis of representation therein shall be reduced in the proportion which the number of such male citizens shall bear to the whole number of male citizens twenty-one years of age in such State.

Section 3. No person shall be a Senator or Representative in Congress, or elector of President and Vice-President, or hold any office, civil or military, under the United States, or under any State, who, having previously taken an oath, as a member of Congress, or as an officer of the United States, or as a member of any State legislature, or as an executive or judicial officer of any State, to support the Constitution of the United States, shall have engaged in insurrection or rebellion against the same, or given aid or comfort to the enemies thereof. But Congress may by a vote of two-thirds of each House, remove such disability.

Section 4. The validity of the public debt of the United States, authorized by law, including debts incurred for payment of pensions and bounties for services in suppressing insurrection or rebellion, shall not be questioned. But neither the United States nor any State shall assume or pay any debt or obligation incurred in aid of insurrection or rebellion against the United States, or any claim for the loss or emancipation of any slave; but all such debts, obligations, and claims shall be held illegal and void.

Section 5. The Congress shall have the power to enforce, by appropriate legislation, the provisions of this article.

Amendment XV [1870]

Section 1. The right of citizens of the United States to vote shall not be denied or abridged by the United States or by any State on account of race, color, or previous condition of servitude—

Section 2. The Congress shall have power to enforce this article by appropriate legislation.

Amendment XVI [1913]

The Congress shall have power to lay and collect taxes on incomes, from whatever source derived, without apportionment among the several States, and without regard to any census or enumeration.

Amendment XVII [1913]

The Senate of the United States shall be composed of two Senators from each State, elected by the people thereof, for six years; and each Senator shall have one vote. The electors in each State shall have the qualifications requisite for electors of the most numerous branch of the State legislatures.

When vacancies happen in the representation of any State in the Senate, the executive authority of such State shall issue writs of election to fill such vacancies: *Provided,* That the legislature of any State may empower the executive thereof to make temporary appointments until the people fill the vacancies by election as the legislature may direct.

This amendment shall not be so construed as to affect the election or term of any Senator chosen before it becomes valid as part of the Constitution.

Amendment XVIII [1919]

Section 1. After one year from the ratification of this article the manufacture, sale, or transportation of intoxicating liquors within, the importation thereof into, or the exportation thereof from the United States and all territory subject to the jurisdiction thereof for beverage purposes is hereby prohibited.

Section 2. The Congress and the several States shall have concurrent power to enforce this article by appropriate legislation.

Section 3. This article shall be inoperative unless it shall have been ratified as an amendment to the Constitution by the legislatures of the several States, as provided in the Constitution, within seven years from the date of the submission hereof to the States by the Congress.

Amendment XIX [1920]

The right of citizens of the United States to vote shall not be denied or abridged by the United States or by any State on account of sex.

Congress shall have power to enforce this article by appropriate legislation.

Amendment XX [1933]

Section 1. The terms of the President and Vice-President shall end at noon on the 20th day of January, and the terms of Senators and Representatives at noon on the 3d day of January, of the years in which such terms would have ended if this article had not been ratified; and the terms of their successors shall then begin.

Section 2. The congress shall assemble at least once in every year, and such meeting shall begin at noon on the 3d day of January, unless they shall by law appoint a different day.

Section 3. If, at the time fixed for the beginning of the term of the President, the President elect shall have died, the Vice-President elect shall become President. If a President shall not have been chosen before the time fixed for the beginning of his term, or if the President elect shall have failed to qualify, then the Vice-President elect shall act as President until a President shall have been qualified; and the Congress may by law provide for the case wherein neither a President elect nor a Vice-President elect shall have qualified, declaring who shall then act as President, or the manner in which one who is to act shall be selected, and such person shall act accordingly until a President or Vice-President shall have qualified.

Section 4. The Congress may by law provide for the case of the death of any of the persons from whom the House of Representatives may choose a President whenever the right of choice shall have devolved upon them, and for the case of the death of any of the persons from whom the Senate may choose a Vice-President whenever the right of choice shall have devolved upon them.

Section 5. Sections 1 and 2 shall take effect on the 15th day of October following the ratification of this article.

Section 6. This article shall be inoperative unless it shall have been ratified as an amendment to the Constitution by the legislatures of three-fourths of the several States within seven years from the date of its submission.

Amendment XXI [1933]

Section 1. The eighteenth article of amendment to the Constitution of the United States is hereby repealed.

Section 2. The transportation or importation into any State, Territory, or possession of the United States for delivery or use therein of intoxicating liquors, in violation of the laws thereof, is hereby prohibited.

Section 3. This article shall be inoperative unless it shall have been ratified as an amendment to the Constitution by conventions in the several States, as provided in the Constitution, within seven years from the date of the submission hereof to the States by the Congress.

Amendment XXII [1951]

No person shall be elected to the office of the President more than twice, and no person who has held the office of President, or acted as President, for more than two years of a term to which some other person was elected President shall be elected to the office of the President more than once.

But this Article shall not apply to any person holding the office of President when this Article was proposed by the Congress, and shall not prevent any person who may be holding the office of President, or acting as President, during the term within which this Article becomes operative from holding the office of President or acting as President during the remainder of such term.

Amendment XXIII [1961]

Section 1. The District constituting the seat of Government of the United States shall appoint in such manner as the Congress may direct:

A number of electors of President and Vice President equal to the whole number of Senators and Representatives in Congress to which the District would be entitled if it were a State, but in no event more than the least populous State; they shall be in addition to those appointed by the States, but they shall be considered, for the purposes of the election of President and Vice President, to be electors appointed by a State; and they shall meet in the District and perform such duties as provided by the twelfth article of amendment.

Section 2. The Congress shall have power to enforce this article by appropriate legislation.

Amendment XXIV [1964]

Section 1. The right of citizens of the United States to vote in any primary or other election for President or Vice President, for electors for President or Vice President, or for Senator or Representative in Congress, shall not be denied or abridged by the United States or any State by reason of failure to pay any poll tax or other tax.

Section 2. The Congress shall have the power to enforce this article by appropriate legislation.

Amendment XXV [1967]

Section 1. In case of the removal of the President from office or of his death or resignation, the Vice President shall become President.

Section 2. Whenever there is a vacancy in the office of the Vice President, the President shall nominate a Vice President who shall take office upon confirmation by a majority vote of both Houses of Congress.

Section 3. Whenever the President transmits to the President pro tempore of the Senate and the Speaker of the House of Representatives his written declaration that he is unable to discharge the powers and duties of his office, and until he transmits to them a written declaration to the contrary, such powers and duties shall be discharged by the Vice President as Acting President.

Section 4. Whenever the Vice President and a majority of either the principal officers of the executive department or of such other body as Congress may by law provide, transmit to the President pro tempore of the Senate and the Speaker of the House of Representatives their written declaration that the President is unable to discharge the powers and duties of his office, the Vice President shall immediately assume the powers and duties of the office as Acting President.

Thereafter, when the President transmits to the President pro tempore of the Senate and the Speaker of the House of Representatives his written declaration that no inability exists, he shall resume the powers and duties of his office unless the Vice President and a majority of either the principal officers of the executive department or of such other body as Congress may by law provide, transmit within four days to the President pro tempore of the Senate and the Speaker of the House of Representatives their written declaration that the President is unable to discharge the powers and duties of his office. Thereupon Congress shall decide the issue, assembling within forty-eight hours for that purpose if not in session. If the Congress, within twenty-one days after receipt of the latter written declaration, or, if Congress is not in session, within twenty-one days after Congress is required to assemble, determines by two-thirds vote of both Houses that the President is unable to discharge the powers and duties of his office, the Vice President shall continue to discharge the same as Acting President; otherwise, the President shall resume the powers and duties of his office.

Amendment XXVI [1971]

Section 1. The right of citizens of the United States, who are eighteen years of age or older, to vote shall not be denied or abridged by the United States or by any State on account of age.

Section 2. The Congress shall have power to enforce this article by appropriate legislation.

Glossary

Administrative rulemaking: A process by which government agencies develop internal rules governing the behavior of their employees.

Bench trial: Trial by a judge instead of a jury. Occurs at option of defendant.

Bill of attainder: A bill or statute extinguishing the civil rights and capacities of a person upon sentence of death or outlawry, usually after a conviction of treason or felony.

Black codes: Refers to statutes passed to create or perpetuate segregation such as the Louisiana *Code Noir* of the antebellum period. The black codes were usually statutes passed at various times and scattered throughout the laws of a state, rather than a distinct, specific code or statute.

Capital punishment: Penalty of death imposed for defendants convicted of serious crimes, usually premeditated murder.

Code of criminal procedure: A federal or state law that specifies the formal steps for processing a criminal case through the criminal justice system.

Common law: A system of law used primarily in English-speaking countries based on previous judicial decision rather than on statute. Often referred to as "judge-made law."

Corporal punishment: Punishment of the body (Latin, *corpus*) by whipping, branding, or maiming. Generally abandoned in the United States criminal law during the nineteenth century.

Coverture: A common law doctrine by which women as of the moment of marriage were said to be "covered" by the legal personality of husbands; a form of legal dependency.

De facto segregation: Racial segregation caused by social and economic factors, rather than mandated by law. For example, the segregation of schools in an urban area resulting from the fact that most whites live in the suburbs or in specific neighborhoods within a city, and that most minorities live in the central city, or in suburbs or neighborhoods that are almost wholly minority. The result is actual segregation, even while the schools are legally integrated.

De jure segregation: Racial segregation required by law, such as statutes creating separate schools for blacks and whites.

Double jeopardy: Being tried twice for the same crime.

Dower: An important legal consideration for women before the twentieth century, dower generally referred to the provision, customarily one-third, which the law made for a widow out of the property of her husband for the support and nurture of herself and her children. Dower has been abolished in the majority of states and materially altered in others.

Due process: A concept that is one of the fundamental principles of the Anglo-American legal tradition. It has never been defined precisely, but in the context of criminal justice, it means that proceedings should be fair and not arbitrary or capricious.

Eminent domain: The power to take private property for public use by the federal or state government, municipalities, and private persons or corporations authorized to exercise functions of a public character.

Enjoin: To impose an injunction; to prevent the execution of a judgment, order, or statute so that lawmakers or judges might reconsider the justice of the rule of legal question.

Equal protection clause: A provision of the Fourteenth Amendment, the clause prohibits a state from denying to any person within its jurisdiction the equal protection of the laws. This clause requires that persons under similar circumstances be given equal protection in the enjoyment of personal rights and the prevention or redress of wrongs.

Exclusionary rule: The prohibition on using illegally obtained evidence against a criminal suspect.

Ex post facto: Latin for "after the fact." Usually used in reference to a law that makes an act criminal after it has taken place.

Expressive conduct: Political statements--including the raising of liberty poles in the eighteenth century, picketing, and even flag-burnings—that mix together the elements of speech and action. A majority of the Supreme Court has protected expressive conduct under a broad reading of the free-speech clause of the First Amendment.

Femme covert: From the Old French, the term literally meant a "covered or protected woman" and referred to a married woman; in other words, a woman "protected" by her husband.

Femme sole: An Old French term meaning literally "a single woman." The phrase included those who had been married but whose marriage had been dissolved by death or divorce and, for most purposes, women who were legally separated from their husbands. Its importance lies in the legal rights it granted to unmarried women.

Fleeing felon rule: The old legal standard that permitted police officers to shoot and kill individuals who were suspected of having committed a felony and were fleeing to avoid arrest. Declared unconstitutional in *Tennessee v. Garner* (1985).

Future interest: Interest in land or other things in which the privilege of possession or of enjoyment is in the future, not the present.

Grand jury: The large (grand) jury that investigates complaints of crimes and issues indictments.

Habeas corpus: Latin for "You should have the body." A legal command (or writ) to someone restraining an individual to bring that person before a judge and show legal justification for the detention.

Incorporation doctrine: The process by which the Supreme Court applied provisions of the Bill of Rights against the states by bringing those provisions under the umbrella of the due process clause of the Fourteenth Amendment.

Incorporeal rights: Rights to intangibles such as legal actions. Incorporeal chattels are a class of rights growing out of or incidental to things that are personal such as patent rights or copyrights.

Indeterminate sentence: A sentence that falls within a legislatively prescribed range rather than for a set term; used to fit punishment more closely to the actual circumstance of the crime and to promote reformation of the offender.

Intangible property: Property that has no intrinsic and marketable value but is merely the evidence of value, such as certificates of stock, bonds, notes, franchises, value in a going business, trademarks, copyrights, and other nonphysical, noncurrent assets which exist only in connection to something else.

Judicial activism: A judicial philosophy holding that the Supreme Court should actively rule on the constitutional aspects of federal and state laws and procedure.

Judicial restraint: A judicial philosophy holding that the Supreme Court should defer to legislatures in matters of constitutional law.

Libel law: Traditional legal action that permits persons to sue publications which damage their reputations. Seditious libel involves criminal prosecution for criticism of governmental policies or public officials. In civil libel suits, people who claim their reputations have been injured, including public officials, sue for money damages. After New York *Times* v. *Sullivan*, both criminal and civil actions must meet strict constitutional standards designed to protect liberty of the press more fully than the old common law of libel.

Majoritarianism: Rule by legislative or popular majorities. The term usually implies scant regard for the rights claims of unpopular individuals or legislative minorities.

Marital unity: A common law doctrine that described the merger of a wife's legal identity into that of the husband. In effect, husband and wife became one and the one was the husband, resulting in several legal disabilities for the wife. See also Coverture.

Militia: A military force consisting of citizen-soldiers for whom the bearing of arms is not a primary occupation.

Personal Property: Everything that is subject to ownership that is not land or an interest in land. Further classifications of personal property are tangible and intangible.

Petit jury: The small (petit or "petty") trial jury, usually composed of twelve members, who determine guilt or innocence.

Plea bargaining: An agreement between the prosecutor and defendant to plead guilty to a lesser crime than the one charged in exchange for a reduced sentence.

Police powers: Powers granted to state legislatures for health, safety, morals, and welfare.

Prerogative courts: Certain non-common law courts in sixteenth- and seventeenth-century England which were appointed and controlled by the King.

Preventive detention: The concept that judges should have the power to deny bail to criminal suspects for the purpose of preventing them from committing further criminal acts.

Prior appropriation: A water law doctrine holding that the first to divert water from its natural channel and put it to a beneficial use has a right to the amount of water diverted and applied. The appropriator need not own real property abutting the water course to hold this right.

Privileges and immunities clause: There are two Privileges and Immunities Clauses in the Constitution, the first in Article IV ("The Citizens of each State shall be entitled to all Privileges and Immunities of citizens in the several states.") and the second in the Fourteenth Amendment ("No State shall make or enforce any law which shall abridge the privileges or immunities of citizens of the United States.") The purpose of these clauses is to place the citizens of each state on the same footing with citizens of other states as far as the advantages resulting from citizenship are concerned.

Procedural rights: Rights that create a mode of proceeding by which a legal right is enforced, as distinguished from a substantive right, which concerns some practice such as free speech or press.

Radical Whigs: Opposition political spokesmen in England during the late seventeenth century and early eighteenth century who distrusted executive authority and looked to the local militia to balance the tyrannical power of a king with a professional military at his disposal.

Real property: Land and anything permanently affixed to it.

Release on recognizance: A procedure by which a criminal suspect obtains pretrial release on the basis of his or her promise to appear in court and without having to post bail.

Relict: Derived from the Latin, *relinquere*, "to leave behind," the term refers to a widow or widower or their survivor. A widow (relict) controlling substantial property as a result of dower right possessed a high degree of autonomy, even before the twentieth century.

Seditious libel: See Libel.

Similarly situated group: Referring to groups having similar characteristics or subject to similar circumstances, the term has been used by women's rights supporters, both historical and contemporary, to draw comparisons between the disabilities of women's situation and the circumstances affecting African Americans, among others.

Standing armies: Professional soldiers in the service of national authorities and feared as an extension of executive power and influence.

Strict scrutiny: A test for determining if there has been a denial of equal protection, "strict scrutiny" places the burden on government to establish the necessity of the statutory classification.

Substantive due process of law: A judicial doctrine that there is a constitutional guarantee that no person may be arbitrarily deprived of life, liberty, or property. As created and defined in the nineteenth century, the guarantee was against legislation that took property from one person and gave it to another without a judicial proceeding such as the legislative outlawry of a profession that had been legal prior to the statute's passage.

Substantive rights: Rights that create, guarantee, define, or regulate some practice such as free speech or press. These substantive rights can be contrasted with procedural rights, such as the right to a jury trial, which guarantee specific ways of proceeding by which a legal right will be enforced.

Suspect class: Generally, a court will employ the "strict scrutiny" test under the Equal Protection Clause in determining the legitimacy of classifications that are based on a trait (race, sex, national origin) that itself seems to contravene established constitutional principles so that any use of the classification may be deemed "suspect." Courts have shied away from terming women a "suspect class" and, consequently, have been reluctant to apply "strict scrutiny" to cases involving sex discrimination.

Tort: A civil wrong that is not a breach of contract (wrongs involving nuisance or negligence, for example). Plaintiffs seek money damages.

Transient necessities: A perception of a majority who feel aggrieved about something and want immediate legislative relief, usually at the expense of the taxpayers.

Venue: The neighborhood, place, county, state or jurisdiction where an injury is declared to have been done, or a fact declared to have happened.

Vested rights: A constitutional law doctrine holding that some rights have so completely and definitely accrued to a person that they are not subject to the actions of individuals or government and that government must recognize and protect those rights by due process of law.

Zengerian Reforms: Popularized by the 1735 prosecution of John Peter Zenger, two eighteenth-century reforms which allowed seditious libel defendants to plead truth as a defense and empowered juries, rather than judges, to determine whether or not publications were actually libelous. They were incorporated into the Sedition Act of 1798 but proved of little value to Jeffersonian defendants in prosecutions under the law.

Index

By and For the People: Constitutional Rights in American History
The publisher's editorial and production team for this text consisted of
Maureen Hewitt, Lucy Herz, Andrew Davidson, and Michael Kendrick. The
text was typeset by Point West, Inc. and printed and bound by
McNaughton and Gunn, Inc.

The cover and text were designed by Michael Methe.
Courtroom sketches by Ida Libby Dengrove.